SMOKIN' JOE

SMOKIN' JOE

The Autobiography of a Heavyweight Champion
of the World,
Smokin' Joe Frazier

JOE FRAZIER

with Phil Berger

Macmillan • USA

MACMILLAN

A Simon & Schuster Macmillan Company
1633 Broadway
New York, NY 10019

MACMILLAN is a registered trademark of Macmillan, Inc.

Portrait of Joe Frazier on title page courtesy of Richard Slone.

Library of Congress Cataloging-in-Publication Data available
ISBN 0-02-860847-X

10 9 8 7 6 5 4 3 2 1

Book design by Scott Meola

Printed in the United States of America

To my father Rubin, called by God early in my life, who has meant everything to me, is always in my thoughts, and whom I miss every day.

To my mother Dolly, the backbone of the family who filled my heart with love for God, love for her, and my fellow man.

—Joe Frazier

To my daughter, Julia, with love . . .

And to my friend, Michael Rakosi, with gratitude.

—Phil Berger

ACKNOWLEDGMENTS

To be successful, you need to have a lot of good people supporting you. I'd like to thank just a few of the folks who've offered me love, encouragement, and advice along the road to becoming heavyweight champion of the world.

First, I thank God for helping me get the job done. I thank Daddy for everything, and Momma for being a good mother who walked tall and carried a big switch. To Tommy, for covering my back every step of the way; to Beck and Flossie, for keeping the home fires burning.

Thanks to my brothers and sisters—Marion and Florence Austin; Eugene and Hazel Frazier; Andrew Frazier and his family; Rubin Jr. and Miriam Frazier; John (Bigboy) Frazier and his family; Tommy and Ollie Frazier; Martha and James Rhodan; the late Julia (Flossie) Frazier; Rebecca Hall; and the late David Frazier.

Thanks to the Preacher (Marvis), the Mouthpiece (Jacqui), Do It All (Natasha), and the Red Head (Denise) for helping me recall some of the best times of my life.

Thanks to the late Yank Durham, for being a loyal friend, my teacher, and a second father. And to Eddie Futch, Milton Bailey, and George Benton for taking up where Yank left off.

Thanks to the people who helped me get my start after the Olympics, including the Cloverlay shareholders, and to Everlast, my sponsor, and my Everlast friends, Ben Nadoff, Jon Toms, and Dennis Clancey.

Thanks to all my boxing opponents, and to all the professional and amateur boxers that stepped foot in Smokin' Joe Frazier's Gym. To my trainers—Val Colbert, Sam Hickman, Eugene Drew, and King Solomon. Thanks to Butch Lewis, Leon and Michael Spinks, the late Jersey Joe Walcott, and especially to my inspiration, the late Joe Louis.

Thanks to Denise, Linda, and Janice for being my great trouble shooters. To Dr. Finton J. Speller, Dr. Nicholas DePace, Dr. Joseph Fabiani, Dr. Myron Yanoff, Dr. Henry Winkler, Dr. Charles Kellman, and Dr. Katowitz for keeping me together over the years.

Thanks to the U.S Olympic Committee; the boxing establishment—the WBC, IBF, WBA; the International Boxing Hall of Fame; promoters Jerry Perenchio, Jack Kent Cooke, Bob Arum, Teddy Brenner, and Don King; Madison Square Garden management, past and present, the late John Condon, Sonny Werblin, the Biondi family, David Checketts, and John Cirillo; boxing commissioners Randy Gordon, Larry Hazzard, Jerry Gormley, and especially Valerie Dorsett; and James J. Binns.

Thanks to all the sportswriters and photographers throughout the years, especially Stan Hochman, of the *Philadelphia Daily News*.

Thanks to my friends—Reverend A. B. Brown; Sherman Helmsley; President Nelson Mandela; Frances Meyers; Daisy Chennssault; Patty Deirfus; the late, great Gypsy Joe Harris; the late William Neil; Julius Irving; Jim Brown; Lee Majors; Dr. John Thompson; LeRoy Neiman; Jon Amos; Donald and Marla Trump; Daisy LeSure; the late Frank Bannister; Bill and Cathy Bailey; Bill Anderson; the Nixes; Kenny Johnson; Julie Lynn; Joe, Chuck, and Lou Verne and family; Joe and Helene Goldstein; Webster Riddick; Richard Slone; Dick Gidron; Theresa Riley; the Figueroa family; the late Norbert Ekassi; the late Jack Fried; Ralph Easley; Andy Quigley; James Connelly; Gene Bonner, James Bonner, and all the Bonner boys; Joe Kelly; the late Sonny Averona; Henry Reed; Lou Yellin; Margaret Boyce; Lou Priluker; the late Bing Parisi; Jacqueline Roberts; Ryan O'Neil; Dickie Murray; Bob Hayes; Richie Allen; Ernest D'orum; Mitch and Ada Mitchell; Bob Goodman and family; Bo Averona and family; Mr. and Mrs. Simon Jinx; Russ and Theresa Hoffman; Legrant and Janette Pressley; and Joseph Shanklin.

Thanks to my whole family—Daralyn Frazier; Peter Lyde; Gary Collins; Ron Gibson; James Frisby; Aunt Elizabeth (Essie) Riley; my late aunt Ida Murray; Aunt Jenny (Sissy) Morrel; Cousin Gloria; Uncle Cadillac and Aunt Bell; John and Frances Morralle; Victoria Riley; Tom and Ginger Bolden; Rivers and Mary Riley; Turkey Benjamin; Joe (Little Joe), Ann, Keith (Little Bubba), Lisa (Midget), Stanley, Rodney, Dannette, and Orhonda Frazier; along with a host of other nieces, nephews, and my grandchildren, and many others close to my heart but too numerous to mention.

Thanks to the folks at Macmillan who put this book together: my fantastic editor, Traci Cothran; Maria Massey; Cheryl Mamaril; Ken Samelson; Scott Meola; Jeanine Bucek; Elliott Ehrlich; Natalie Chapman; and Alan Oakes. To Phil Berger, for his talent of putting together the story of my life. To Linda Ronan and Linda Wachtel at the Sports Illustrated Library. And thanks to Madison Square Garden Photographer, George Kalinsky, for arranging this deal, and for the love and support he and his wife, Ellen, have given to me over the years.

And, finally, thanks to all my fans, who were in my corner all around the world.

CONTENTS

1

"That Boy Is Gonna Be the Next Joe Louis"

Where I come from, folks don't know me as Joe Frazier.

I was always Billy Boy.

That name was given to me by my daddy, Rubin Frazier. He owned a 1940 Ford that he drove the hell out of—over rough terrain, along back-country roads, on streets all over Beaufort County, South Carolina. The particular Ford model—known as a "Billy"—was a beast. No matter how hard Daddy drove that sucker, the Billy always got him to where he had to go, never breaking down. In Daddy's mind, the car stood for reliability, the same sort of trustworthiness that he saw in me.

See, we were as close as father and son could be. I like to say I went from my momma's belly into my father's arms. Yeah, my daddy was my hero, my heartbeat. We were always together. From the time I was a toddler, Daddy used to carry me wherever he went—over the ten acres of farmland we Fraziers owned, to the still where he made bootleg corn liquor, and into town on Saturdays to buy the necessities that a family with eleven children needed. And wherever we went, Billy Boy wasn't along just for the ride.

From the time I was able to walk, I not only hung out with him but also helped any way I could. My daddy was broad-shouldered and big-beamed like I am, but strong as he was he sometimes needed help because he'd had his left hand and part of his forearm amputated about a year before I was born on January 12, 1944. He'd lost the hand as the result of a shooting incident.

My momma, Dolly, told me what happened. It seems that she and Rubin were sitting in a little pickup truck outside a club one Saturday night when along come a fella named Arthur Smith. Now my momma and daddy loved one another, but Rubin had an eye for the occasional other woman as well . . . and one of those other women, it turned out, Arthur Smith was sweet on.

Understand this: Smith and my father were friends, but on this night and with a bellyful of liquor in him Smith got to thinking badly about his love rival. And as my parents were getting ready to drive home that night, this scamboogah Smith pulled out a pistol without my daddy seeing it.

As Rubin said good night, Smith fired several times. One of those bullets hit my momma in the foot. But the greater harm was done to Daddy. His left arm was hanging out of the cab of the truck, alongside the door, when bullets smashed into and destroyed his hand and forearm.

Arthur Smith went to jail for the shooting, but he didn't stay there for long. As my momma put it: "If you were a good workman, the white man took you out of jail and kept you busy on his farm."

🥊　🥊　🥊

Both my parents knew about working on the white man's farms. While we had those ten acres, and two mules, Buck and Jenny, to work them, the land was what country folk called "white dirt"—which is another way of saying it wasn't worth a damn. We couldn't even grow peas on it, which grow just about anywhere, and the same was true for corn. On the Frazier spread, all we could get to come up was cotton and watermelon.

So that made life a scramble for survival. And in that part of South Carolina it meant you worked on the white man's land for a day's wages. Momma had done it since she was a girl of five. For fifty cents a day, she'd work from sunup to sunset pulling radishes, cutting cabbage, and digging potatoes for a white man named Trask. Every morning, to gather his field help, ole Trask would send a bus through the Laurel Bay section of Beaufort (pronounced BYOU-fert), where black folks lived and where I was later raised.

Dolly worked shorter days while she was going to grade school, but things being what they were, her schooling didn't last long. Dolly's parents were not young anymore; they needed help from their ten kids if they were to make a go of it. So Momma quit school in the fourth grade and went full-time into Trask's fields. By the time she was a young woman she was earning the grand sum of one dollar a day.

By then Rubin was courting her nights while working days in fields belonging to two white brothers named Jim and Mac Bellamy. Daddy had grown up practically next door to Momma—"the next ten acres," she called it. They'd played hide and go seek as kids. As teenagers, she'd watch him compete as a catcher for the Laurel Bay hardball team. And after those ballgames the two of them would picnic and go dancing until midnight, back when the Charleston was all the rage.

Rubin and Dolly were married in 1930, in the midst of the Depression. I was the twelfth child they would have. Another one, David, followed, but when he died of diphtheria as a nine-month-old infant, I became the baby of the family. Whether that event contributed to the special treatment my daddy gave me, who can say? All I can tell you is that it was no secret that I was his favorite.

And I was not shy about taking advantage of my position. As a little boy, if I wanted more food, or didn't want to do a chore—and any of my brothers or sisters tried to say otherwise—I'd just use the magic words: "I'll tell Daddy." It was usually enough to get my way. Not that my siblings—Marion (Bubba), Eugene (Skeet), Andrew (Bozo), Rubin Jr. (Jake), John (Big Boy), Thomas (Tommy), Martha (Mazie), Julia (Flossie), and Rebecca (Beck)—were happy about it. "You're spoiling him, Daddy," Flossie would say. "We're tired of that. Billy can have this and that, do this and that. Everything Billy." Sometimes—say I wanted a second helping of crab stew, a favorite dish of mine—he'd defend me, saying: "The boy can't eat but a stomachful." Other times he would just fix Flossie with a look, and that was that. In those days, you didn't talk back to your parents; you better swallow your words 'cause Daddy didn't play no backtalk.

Those were hard times. Our house—six rooms and a porch built by Daddy and my brothers and sisters—was set on oak blocks and had a wood roof reinforced by tin. But that still wasn't enough to keep the elements from fooling with us. I mean, I could look up and tell you what time of day it was from where the sunlight shot through. And when it rained hard, we'd spend half the night putting buckets out to keep it from flooding us.

In those days, we had no telephone, no running water, no plumbing. The outhouse was seventy-five yards from the back door. For me that outhouse was a particular problem on nights there was no moon. I was scared as hell of the dark; still am. City folks have no idea what nights in the country can be like, particularly in Laurel Bay, where there were no street lamps.

Step out there on a night when there was no moon up in that sky, and you couldn't even see your hand in front of your face. It felt like the air was full of danger—mosquitoes whooshing by your face; an owl hooting; a cow moaning; a rabbit or coon making a run for it at your feet. And if you'd been brought up, as I was, by a mother who'd scared you practically out of your britches with ghost stories, well, you'd just as soon stay indoors, where there was light . . . and what we called a "slop jar." Every room had a slop jar—a five-gallon can with the tar burned off. If it was raining outside, or dark, or you simply didn't want the bugs to bite your butt, well then you did your business in that slop jar.

With eleven kids to provide for, it was not enough for Rubin and Dolly to farm their land, raise chickens, hogs, and a few cows, and work the white man's fields for low wages. It took a lot more; it took unending hustle to keep the family going, and neither Momma nor Daddy shirked the responsibility.

Some nights Momma would come back from Trask's fields and go crabbing or fishing. On the Broad River, she'd catch whiting, catfish, blackfish, croker, spottail bass, flounder, anything she could coax into biting her line. What we didn't use for ourselves, she'd sell to people in the neighborhood. She'd put seven or eight fish on a string and offer them up for fifteen cents a string.

In the woods near our house grew a leafy plant. Momma and some of us children would scavenge for this plant, which in those days we called "musk" . . . don't ask me why. We'd collect the plant and then dry it in the sun. The stuff would crumble and the scent of it would be so strong you could get high on it if you inhaled. This musk, which I figure now must've been tobacco or marijuana, was a cash crop for us. A guy from down the road in Orangeburg would come by every so often and give us nineteen or twenty cents a pound for what we had collected.

At certain times of the year, the crab factory and tomato factory would get to canning, and Momma would go to work there. It was seasonal work. She'd take up her spot on the line as the trucks rolled in with the tomato harvest from the small farmers of Beaufort County, or with the crab haul that fishermen brought in from the Broad River or over in nearby Hilton Head. The crab, of course, came in a shell and in those days they didn't have an automatic picker to separate the meat out. Women like my momma were hired to do that.

When they were first married, Rubin would cut wood by the cord, and a truck would appear and haul it away, paying my daddy a few bucks for his trouble. By the time I came along, he was a one-armed man and couldn't swing an axe quite like he used to, but that didn't stop him. He would take orders from folks around Laurel Bay and then the two of us would grab our axes and chop down what was needed. Daddy would swing away one-handed while I'd use the conventional two-handed grip. Some of the wood we'd keep for our fireplaces, particularly pine that had gotten a little rotten. Pine like that would have gas in it that lit up fast when you put a match to it.

Anyway, I was no more than six or seven years old when I stood alongside my daddy, hacking down trees in the woods on our property. As I'd tell folks a long time after: "I never had a little-boy life." Hell, a year later I was getting up at four in the morning ("Wake up, Billy Boy," Daddy'd whisper) to help cook that bootleg liquor.

The still was on those ten acres of ours, out a ways in the woods. To make liquor the way we did you'd need to let corn, water, and sugar sit for a week in a fifty-five-gallon drum that we kept buried in the ground. Ten pounds of corn, five pounds of sugar, and all that water would turn sour over that period of time. After you collected it all in five-gallon cans, you'd haul them to the still, which was about five hundred yards from the buried drum.

The still was where we cooked that sour mash. You'd pour it into the pot, put the pot on the fire, and cap off the still. My job was to keep the smoke from rising by redirecting it with a piece of carboard. That way people would never get wise to where the still was.

While I was doing that, a pipe that ran from the pot through a trough that was filled with cold water was conveying the vapor. At the end of the trough the pipe turned south, where a bottle would catch the now-vaporized liquid that emerged. That liquid would turn out to be about five gallons of good strong liquor. How strong? Well, I'll tell you this much: There were times the Fraziers of Beaufort used it like kerosene to start a fire in our fireplace.

Daddy and I would put the liquor in see-through glass jugs for the sake of the customers. Those folks insisted on the glass jugs so they could shake up the liquor and watch how long it held its beads. The longer it did, the better that corn liquor was thought to be. They'd shake the jug and say, "Ah. That's good stuff."

We sold our corn liquor for seven dollars a gallon. Sometimes I'd sit alongside Daddy as he drove the route his clients were on. Other times, if he was busy, I'd drive the route myself. I wasn't more than ten years old, but I'd been driving his cars and trucks from the time I was seven. No big thing. It'd be about five in the morning when I'd get started, taking back roads. I wasn't worried about the law. The state troopers and sheriff didn't travel those roads unless some scamboogah had given them a tip about illegal doings. And even if they'd have stopped me, what could they have charged me with? I was just a boy.

Tell you the truth, though, it was more fun when my daddy drove. On this liquor run were a couple of woman customers that he kind of liked. When he'd get to one of their houses, he'd cut the engine and stammer, "S-s-son, I'm going to get the money."

Well, he'd be a long time getting that money, a damn long time. And lucky for me these women had daughters. They would spot me in the truck and signal to me. So while Daddy went in the front door to "get the money," twelve-year-old Billy Boy went in the back door and had fun with those sweet country girls. I don't think Daddy ever caught on.

By the time we'd get back home, Momma would be up and cooking breakfast. Then Trask's bus would show up and she'd be gone for the day. While she was out in the fields, my sisters Rebecca and Flossie prepared dinner and cleaned the house. All of us had chores. Me, I might have to go to the pump we had in the backyard and crank it for water and then feed the animals.

Daddy was an overseer on Bellamy's place, making about fifty dollars a week. People picked tomato, cucumber, squash, and lettuce, getting paid by the box. Each day Daddy would mark down how many boxes they had gathered and give the worker a ticket that stated the amount. At the end of the week the worker would cash in his tickets. When the work day was over, he'd drive the field hands home in a truck or bus the Bellamys provided.

In the morning, before he picked up the workers to haul them out to Bellamy's, we'd drive out three, four miles to the government pump house, where you could get water for free. Daddy and I would load fifty-five-gallon drums with water and take them back to the farm to irrigate the fields.

No surprise, I began working for the Bellamys early on, making three or four dollars a day. I was a big stocky kid who didn't mind hard work and responsibility. By the time I was twelve, I was driving a tractor along those fields, collecting the boxes of tomatoes and cucumbers and squash that field hands would leave at the end of each row and then loading them onto the tractor. Then I'd drive the boxes to the packing house, where other workers would sort out the good from the bad stuff and pack the boxes into crates that would be loaded onto eighteen-wheelers.

Lots of times my work day would begin after school and run past midnight. That packing house operated damn near through the night at Bellamy's. As a result, I'd be too tired to pay much attention the next day in school . . . after walking four miles to get there. Not that I was any more eager for learning when I was rested. Truth is, I wasn't much for school, which in those days wasn't all it could have been for the colored.

To begin with, the schoolhouse back then was segregated, which in the Beaufort of that time meant separate and unequal. Unequal in every way. The length of the school term for blacks was shorter than it was for whites, and what public money there was for education went mostly to white schools.

Not that I felt deprived. The fact is I just didn't learn quick, and I didn't learn easy. My mind wanted excitement. More often than not I'd be out in the woods with other truants, shooting dice or playing cards for nickels and pennies. Or I'd meander over to Bellamy's place and put in a long work day. While I felt a restlessness about what my future held, I never saw school as holding the answer.

🏃 🏃 🏃

As it turned out, one of my kin would provide a clue to what my life would be about. When my daddy got a black-and-white television in the early 1950s—the first family in Laurel Bay to have one—my mother's brothers, Manson and Israel, and a few other adults from the neighborhood would come by to watch the boxing matches on that snowy fifteen-inch Philco screen.

Daddy and the men would sit on the porch, drink the corn liquor, and speculate on the night's action.

"What are the odds, man?"

"Oh, shoot—that boy can't fight: I'll put money on the other guy."

"What the hell do you know? You don't know no boxin'."

"I'll box your damn ears off if you don't quiet down."

They'd fuss like that until the opening bell.

In the early days of TV, boxing was on the screen damn near every night. On Fridays, NBC and Gillette razor blades presented fight cards from Madison Square Garden in New York, with Jimmy Powers, a newspaper columnist, delivering the blow-by-blow. Middle of the week, CBS and Pabst Blue Ribbon beer had fights from all over the country, with Russ Hodges or Jack Drees announcing. The Dumont network had Dennis James calling matches from small arenas around New York like Sunnyside Gardens, and later Ted Husing or Chris Schenkel delivered the action from Eastern Parkway in Brooklyn. ABC did not ignore boxing either, televising matches regularly in prime time, including the last nighttime network boxing series, which ran until September 1964.

The way it was at Rubin Frazier's place, Momma sold drinks for a quarter as we all watched great fighters like Sugar Ray Robinson, Rocky Marciano, Willie Pep, Rocky Graziano. One night, as I walked onto the porch to go into the house, Uncle Israel looked at me and, noting my stocky build, told the others: "That boy there . . . that boy is gonna be another Joe Louis."

Well, those words made an impression. Eight years old at the time, I thought: why not? Boxing fit with the rough-and-tumble character I was. At school, classmates would give me a sandwich or a quarter to walk with them at final bell so that bullies wouldn't mess with them. Bullies would see me and say: "Oh, okay, Billy. I didn't know you were friends with him." Around Laurel Bay, any scamboogah (a disrespectful, low-down and foul person) who got in my face soon regretted it: Billy Boy could kick anybody's ass.

Another Joe Louis. That sounded dead right to me. From the moment that Uncle Israel spoke those words, I took them to heart. The next day, I got an old burlap sack and filled it with rags, corncobs, a brick in the middle, and Spanish moss that grew on trees all over Beaufort County. I tied a rope to it and then hung this makeshift heavy bag from an oak tree in the backyard lot where the mules were kept. And for the next six, seven years damn near every day I'd hit that heavy bag for an hour at a time. I'd wrap my hands with a necktie of my daddy's, or a stocking of my momma's or sisters', and get to it.

I told folks I was destined to be a world champion, the next Joe Louis. They looked at me as if I was from Mars. My sister Flossie would laugh at that boast.

"Yeah, you're just foolin' yourself," she'd say.

"You'll see," I'd say. "You'll see."

"You can't even do your homework, boy. How you gonna be champion of the world?"

"What's that got to do with anything," I'd say.

Sometimes relatives would stop by and see me whacking away at that bag, and they would take to laughing too.

"You all can laugh," I'd tell them. "But I'm gonna be world champion some day."

Momma never said anything about my ambition to be the next Joe Louis, but she'd never been crazy about her baby boy risking life and limb. When I'd had a chance to play football in school, she'd refused to sign the permission slip. "They want to kill my child," she said. "No thank you."

But hitting a defenseless burlap sack—what harm could come of that, she must have figured. Eventually, she probably thought, I'd give up that fool notion of fighting for a living and that would be that. But for now, I had her permission to work out on the bag for an hour a day when I got home from school or from Bellamy's.

There were no boxing gyms in Beaufort, and no organized competitions. Colored kids couldn't even use the playgrounds in Beaufort—it was whites only. All I had to build my dream on was that homemade heavy bag.

But I'll tell you this. The fighter that became Smokin' Joe Frazier started there. I didn't lollygag when it was time to work the bag. In that daily hour that Momma allowed me, and with only a short break or two, I'd work myself into a lather pounding away at the bag.

And from the git-go, the left hook was my weapon of choice. Boom boom boom: I'd throw it like a wrecking ball against that burlap sack and feel a tingle from head to toe from the impact it made.

But it wasn't long after I began working out that my left arm was seriously damaged because of an ornery three-hundred-pound hog of ours. Sounds weird, I know, but it's true. This boar hog of ours was so nasty that from time to time I couldn't resist teasing it. Well, one day when I was about eight, I poked it with a stick and ran like hell. Unfortunately, somebody had left the gate to the pigpen open and that damn creature ran straight through, chasing my sorry ass. Scared? Oh, yes. I ran like hell and, in my hurry, fell and hit my left arm on a brick.

The fall tore up my arm bad. But we were too poor to see doctors, so the arm was left to heal on its own. It did, but I would never be able to fully straighten it as I had before the accident. The left arm was now crooked, and lacking full range of motion. But as it existed, it was as though it was cocked for the left hook—permanently cocked. Strange for a guy whose success in the world would later depend on what that left could generate.

My momma was not pleased that I had provoked the hog and gotten hurt in the process. When Momma was not pleased, watch out. She was a tough, no-nonsense lady, with a deep religious conviction. She believed in the Lord and on Sundays her voice would blow the doors open when she lent it to the congregation at St. John's Baptist Church in Billy Hill. But on God's ten acres there in Laurel Bay, she didn't need divine intervention to get her children to do right. All she had to do was put her word out there, and we listened up. If we didn't, there'd be hell to pay.

Like the time she told me to go to the mailbox, half a mile down the road, and see if a shipment of tangerines she was expecting from family in Florida had arrived. "And don't dally, Billy Boy," she said. "You get on back right away."

Well, on the way I ran into friends who were shooting marbles. I joined their game, figuring I'd sneak a few minutes and then hurry back, double-time, with those tangerines. Trouble was I began losing and couldn't resist trying to get even. *I got to get my marbles back,* I told myself.

All of a sudden I heard, "Biiiillllllly!"—my momma shouting my name. I started crying on the spot, knowing I was going to get a butt whupping.

"Did I say not to stop?" my momma asked when I got back.

When she grabbed for her switch, which was really three switches of tree vines that she'd braided together, I panicked. I told her, "I'm leaving this place," and started running.

She chased after me, saying, "You're leaving, huh? Leaving your dear Momma that raised you up this far."

She was faster than an Olympic sprinter, and not only tracked me down, but proceeded to apply that switch to my black butt. Child abuse with love.

I laugh now, thinking about it. But she was and, at age eighty-six, still is a unique lady, determined and spiritual and loving all in one. She was superstitious, often smoked a corncob pipe, and had all these voo-doo stories and sayings. When she'd see a flock of crows in the sky, she'd say, "There's going to be a big funeral." If you walked by a graveyard and heard strange noises, she'd tell you, "That's people they buried alive." When an owl hooted or a bull moaned, she said it was sadness.

Tough as she can be when she has to, she is really a very loving woman. She is very kind to people, very sweet. Dad, being a man who liked women, begat (as they say in the Bible) a whole slew of half-brothers and sisters for me. (He once told me he had twenty-six children in all.) Well, when these children stopped by, Momma accepted them. They came into our house, spent time in our midst. They belonged to Daddy, but Momma loved them. She cooked for them and took care of them like they were her own. She was a righteous mother, with that abiding faith of hers in the Bible.

Lots of times, she wouldn't wait for Sunday to praise the Lord. If she felt the Lord had blessed her—if, say, she went to work and got over the quota and made extra money doing it—she'd come home and have church in our own backyard. She'd invite relatives from nearby and neigh-bors, and they'd gather at our place, sing and shout and have, as they called it, a hallelujah good time.

And she never lost her faith. Years later, when she was all stooped over from those long days in the field, I urged her to let me take her to a doctor who could perform an operation to straighten her back.

"No thank you," she told me. "I'm satisfied with the way God is keep-ing me. If I get straight, I'd be too tall for God."

That's Momma, a woman who never strayed far from her religion. When we were growing up, sometimes rather than applying that switch to our butts, she'd quote Scripture to get us to do right. Like, "Honor your mother and father . . . that your days may be long upon the land which the Lord thy God giveth thee." Or, "A humbled child will taste the grace."

Of course, Sunday was *the* day for church things. At church Momma usually had me sit next to Miss Grace. Sometimes the spirit would hit her and she would jump all over the place; at those times it was my job to keep Miss Grace from hurting herself or anybody else because she weighed 300 pounds. And dinner on Sunday was always a bit more special. We'd cook one of our chickens and eat a hearty meal with butter beans, rice, and fried bread. If Momma had had time that week to pick wild huckleberries, we'd have huckleberry pie for dessert.

During the week, we had to stretch our dinners. We had big pots of peas and fried corn bread, or crab stew. It wasn't easy feeding a family as big as ours. But in Laurel Bay people looked out for one another . . . and that helped.

Say a farmer butchered a hog. Lots of times he'd drop by with a little meat for us. It's how I developed a liking for all the delicacies from a pig, like chitlins, pig's feet, tails and ears. Folks that harvested potatoes might leave a bag of spuds in our doorway. Those that grew cane would grind it up to get the juice, then take it to the mill to cook it into syrup. And afterward drop a jar of syrup with us.

That's how people were in those times. There was a strong sense of community, of poor black people looking out for and helping one another.

On weekends, the one I'd be looking out for would be my daddy. Weekends were party time, and Rubin would be out there having himself some fun. Folks would throw house parties: booze, dancing, and Friday night fish fries, or maybe they'd barbecue a pig. As Daddy's right-hand man, I'd go along with him, sitting in a corner while making sure nobody was looking at him funny. If I suspected someone was, I'd warn Daddy, "Watch out for that guy."

Often those parties went late into the night, and I'd get too tired to stay awake. Those times I'd just go sleep in the car until he woke me. Then, because he was tired and had had too much to drink, he'd set me in his lap in the driver's seat and let me steer the car home. "You doin' good, Billy."

When we'd get there, Momma would say, "Where you and your father been?"

"I don't know nothin'," I'd say.

She'd fix me with a look and say, "You're gonna grow up to be just like that daddy of yours."

She was right. I wasn't no more than thirteen when I dropped out of school and began chasing the ladies real hard. In most places, thirteen's a boy. But at that age I had a man's perspective. Fact is by the time I was ten, eleven years old, adults in Laurel Bay would steer their kids clear of me. And with good reason: I was advanced for my age, and a bad influence if you were raising your young ones to be goody two shoes.

Big for my age, and experienced, I worked long hours on the Bellamy farm and in the evenings ran with an older crowd. Most nights me and my friends B. A. Johnson and Dickie Murray would pile into my car and hit the road. Because I was underage and because he had a license, Johnson would drive. We'd go everywhere, down to Jasper County, near Hilton Head, or closer to home. Sometimes we'd steal potatoes from a potato bank and cook them in the woods, other times we'd steal fruit from an orchard.

But mostly it was about the ladies—we'd go to clubs, to parties, anywhere where folks hung out. In some places, the local fellows were not awfully happy to see us. They wanted the ladies to themselves. But if they tried to muscle us, they ended up with bloody noses or worse. We were handy with our fists—no one had knives and guns then—and we'd bust those scamboogahs up and take their ladies with us.

With no motels for us back then, we'd drive out into the woods. Since the car was mine, I had dibs on the backseat. I'd lift it out of the car and carry it off so my girl and me could have some privacy. Dickie and Johnson had their choice of romancing their ladies on the hood of the car or off in the woods on what we called "a pine straw mattress."

We hung around some pretty low-down places, where God wouldn't even go, and where sometimes things could get dangerous. I remember one club where a woman showed up with what we called "a ten-cent pistol." That's a jug full of Red Devil lye, human piss, and honey. She had heard her husband was messing around on her, and when she saw the evidence that he was, she started unloading that ten-cent pistol—slinging the stuff in his direction. That place cleared out in a New York minute.

I was thirteen and a half, nearly fourteen when I first saw Florence Smith. She was sixteen, and still going to school. We met at her grandfather's wake—her uncle James is married to my sister Martha. I took one look at her and said: This lady is for me. We snuck into my car and talked. I told Florence I just had to see her again; she said she'd like that.

Easier said than done. The trouble was the Smiths had no telephone and lived on Lady's Island, which was twenty-five miles from Laurel

Bay. That meant driving out there without knowing whether she'd be home, much less whether her parents would let me see her. In those days, see, you had to ask the parents for their daughter's company. Well, the first time I showed up, her father, who was an electrician at the U.S. Marine base at Parris Island, told me his wife, Elsie, wasn't there to give her permission.

"Can I wait outside 'til Mrs. Smith gets home?" I asked.

"No, sir," he said. "You can leave the house right now."

Same thing happened the next time. But the third time I appeared at their door, both of them were there.

Florence's father proceeded to give me the third degree.

"How old are you, son?" he asked.

"Fifteen," I lied.

What the hell. I had my own car, my own money. By my reckoning, I was no boy.

I was crazy about Florence, and would see her every chance I could. On Friday nights I'd pick her up early and go out dancing at one of the clubs, getting her back to her place by around 9:30 so I could take advantage of the rest of the night.

Because I was also crazy about a girl named Rosetta, who lived near Parris Island, only fifteen miles from Florence's home. If Rosetta's father wasn't there, we could sneak an hour or two on the couch. But I'd keep an eye on the driveway and be sure to be leaving by the time her father was coming home.

All that driving was death on my gas tank. The Fraziers' cars were pieced together by my daddy. Aside from everything else he did, Rubin would collect the hubs of autos left to rot away in backyards or on the side of the road. Then he and I would salvage what we could and, like Dr. Frankenstein, revive a car that, missing a crucial part, just wouldn't run. Once we got to working on it, presto—the damned thing was suddenly an automobile that would get up and go. But it wasn't necessarily cost efficient, as the gas-guzzling son of a bitch that I drove could show you.

Well, Johnson and I solved that gas shortage. We took to staking out the roads around Laurel Bay for cars that broke down. Usually they belonged to Marines who didn't get paid until the end of the month. That meant those Marines wouldn't be coming 'round soon to take back their cars. And that meant their cars were soon ours.

We siphoned the gasoline in their tanks and emptied it in a fifty-five-gallon tank that we kept hidden in the woods. Then we took apart the car, keeping what we needed—tires, batteries, whatever—and selling what we could. It wasn't something I was awful proud of doing, but necessity turned me into a car-stealing scamboogah for a while. Momma and Daddy, I'm glad to say, never did find out.

One afternoon back in Beaufort, I walked into a black social club called the Milton Club, looking for Johnson. I found him . . . and—surprise, surprise—Rosetta as well.

She threw her arms around me, but when I didn't respond with the gusto I usually did, she asked what was wrong.

"Well," I told her, "Florence is waiting for me in the car. I've got to drive her back home."

"Who's going to take *me*?" she asked, getting all steamed up. Then she decided: "I'm going with you."

And she walked right to my car, and got inside. Florence sat in front and Rosetta sat behind her, next to me.

Well, as you can probably imagine, the air was tight in that car as Johnson drove the twenty-five miles to Florence's home.

At one point, Florence turned to me and asked, "Billy, who do you love?" Meaning her or Rosetta.

I told her: "I love my mother and father and my brothers and sisters."

"You're not telling me anything," Florence said.

"I'm doing the best I can, darling."

"Who you calling 'darling'?" Rosetta asked.

And that's how it went for the next twenty-four and a half miles.

When we reached Florence's house, she told me: "Don't come back 'les you can tell me who you love."

And when we dropped off Rosetta, she said the same.

Well, I know they say a man can't love two women at once, but I have never subscribed to that. My feeling is a man can love as many as he can love.

As far as Florence and Rosetta . . . I ended up marrying one of them and having children by both.

Beaufort is in the center of Beaufort County, a cluster of sea islands on the southeastern tip of South Carolina. That's where it stood geographically.

Where it stood racially . . . ? Well, let's just say that its attitudes had me wanting to leave there from the time I was a boy. I remember when I was thirteen getting on my knees at night and saying, "Lord, when is this going to change? I've got to live. I've got to get out of here."

Beaufort was a beautiful enough place—endless waterways offering picture-postcard views, streets with canopies of trees laced with Spanish moss, big fancy homes. The grass was green, the air was fresh.

Filmmakers whose movies were set in the South often shot them in Beaufort on account of the city's scenic quality—the salt-water swamplands, oyster creeks, the backcountry of thick pine forests, with their dusty roads and wooden shacks. *The Big Chill, The Great Santini, The Prince of Tides, Forrest Gump,* and *Daughters of the Dust* would all be filmed there.

And yet for all that, there was no escaping that Beaufort was the Deep South, rotten with the exploitation of blacks. Slavery had existed here, and the reminders of that were everywhere. Almost all black communities were named after the plantations around which they rose up— Coffin Point, Fripp, Gray's Hill, and, yes, Laurel Bay.

In the cotton fields where blacks once served as slave labor, the tiny "praise houses" they built to hold their shouts during the work day were still visible when I was growing up—small, crumbling frame structures sitting in the middle of fields.

Nearly a century after the Civil War had ended, life was still hard for colored folks. A black growing up in Beaufort couldn't use the same bathroom, lunch counter, or water fountain that white folks did.

When a black boy went to the Breeze Theater on Bay and Charles, he sat up in the balcony while the white folk sat down below.

When he awaited a bus, he sat at the back of the station.

When he walked the city's sidewalks, he crossed to the other side to let a white man go by.

I can remember shopping in downtown Beaufort on Saturdays in a store where a parrot had been taught to say, "Niggers teefing, niggers teefing"—niggers stealing, niggers stealing.

Big things, little things: Beaufort never stopped letting you know you were a nigger. I had a cousin named Jacqueline Brown who, when she was five, went with her grandmother to the doctor. Grandma needed looking after by the doctor. So while the old lady sat with a sheet over her in an examination room, Jacqueline waited for her in the colored waiting room. The way things worked back then was the doctor took care of all his white patients first, then would deal with the black ones. So it was a long wait for Jacqueline, sitting alone in that waiting room. From where she sat she could see the children in the whites' waiting room had books that they could read. So she got up, walked to where the books were and began reading one. The white children said nothing— they didn't care—but the doctor's nurse sure did.

"What are you doing in here?" the nurse said. "Get out of here, you little nigger."

If that was not bad enough, her grandmother—afraid that the doctor might not see her now—took Jacqueline by the hand and sat her roughly in a chair back in the colored waiting room. Jacqueline, who today is executive director of the Youth Future Authority in Savannah, never forgot or forgave the society that would treat a child like that.

That was the South I grew up in, and why I felt stifled in Beaufort. I sensed a world beyond Beaufort of comforts and joys that I'd never know if I didn't leave there. And day by day, things happened that added to my frustration and unhappiness . . . and nudged me closer to that hour I'd be hauling ass and heading north.

One night when I was fourteen, I was hanging out in the street with Johnson and Dickie Murray in front of the Milton Club, when a white boy came driving by.

"Get out of the street, nigger," he shouted at me as his car passed inches from me.

"Come and do something about it, cracker," I hollered back.

"I'll meet you the next street over," he told me.

He parked the car and got out. And pretty soon a bunch of us from the Milton Club came walking on up.

"Where's that bad nigger?" the white boy hollered out.

By now there was a small crowd—maybe twenty of his friends and mine.

"You must be lookin' for me, cracker," I told him.

I'd never seen him before, but he must have been a local boy, about five feet eleven inches and eighteen years old. In the next second him and me were locking butt . . . right there in downtown Beaufort, with everybody hollering like hell.

Well, I hit him with that left hook that I'd been perfecting on that backyard heavy bag, and he went down like I'd leveled a shotgun on him. I jumped right on the scamboogah and continued to work him over while my Milton Club guys shouted: "Finish him, Billy. Kill his ass."

All bleeding and scared now—you could see it in his eyes—he says to me: "Hey, friend. Let's talk this thing over."

I'd just wanted to show him I was as much a man as he was, and I knew there was no longer any question on that count. So that was that. I let him up. We shook hands and went our separate ways.

But it wasn't the end of my problems with the racial attitudes of Beaufort County.

I'd been working on the Bellamy's spread for . . . oh, maybe six, seven years, and had never had no trouble with either Mac or Jim. I did my job; they treated me okay—as okay as a black man was treated in those times. I mean, face it: Blacks in Beaufort were underpaid and made to feel like second-class citizens. Come time for lunch at Bellamy's, you didn't wash up and sit in a dining hall. Uh uh. You ate where you worked, like some bow-wow. Me, I'd break out lunch and have it right there on the tractor.

While the Bellamys were people we saw every day, we didn't expect much consideration from either Mac, who was the younger of the two and easy-going, or Jim, who was a little rougher and a lot more redneck-nasty.

One day, a little black boy of about twelve screwed up one of the Bellamy tractors without meaning to. Well, Jim became so enraged that he took off his belt and proceeded to put a whupping on this child right there in the field.

I went back to the packing house and told the black brothers there what I had seen.

"Wasn't right Bellamy doing that," I told them. "A white guy taking a strap to a black kid."

Soon after, Jim saw me and said: "Hey, Billy. What the hell you shootin' your mouth off for?"

I asked him what he was talking about.

"Don't give me that shit, Billy," he said. "You come up here telling these colored guys this and that about me. Tell you what, nigger. I want you off this place before I take this belt off again."

"No," I told him. "You better keep the belt to hold your pants up 'cause you're not going to use no belt on me."

He looked at me a while, as if trying to make up his mind whether to mess with me or not. Then finally, he said: "Go on. Get the hell outta here."

From that day, from that moment, I knew it was time for me to leave this place where I'd been raised up. There wasn't nothing ahead but bad times and a low-rent life for a man like me. Even Momma could see it. She told me, "Son, if you can't get along with the white folks, then leave home because I don't want anything to happen to you."

But the train fare out of Beaufort to the cities up north was pretty steep. The bus? Well, for a long time the closest the Greyhound had gotten to Beaufort was Charleston, some ninety-six miles away. But by 1958, the Dog—as we called Greyhound—had finally made Beaufort a stop on its South Carolina route. I figured if I worked a while I'd have enough to pay that bus fare and still have a little for my pocket when I got to New York City.

My brother Tommy lived in New York, and had told me I could stay with his family and him. So in the months that followed my run-in with Jim Bellamy, I began thinking real hard of life beyond Beaufort— and what it could be like. I wanted all the nice things I saw some folks had no trouble acquiring—the clothes, jewelry, cars, homes. And I knew there was no way in hell that any of that could happen if I stayed in the South.

I went to work for the local Coca-Cola plant. The white guy who drove the truck would write the receipt for each place we delivered to. And then old Billy would do the real work, stacking and unloading the crates. I stayed with Coca-Cola until the government began building houses for the Marines stationed over at Parris Island, when I got myself on a work crew.

Our job was to raise the rafters that would hold the roof up. There were seven rafters to a roof. We were four guys working from 6:00 A.M. to noon for $140 per man a week. Rafter after rafter we shouldered into place, and at the end of each week I'd have a little more to stick in my pocket.

Nine months or so had gone by from when I'd gotten the boot from Bellamy's place. And then one day, with no fanfare, no tearful goodbyes, I packed quickly and caught the first thing smoking northward. Yeah, I climbed on the Dog's back and rode through the night . . .

It was 1959. I was fifteen years old and on my own.

2

THE OLYMPIC GAMES

The expectations I had of a brand new, grand new life were pretty quickly shot to hell.

New York was hard going.

I stayed with my brother Tommy and his wife Ollie in their three-bedroom apartment on West 110th Street, but it wasn't long before I felt like a mooch.

Since most of the time I was without a job, I had to rely on Tommy, who worked in the garment center, to lay a few bucks on me every once in a while to keep me going. It embarrassed me to have to ask my older brother for money. He had two kids to support and didn't need a tenant without prospects to complicate his life.

Occasionally I'd find work—odd jobs that I got by bribing someone to slip me onto the payroll. That happened with a fellow in a sheet metal factory in downtown Brooklyn. The money—$150 a week—was good while it lasted. Trouble was as soon as I'd paid off the rip-off artist, the scamboogah went and got me fired. The same thing happened with an electrician's job I had in Brooklyn. Pay the joker off to get me the work, stay a month and then get shitcanned so he could get a kickback from some other man out of a job.

It wasn't a question of how good a worker you were. It was a matter of being in luck. And luck was avoiding me like crazy back then. After a while, as my days without a job lengthened into weeks, I got a bit desperate.

By now my old Beaufort friend B. A. Johnson had come up north to live with relatives he had in the Bedford-Stuyvesant section of Brooklyn. The both of us found out about a junkyard in Far Rockaway that would give you fifty dollars a car no matter what condition the car was in. Late-model beauty or old bomb, them junkyard boys didn't care. Here's fifty bucks, see ya. So we began scoping the streets of Bedford-Stuyvesant, the way we had in Beaufort, and when a car sat out there too long, we'd mark it as ours. Johnson would borrow a car from his kin, and we'd push that other car straight to the junkyard, get our fifty bucks, and be gone.

We stole one car a week for a few months while searching without success for legit employment. On weekends, there was nothing for Johnson and me to do but party. Brooklyn, Harlem, Queens: There were parties everywhere. Lots of times folks would organize what they called a rent party. They'd sell you booze and sandwiches so that the party would cover the rent that was coming due.

Partying took the hurt off of being on my own with nothing happening. But it got to a point, finally, where I was just too embarrassed to keep leaning on my brother. I decided to head to Philadelphia, where I had relatives that would put me up, and see if my luck would change.

My aunt Evelyn Peeples had a three-story house in north Philadelphia: 1845 Thirteenth Street. She worked as a domestic in the suburbs, so she had to sleep over there several days of the week. For her, having kin like me to watch the house while she was gone was a relief. For me, it was rent-free lodgings that were just as welcome.

One of my relatives in Philadelphia, James Martin, was working at Cross Brothers, a kosher slaughterhouse in the city. Through him I got through the door and talked myself into a kind of audition for a job. For three years, from 1961 to 1964, I would work for Cross Brothers without ever being on the payroll.

I was putting in forty or more hours a week to learn the job and earn the right to have it, eventually, full-time. My remuneration? Well, sometimes I'd get paid for six hours of that forty-hour week. Then again sometimes Cross Brothers might be a bit more generous . . . but never to where I confused myself for a rich man.

It was not a great situation. But unable to find other work, I kept punching the clock at the slaughterhouse. At least I could count on making a buck there. And given the fact that back in Beaufort, in September 1960, Florence Smith had given birth to my first child, a son named Marvis, every little bit helped.

So for roughly twenty-five dollars a day I did a little of everything at Cross Brothers. I would sweep the floor, wash blood down the drain, and dump the steers' guts through a chute so it could be ground up. There were times they'd have me wheel sides of beef into the refrigerated lockup, where I'd practice my combinations, like you saw Sly Stallone do in *Rocky*. He got that off me, as he did my habit of running the steps of the art museum.

Other times I might do a little butchering, but I never was too crazy about working with those knives. I also handled what they called the "weasel machine"—a device that went up the steer's neck and separated the lung from the stomach. Friends would ask me whether doing that was unpleasant. Not for me, I'd tell them jokingly; maybe for the steer.

Actually, it must have been pretty damn scary for those animals. They'd bring them onto the killing floor in trucks. And bam, a shute would pick the creature up by the belly, shackles would drop behind its neck, another device would raise the animal up by the chin so the throat would be fully exposed for the rabbi to slit with his knife.

Don't think those steers couldn't sense what was coming. Every once in a while, one of them would get loose—say the guy would forget to drop the shackles around its neck—and, man, that bull would run the floor like an NFL fullback, hitting everything in sight, bouncing off walls, ramming sides of beef, and going after any human son of a bitch unlucky enough to be in his path. That scamboogah was desperate to get off that killing floor; he never made it, though. Cross Brothers stored guns there for the occasional emergency like that, and, bang, they'd shoot the crazyass bull in the head. And that would be that.

🥊 🥊 🥊

Being on my own took some getting used to. In New York, and for a while in Philadelphia, I just couldn't get a grip. All the vows I made, the dreams I'd had in Beaufort about a better life . . . well, all that seemed beyond me. During the time I was in New York, I never walked into a gym, or did any training. I just couldn't get focused. But as I settled into my life in Philadelphia, things changed. I began to feel those stirrings again to be more than just another guy. I hated being ordinary, hated having a job that was just a job.

By December of 1961, my weight had ballooned to 220 pounds, or about thirty pounds more than what I should have been. I felt disgusted about how sloppy I looked . . . at the same time I was kicking myself for not having acted on that dream of mine to be the next Joe Louis. Two years out on my own and what did I have to show for it? A big butt and no life to speak of. It was time to get serious.

One day around Christmas 1961 I walked into the Police Athletic League gym on Twenty-second and Columbia in Philadelphia. The fellow that ran the place, a retired cop named Duke Dugent, gave me an application for joining the gym and told me come back when I'd filled it out.

After the New Year 1962, I was back and ready to rumble. A relative of mine, Rivers Riley, who ran a barbershop in north Philadelphia, gave me the money to buy the high-top shoes fighters wear as well as hand wraps and a gym bag. I really appreciated that, because I didn't want to walk into that gym looking raggedy.

It didn't take long to find out that being the chief ass-kicker in Beaufort, South Carolina, didn't count for much in that PAL gym. The first time I got into the ring to spar I went up against a big strong guy that they called Georgie Boy. Georgie Boy proceeded to hit me with a right hand to the chest that even now, all these years later, feels like it left a permanent dent on my sternum. Man, he put a lick on me.

I took his shot and, though I felt sick from the impact, I never let him know it. I fought Georgie Boy best as I could. In truth, the best I could was a long ways from being worthy of anybody's attention. I was just a short-armed, overweight boxing wannabe.

But man I did want to be a fighter. And with that first exposure, I was hooked. The PAL gym felt like my room, my place to shine. After that first day, I knew I had a long way to go to become a fighter, but like the little boy banging away at the burlap sack in the backyard, I was confident that in time I would succeed. And I backed my confidence with the old standby—hard work.

Every morning I would get up at four o'clock and do three, four miles of roadwork in Fairmont Park, away from the fumes of traffic. Then off to Cross Brothers for a long work day. Leaving the slaughterhouse, I'd head for the PAL gym and a two-hour workout—jumping rope, hitting the bags, doing situps and pushups, and then strengthening my neck muscles by arcing my back for neck bridges. The first time I worked the heavy bag I could see Duke Dugent stir. He saw a fat boy banging the bag with an authority not often seen in a newcomer. He saw a fat boy who had heavy hands. He saw a prospect.

"You just here to get a workout, son?" he asked. "Or are you—"

"I want to do this for a living," I told him.

"Uh huh," he said, measuring me with his eyes.

With each day's training, I was improving rapidly. And when Georgie Boy and the eight or nine other heavyweights in the gym stepped in the ring with me, it was no party. I pounded on those boys, always moving forward and throwing punches. It wasn't long before Georgie Boy would show up and, craning his neck this way and that, be looking to see if I'd shown up.

"Joe here?" he'd ask, nervously.

"Ain't seen him."

But I'd be there all right; I'd be sitting in Duke Dugent's office, talking boxing. Georgie Boy would have rather I'd stayed away. But I was there every day, ready to give him and anybody else that wanted it another asswhupping.

And believe me I handed out asswhuppings like lollipops at the doctor's office or corsages at the senior prom. Pretty soon I'd run all the heavyweights out of the gym, and had to work against the smaller boys, like Gypsy Joe Harris (who eventually became a world-ranked welterweight and might have become champion if the boxing commissions didn't discover that Gypsy was blind in one eye, obliging them to revoke his license).

I'd work with them little guys, trying my damnedest not to hit them with any hurting shots. The idea was just to move against their speed to sharpen my reflexes and dodge their punches to improve my defensive instincts. Trouble was, when I am in a boxing ring it is unnatural for me to pull my punches.

With a shortage of heavyweights to spar with, these smaller guys were a reasonable Plan B . . . except for the fact they didn't like getting hit with the kind of punches I could lay on people. To avoid getting them hurt, one of the trainers in the gym, Yancey (Yank) Durham, came up with the idea of tying my left hand around my neck with a hand wrap, tie, or belt. It worked. Now I was forced to concentrate on movement against these quick little guys.

Sometimes, the job at Cross Brothers would hold me beyond closing time at the PAL gym. But that didn't stop me from keeping up with my training. By now, Duke Dugent had become convinced I had a future in boxing, and he gave me a key to the gym for those occasions when I got caught up late at the slaughterhouse.

On those nights I'd bring a little thirty-dollar record player to the empty gym. With that and a stack of 45s—James Brown, Otis Redding, Sam Cooke, the Drifters, Aretha Franklin—I'd work out by myself, to the best of the soul sound. Each record ran about three minutes, the length of a round in boxing. So I'd hit the bag, or shadow box, or skip rope until the music stopped. Then wait 'til the next record descended, and go again.

I was nothing but diligent about boxing. I was eating right—Duke had sold me on the virtues of fat-free, vegetable-filled meals—and I was no longer staying out late. Come midnight, man—I was in bed. I was treating my body like the resource I knew it was, giving it all the rest and nourishment it needed. Fat-boy Frazier was long gone and in his place was 190 pounds of lean, mean fighting machine. And I was getting better by the day. Late that year, 1962—my first year in the gym—I won the city's Golden Gloves novice title as a heavyweight.

For me that was just a start, a sign that if I gave my all I could rise to the top, but I knew to do that I would have to stay dedicated—that hard work was not a part-time deal. Good times, bad times—I had to stay at it . . . to never let up. I remember showing up one night at the gym with the pinky of my left hand heavily bandaged.

"What happened?" Dugent asked.

"Little accident on the job," I told him.

In truth, the injury was more serious. With a butcher's knife, I'd sliced off a piece of pinky while working at Cross Brothers. Nine stitches later they'd grafted the skin back on. But I figured if I told Duke Dugent what really had happened he might suggest I take the day off. I didn't want time off. I was eager to keep making progress. So I played down what had happened in the slaughterhouse.

By now, Florence had come north with Marvis, and was staying in the same house, separate rooms, as I was. The separate rooms was Evelyn's doing. Aunt Evelyn had the old-fashioned belief that only married folks slept together. Of course, when Evelyn wasn't around, Florence and I didn't have trouble finding one another.

But Evelyn stayed at us, preaching the virtues of married life. She'd talk to Florence—give her a whole long spiel about the pleasures of a life sanctified by marriage—and then she'd come after me with the same speech. Eventually, in September 1963, Florence and I were married at City Hall.

Back in the gym, Yank Durham had begun to watch me with keen interest—Duke Dugent had told him Joe Frazier was the real McCoy. Yank was a former amateur fighter, whose hopes of turning pro had ended in an air raid in England during World War II, when a jeep ran him over, breaking both his legs and requiring him to be hospitalized for almost two years.

When Yank was mustered out of the army, he came back to Philadelphia and began working for the Pennyslvania Railroad as a welder. In his spare time, he managed and trained fighters, none of whom had amounted to much by 1962. But Yank knew his business. He knew how to build a fighter and maneuver him. He just needed a Joe Frazier to show it.

"Think we can get along?" he asked me one day in the gym.

"Yeah," I told him.

"Then let's go to work."

I liked, and trusted, Yank from the git-go. We had no written contract—ours was a handshake deal. As long as we were together, Yank was on the up-and-up with me. Later, when I turned pro, Yank sometimes managed a side deal to sweeten his pocket while negotiating a fight for me. But when he did, he would let me know the details of how much he was making—a damn unusual practice for boxing guys.

Yank was a big man, with a deep, booming voice, hair flecked gray, and a salty manner of expressing himself that would crack me up. He'd jam obscenities into his sentences in a way that sounded perfectly natural. "Cocksucker, let's get this guy out of here," he'd tell me between rounds of a fight. Meaning, knock this guy out ASAP. Or, if I walked into a punch because I was carrying my hands too low: "Whatchoo doin'? Cocksucker, get your hands out your ass."

Yank was no shrinking violet. He was a grand character who went through life with a twinkle in his eye. Like my daddy, Yank was a hustler, doing what he had to in order to make a living. That included cooking up bootleg liquor. As I had in Beaufort, I would deliver the homemade brew. As a favor to Yank, I'd go to the customer's address and drop the liquor, without any money ever being exchanged. I'm not sure how the transaction got concluded, but knowing Yank I'm sure he got paid.

The newspaper guys were amused by Yank's habit of expressing himself in the first person singular when he was talking about *me*. "I'm gonna knock this guy out, no question," Yank would say. Meaning that his fighter, Frazier, was going to score a knockout.

Yank worked me hard, and I came on as a fighter, developing the little wrinkles or techniques that would enable me to best use the strengths I had—like a left hook that could knock a man into another time zone, bottomless energy, and a take-no-prisoners attitude.

To exploit those assets, and overcome my lack of height or reach, I needed to get in the other guy's face without getting clobbered as I walked toward him. It meant I had to learn to slip that man's punches—moving my head and shoulders sideways to avoid that punch as I moved forward. I worked on slip moves by myself, and with Yank. I worked on them with the little guys in the gym, bending at the knees and, as they fired at me, moving my head to one side or the other and getting myself in position to fire back.

Slip to the right, I'd go to the body. Slip to the left, I had my choice—whack him upstairs or downstairs.

Yank liked to say my offense was my defense. The idea was that when I whaled away at a guy, throwing punches nonstop, the other man had all he could do to defend himself. He was so busy trying to survive he couldn't muster any show of force on his own.

It was an approach that fighters like Rocky Marciano and Henry Armstrong had used with great success before me. (Armstrong was known to have thrown 200 punches in a round.) Marciano had retired undefeated as heavyweight champion in 1956 and Armstrong had won world titles in several weight divisions—as a featherweight, lightweight, and welterweight. Both of them were ultra-aggressive fighters, who wore an opponent down with the volume of punches they put in his face. Yank got hold of films of their fights for me to watch, the idea, I guess, being to reinforce my approach of rapid-fire destruction.

I admired both of those guys, Armstrong and Marciano, but in the years that followed it was to Marciano that I would most often be compared. There were certain similarities. Both of us were unrelenting undersized aggressors, convinced that we were the stronger, tougher man. And while on the surface we appeared to share the same style, there were differences. Rocky stalked a man from a low, awkward crouch where I would bob and weave my way past his reach. Marciano demolished foes with sledgehammer right hands usually, where my haymaker was the left hand.

Just as I had when I was growing up, I wasn't shy about telling folks what lay ahead. At Cross Brothers, they took it as a joke when I told them I would be champion of the world. But Yank didn't. Like my daddy, Yank liked to drink and party. And wherever we went, he would tell all those happy souls that I was going to be the next Olympic champion and, further down the road, champion of the world. They would nod and smile politely, obviously not believing a word of it.

It didn't matter. We believed and kept working toward our goals.

When there was no sparring available, Yank would hold a big medicine ball against his body and I would punch it. Yank worked on making my left hook more lethal by shortening its arc. While wide-arcing punches are photogenic, they take more time to arrive at the target and leave a fighter susceptible to counterpunches. Compact punches, thrown with leverage, usually do more damage. As that old boxing saying goes: It's the punch a man doesn't see that renders him senseless. And logically a punch traveling a short distance was more likely to get past the opponent's radar.

So when Yank had the medicine ball I'd throw that left hook again and again, in various combinations—off the jab, or following a right hand, or in succession . . . what's called "doubling up" the hook.

Opponents were aware that if they were going to get hammered by Joe Frazier, the left hook would do the damage. They knew it but couldn't do an awful lot about it because I delivered the punch with speed and accuracy, and kept it coming. I wore a son of a bitch out with that hook.

And when I worked out on Yank's medicine ball, or on the heavy bag, I was constantly trying to sharpen my delivery of the punch. The short arc, the variations on combinations that would disguise the moment when it was coming—that was my objective.

In that respect, my attack followed the philosophy of Green Bay Packer football coach Vince Lombardi, who didn't believe in having an offense with fancy flourishes. Lombardi's teams would run a few simple plays again and again, and if the other team knew what was coming . . . it didn't help. The Packers executed with precision and with a stop-us-if-you-can attitude.

That was the way I was. Straight-ahead, all cylinders turning. There was no way in hell I'd let you off the hook once I'd hurt you. And with every day I was getting just a bit sharper at bringing that hurt. With a feint, I could bait my man into exposing that jaw. Or I'd whack him a no-mercy left to the rib cage and, when he brought his elbows in to protect those ribs, lowering his guard in the process, I'd fire off another hook, but this one to the now-unprotected jaw. Bing, bang: downstairs, upstairs. Doubling the hook. Like a time-charge it went off.

Sometimes, when I'd be punching that medicine ball, I'd purposely miss and whack Yank a shot or two, just to bust his chops. It cracked me up to hear him, in that deep and solemn voice of his, say: "Cut it out, god-dammit. That hurts." Yank was my boxing mentor, but we had lots of laughs as well.

Meanwhile, I was traveling around the country, fighting regularly and getting a reputation as a top amateur fighter. I won the Middle Atlantic Golden Gloves heavyweight championship in 1962, 1963, and again in 1964. My only loss in my three years in the amateurs—and I was convinced it was a bum decision—was to a fighter from Grand Rapids, Michigan, Buster Mathis.

Buster was a curious sight for a fighter. He was six foot three and weighed in excess of 300 pounds, but in the ring that fat boy was nimble and slick beyond anybody's expectations. That a guy with a protruding belly and jiggly chest could move so smooth and box so clever made him a big favorite with amateur officials and spectators alike. Watching ole Buster was like watching a dancing bear. He was a spectacle.

He was also the man who would be my biggest obstacle to making the U.S. Olympic Boxing Team that would go to Tokyo for the 1964 Games.

Mathis and I met in the finals of the U.S. Olympic Trials at the New York World's Fair that summer of '64. Our fight was scheduled for three rounds, and we fought in headgear and ten-ounce gloves, even though the boxers who made it to Tokyo would compete with eight-ounce gloves and no headgear.

I was eager to get back at Mathis for his handing me my only loss as an amateur. I had knocked out two opponents to get to the finals and intended to give Mathis the asswhupping he deserved. But once again, when the dust settled, the judges had called it for Buster, undeservedly I thought. All that fat boy had done was run like a thief—hit me a peck and backpedal like crazy.

But amateur boxing is strange. By its rules, a flimsy jab counted as much in the scoring as a punch that knocked the other man down. The emphasis was on the "art" of boxing, so-called, which sometimes distorted the result.

Not only that, Buster had worn his trunks damn near up to his titties, so that when I hit him with legitimate body shots the referee had taken a dim view of them. In the second round, the referee had gone so far as to penalize me two points for hitting below the belt. In a three-round bout a man can't afford a points deduction like that.

Well, I returned to Philadelphia feeling as lowdown as I'd ever been. I was even thinking about giving up boxing. But Duke Dugent and Yank were able to talk me out of my doldrums and even suggested I make the trip to Tokyo as a sparring partner and an alternate to Mathis.

"But what about my job at the slaughterhouse?" I asked, afraid that Cross Brothers would fire me for taking leave like that.

But Duke, as an ex-policeman, was tight with the city's police commissioner, Frank Rizzo, who phoned Cross Brothers and got them to agree to hold my job. I still wasn't sure that I could afford the time off. By now, in addition to Marvis, we had two daughters, Jacquelyn, two and a half years old, and Weatta, thirteen months old, and money was tight for us. Florence was working for Sears Roebuck, bagging orders there, but even with her holding down a job it was a battle to make ends meet.

In the end, though, we decided to roll the dice: Off I went to the Olympic training camp in San Francisco at Hamilton Air Force Base.

While there, I was a workhorse, sparring with any of them that wanted the action. Middleweight, light heavyweight, it didn't matter to me: I got in there and boxed all comers. In contrast, Mathis was screwing off. In the morning, when we'd do our roadwork, he'd run a mile, then start walking, saying, "Go ahead, big Joe. I'll catch up."

Catch up, my black butt. He just didn't want to put the work in. Every day it was one lame excuse or another.

"I don't want to box today. My legs hurt."

Or, "I need to lose a few more pounds: I'll be ready to go tomorrow."

The guy didn't train, didn't box. The coaches were disgusted with him. I couldn't figure it out: a chance of a lifetime, and the big man was acting like he couldn't care less. It was strange, 'cause you couldn't meet a nicer fellow than Buster.

Whenever he'd see me, he'd give me a warm smile and a big hello and invite me to come by his room: "Big Joe! How you doing, man? Everything okay? Come on in. We'll talk."

He was a burly bear of a guy you couldn't help but like. But talking to him left you with the impression that his mind wasn't on Tokyo. It seemed like he was powerfully homesick, talking about friends and family back in Grand Rapids and the girl from there who wrote him every day. Those letters were dogeared from Mathis' reading them over and over.

Grand Rapids, Grand Rapids: He was constantly talking about going back there, and what he'd do once he got home. He never talked boxing, never talked Tokyo, or a professional career after the Olympics. My feeling was that Buster Mathis wanted out—he didn't want to be in the Olympics. And that just didn't make sense to me.

And it didn't make sense to the coaches. One of them, Freddie Lenn, thought I was the better, hungrier fighter, and he would tell me: "Stay ready, Joe. If something happens to this guy, if his fingernail hurts, you'll be going."

Toward the end of training camp, arrangements were made to put on an exhibition for the military brass at Fort Hamilton. That night, Mathis hit me with a shot on the head and felt pain in his hand. The next day they said he'd busted a knuckle. That meant Mathis was out and I would be going to the Olympics in his place.

Tell you the truth, I wondered whether the hand was really busted or whether the coaches persuaded him it was. It wouldn't have taken much to convince the fat man. Whatever; Mathis was out, and it hardly seemed to faze him. The next morning, when he saw me, he was as chipper as could be:

"Biiiig Joe. I ain't goin' to make it. You carry on. I'm going back home. Joe, man, you can do the job. I know you can do the job."

You never would have guessed that here was a guy who had just lost his chance to be in the Olympics. The big man was happy as a hog at the trough. Unbelievable.

Meanwhile, I phoned back home to give Florence the news. She was thrilled, and told me: "You win that gold, Joe. Then hurry back." My parents had no phone, but Florence passed word to relatives that did, and down the line it went until Rubin and Dolly Frazier heard their Billy Boy was fighting for the U.S.A. With that done, I packed my bags for the long flight to Tokyo.

The Olympic living quarters were divided into compounds—American village, German, Russian, and so on. Each country brought its own food. Some of the athletes would try the cuisine of competitors' countries. Me, I hadn't come those thousands of miles for the dining experience. I wasn't about to take any chances with my stomach. I ate the old standby diet of peas, potatos, rice, carrots, steaks—the food I'd grown up with.

Mornings, I'd do roadwork on the streets within the Village, or at the quarter-mile track in the stadium. Afternoons, I'd go to the gym and train. Tokyo was unlike any place I'd ever been—an exotic city with all kinds of sights to see. But I wasn't there to play tourist. I'd come this far for one reason only—to win the gold medal. Unlike Buster Mathis, I wanted to be here and wanted to show the world what I could do.

So I kept to myself, gearing up for what I had to do. This was an Olympic team with great athletes: runners like Bob Hayes, Henry Carr, Mike Larrabee, Billy Mills, and field men like Al Oerter (discus), Fred Hansen (pole vault) and Dallas Long (shot put), all of whom would win gold medals. But when push came to shove, it would depend on Joe Frazier to keep the U.S. from being shut out from a boxing gold medal in these Olympics.

See, by the time I had knocked out George Oywello of Uganda in one minute thirty-five seconds of the first round and then knocked out Athol McQueen of Australia in forty seconds of the third round, and stood ready to fight a huge Russian, Vadim Yemelyanov, in the semifinals, all other American fighters had been eliminated. That night I gave the six-foot-four, 230-pound Yemelyanov a beating. My left hook was a heat-seeking missile, careening off his face and body time and again. Twice in the second round I knocked him to the canvas. But as I pounded away, I suddenly felt a jolt of pain shoot through my left arm. *Oh, damn. The thumb.*

I knew immediately the thumb of my left hand was damaged; to what extent I couldn't be sure. In the midst of a fight, with your adrenaline pumping, it's hard to gauge such things. My mind was on more important matters. Like how I was going to deal with Yemelyanov for the rest of the fight.

Fortunately, there was no rest of the fight. The Russian's handlers decided their man had no chance, and they threw a white towel of surrender across the ring. At one minute and fifty-nine seconds of the second round the referee raised my injured hand in victory.

One more fight for the gold.

Although my thumb was throbbing with pain, I didn't say a word about it to the coaches, or my teammates. Later that night, I made my way to the medical clinic to have it examined. I was hoping to get a painkiller. But all they could do was ice it down and then wrap the thumb. When they offered to x-ray it, I said no. I wasn't about to blow my shot at the gold by having some medical official discover a fracture and scratch me from the competition.

I went back to the room and soaked the hand in hot water and Epsom salts. Pain or not, Joe Frazier of Beaufort, South Carolina was going for gold.

The opponent was a German named Hans Huber. Huber, a thirty-year-old bus mechanic, had tried to make his Olympic team originally as a wrestler. Failing that, he had competed for a spot on the boxing team and gotten it. He was taller and heavier than I was, but by now I was used to fighting bigger guys. What I was not used to was doing it with a damaged left hand.

But when the opening bell rang, I walked out and started winging punches. There would be time to heal later. Now was for the glory. More than I usually did, I threw the right hand that night. But I didn't discard that left. Every so often I'd crack the German with a left hook, even if it sent a spasm of pain up my arm. But nothing landed with the kind of impact I'd managed in previous bouts. With the limitations of my left hand, it wasn't an easy fight. But I went out there acting like I wanted to win.

Under Olympic rules, five judges scored the fight. That night three of them favored me, and the other two voted for Huber. By the narrowest of margins, I had won gold. And I was now the fourth American to win the Olympic heavyweight gold medal, and I would become the first American Olympic heavyweight champion who would go on to become Heavyweight Champion of the World.

Other Americans who would become heavyweight champions as professionals had won gold medals but in lower weight classifications—Floyd Patterson as a middleweight in the 1952 Olympics in Helsinki, Finland, and Cassius Clay as a light heavyweight at the 1960 Olympics in Rome, Italy. But nobody until me had done it as a heavyweight.

The thrill of representing the U.S. and winning despite a handicap—well, there was no feeling quite like that. I had taken a giant step toward my uncle Israel's casual prediction that Billy Boy would be the next Joe Louis. At the awards ceremony, I had a grin wide as a sunset, as four of Tokyo's prettiest girls, wearing beautiful kimonos, came into the ring with the medals on lacquered trays and hung the gold medal around my neck.

That night I celebrated by taking a few guys from the team out for *sake,* an alcoholic beverage the Japanese make from rice. As we downed shot glasses of the warm drink, I remember laughing a whole lot and feeling ten feet tall. What the hell. I had done it. I had made my mark on this world, and surely there were more good times to come. At that moment I figured that the gold medal was going to be my ticket to instant riches.

I couldn't have been more mistaken.

By Christmas that year, the Fraziers of Philadelphia were in trouble.

My thumb was dislocated and fractured in several places and would require two operations, several months apart, to fix. With my thumb in a cast, I was unable to do the work I'd been doing at the slaughterhouse. I thought maybe Cross Brothers would find other, easier work for me to do. After all, I'd won the gold for the United States. I figured that might be worth some consideration. But Cross Brothers didn't see it that way. Come back when your hand is healed, they said. Which was, it seemed to me, pretty damn cold.

That left us to live on the one hundred dollars a week that Florence was earning at Sears. And that left me to see if I could find a sponsor to help launch me as a professional fighter.

A car dealer from Boston, Peter Fuller, proposed managing me, but he wanted me to relocate to Boston—and relocate there without Yank. Fuller, who had managed Tom McNeeley, a white heavyweight who'd fought and lost to Floyd Patterson for the title, as his son Peter McNeeley would lose years later to Mike Tyson, said Yank could come later. But that sounded like baloney, like Fuller would try to shoehorn another guy in there as trainer. Without Yank, it was no-go for me. Yank was my man. I believed that together we had magic. But even though I declined his offer, Fuller and I remained friends. In fact, years later Fuller, who owned race horses, named one of the nags after me.

What I was looking to do was find a group of backers, like the ten rich white businessmen from Louisville who had bankrolled the heavyweight champion, Cassius Clay, when he had come back from the Olympics four years earlier. They had guaranteed Clay, who now called himself Muhammad Ali, a weekly salary of $150 and a percentage of his earnings. And he had done fine by them. I figured I'd be able to find a similar deal.

But when Yank approached some black businessmen from Philadelphia, they turned him down cold. The way they saw it was that Joe Frazier, gold medal or not, was nothing special. They figured my short arms, my lack of height and weight—at five foot eleven and one-half inches, two hundred pounds, I was small for a heavyweight—would be too much for me to overcome against the big guys that were campaigning as heavyweights. Guys that went six foot two, six foot three and weighed 220 or better.

That brush-off ticked me off; I won't pretend otherwise. I hadn't the least doubt I'd hand out asswhuppings to whoever was out there, and that included Clay his own damn self. I'd seen Clay on closed-circuit when he'd won the title from Sonny Liston in 1964 in Miami Beach, and followed his career since. He didn't strike me as the superman some folks made him out to be. Even while I was fighting amateur I was telling myself I could whup him . . . and some day I would.

Sure I had short arms. My reach was seventy-one inches, which, compared to some of boxing's all-time greats, was a joke. Sonny Liston's reach was ninety-four inches, Clay's eighty-two, Joe Louis' seventy-six. But reach doesn't win fights; men do. And I was all man, and never had trouble getting close enough to the guys that stood in front of me to put a hurt on them.

The doubt that those black brothers had . . . well, for a long time, folks just couldn't, or wouldn't, give Joe Frazier his due. I don't know why. They saw me different than I felt—they saw me as nothing really special. I look normal. Talk normal. Walk normal. But I'm different. I had the will to be a fighter—a fire burned inside that made no matter about reach, height, weight. Numbers, just numbers was all that was. A load of crap.

Come that Christmas season, things couldn't have been worse. I didn't even have money to buy Florence and the children gifts. But somehow, just before the holiday, newspaper reporter Jack Fried got wind of my situation and wrote a story in the *Philadelphia Bulletin* that the guy who'd given his all at the Tokyo Olympics was hurt both physically and financially.

Well, suddenly things began happening. Cash, checks (none of which bounced), and gifts started arriving. It was amazing.

A local radio station found out my address and sent a basket of fruit and gifts for the kids.

The aide to city councilman and attorney Cecil B. Moore appeared at my door with a golf bag full of five-dollar and one-dollar bills. Mister Moore had taken up a collection.

When a man walked into a radio station and gave the morning disk jockey twenty dollars for me, the deejay added another twenty dollars and sent it along to me.

A restauranteur named John Taxin gave five hundred dollars.

A group of sports fans from an investment firm raised one hundred dollars, as did a group from the Haddonfield (New Jersey) Methodist Church.

The holiday season that had been so bleak turned out to be as merry a Christmas as a man could want.

But it's funny: When you live in the spotlight, your money is an invitation for every dirty rotten scamboogah who's down on his luck, and you quickly learn to be on guard. When that unexpected money began raining down on us, and word of it appeared in print, I figured there was a chance it might attract some thieving rascal, looking to take what was ours. So I did what I could to protect ourselves, stuffing the cash in ceiling joists in case someone decided to pay a visit when we weren't around.

On the other hand I recognized how kind folks had been to us, many of them strangers. So when a neighbor showed up the day after Christmas needing a little help, I heard him out. This fellow said he lived down the street at such-and-such address and that a stove was being delivered there as we spoke. He told me his wife had the money to pay for the stove but had gone shopping—a case of bad timing. Could he, the man wondered, borrow the couple hundred dollars he needed to take possession of the stove.

"Don't worry," he said. "When the wife gets back, I'll get you your money."

Well, I'd been blessed. People had been so generous to me that I figured—what the hell, I'll help this neighbor out.

"Okay, brother. You got it. Just wait out there."

I had him wait outside so I could get the money without his seeing where I'd stuffed it. As I was pulling the money out of the ceiling, this neighbor shouted: "Hey, Joe. Hurry. The delivery guy's at the house."

I got the money and gave it to him. Once again, he assured me he'd be back to repay my loan once his wife got home. Well, you've probably figured it out by now: The address was a phony and so was he.

Florence was upset with me for being such a chump, and I couldn't blame her. For a while I would get steamed up thinking about how easily this fellow fooled me. But it didn't take much to cool me out. The hand was healing. Pretty soon I'd be doing what the Lord meant me to do.

Yeah. By spring I was back in the gym again, and raring to go. Yank and I agreed that rather than waiting for someone to back my career, we should go ahead by ourselves. The hell with arms-too-small and all that.

"We'll go it ourselves," said Yank, "until somebody steps forward. Okay?"

"Do you believe in me?" I asked.

"Goddamn right I do."

"Then let's get the job done."

Yank and I went to work. In the gym, he emphasized keeping that hook tight—as much for the damage I would avoid from counterpunchers as for the split-second advantage it would give me when I threw it. When I threw the hook too wide, he'd say: "Get your hand out of your ass." Yank had me keeping my hands up by my chin, and throwing the punch from there. Thrown from there, the arc was guaranteed to be tight. It was when I got lazy and let my hands down that the arc grew wider.

"You don't keep your hands up, you're gonna get dropped," Yank warned.

I continued to work out against little guys, and by now there were some pretty good ones in the gym—like Bennie Briscoe, Cyclone Hart, George Benton, Kitten Hayward, Willie (the Worm) Monroe, and Bobby (Boogaloo) Watts. All of them became top-ten-ranked fighters, and Worm and Boogaloo were among the few guys who beat Marvelous Marvin Hagler during his professional career.

With no sponsor, I did what I could to bring some money in. I worked for a moving company at two dollars and fifty cents an hour, and for the Reverend William H. Gray's Bright Hope Baptist Church as a janitor for even less. But they were jobs. They added to what Florence made at Sears and put food on the table for the kids. And pretty soon, I figured, I'd be giving back these jobs 'cause the money would be rolling in.

𝄡 𝄡 𝄡

Tell you this, though. It didn't roll in right away. From my first pro fight, on August 16, 1965, in Philadelphia I ended up with about $125.

The deal went like this: The promoter gave us a number of tickets to sell and said, "Whatever you sell, you keep." That was how Olympic gold medalist Joe Frazier got paid for his pro debut.

If the money wasn't much, neither was the opponent. Originally, I was supposed to fight a guy named Don Hobson. But Hobson changed his mind, as did the fellow they got to replace him, Roy Johnson. I read later that the guy that ended up across the ring from me in the Broadway Hotel, Elwood Goss, was a steamfitter who was recruited the day of the fight. The story goes that when they asked Goss, who supposedly had had a few pro fights, whether he would face me, he said, "Sure. Who knows. I might get lucky."

He was lucky, all right—lucky to get out of the ring in one piece. I hit him a left hook early in the first round and he went down in sections. That punch showed him that while luck pertained to dice and playing cards it had nothing to do with fighting Joe Frazier. Ole Woody Goss got over that fairy tale in a hurry, and for the rest of the round was clinging to me like last dance at the Milton Club. The ref, a former pro basketball player named Zack Clayton, got disgusted with the excessive holding and the ease I had hitting Goss and stopped the fight at one minute forty-two seconds of the first round.

"If they want a fight," Clayton told newsmen afterward, "let them get somebody who can fight. This guy can't fight at all. One punch will kill him."

In the dressing room after, Yank said: "We got him out of there. That's how we're gonna do 'em all. Get 'em the hell out of there."

Funny how things go. On the day I made my pro debut, fighting for chump change, my old nemesis Buster Mathis was at the Four

Seasons, one of the fancier restaurants in New York, announcing he was turning pro with a group called Peers Management. Peers was paying him a salary plus a percentage of his purses, just the arrangement I'd been looking for.

Even though I'd won the gold medal, fat lazy Buster was already ahead of me in the pro game. When would I catch a break?

I caught hell in my next fight, a month later, when the opponent, Mike Bruce, knocked me down in the second round. Embarrassed, I got up and made it through the round. But Yank told me, as he'd told me before, to get my hand out of my you-know-what.

I did: I knocked out Bruce in the next round.

A week later, another knockout . . . in two rounds over Ray Staples.

Abe Davis was next, on November 11, 1965. The poor guy stepped into the ring wearing tennis shoes, and trunks that looked like they came from a rubbish sale. When you're starting out, you get guys like that, who look like they don't have a clue about what they're walking into. Davis walked into my left hook and was counted out in one round—my fourth straight knockout victory.

But the thrill of victory was real short-lived. That night I got word that my daddy was in the hospital, and dying—hurry home. I took off in the middle of the night for Beaufort. By the time I got there the next morning, he had passed away. Dead of cancer of the lung at the age of fifty-three.

I hugged my Momma, and the tears fell.

"Well, son," she said. "Your pa's gone, and I don't know how I'm going to make it without him."

I tried to comfort her, but his passing hurt like nothing ever had in my life. It was so hard to think of him as being gone. He'd been everything to me. The images that played in my mind were of the man who could do the work of two men even with his one good arm. He could lift a hundred-pound sack of potatoes, drive a truck, drive a tractor, saw wood—you name it—with that one hand. He never once complained, and seemed satisfied it had to be that way. In fact, until I was about eight or nine I didn't actually realize there was anything unusual about Dad.

At least he'd been alive when I won that Olympic gold. That took a bit of the sting off it. Not enough, though, to lift my heart.

I didn't stay long in Beaufort after the funeral. With time passing and the progress I'd made since leaving, I had less and less desire to spend time in the South.

I'd do my grieving away from this place.

🥊   🥊   🥊

When a fighter starts out, if his manager is looking out for him, the guys he fights tend to be of limited skill. That was the case with my early opponents. They were what boxing insiders call "tomato cans" or "shmear cases." In Philly gyms, we refer to them as "dogmeat." Whatever. The idea was to let me settle in for a few fights and get comfortable with the pro game. There'd be time enough for getting it on with the badass boys.

The odd thing about these early fights was that because I was known as a vicious puncher, it wasn't easy to scare up opponents. And those that would agree to fight me wanted more than the going rate, knowing they'd likely be getting their bones dented. So the promoters would end up paying them more than the couple hundred dollars they paid me in those first four fights.

But my money problems were about to end. The Reverend Gray knew Dr. F. Bruce Baldwin, who'd been president of a local dairy and had acquired his Ph.D. with a thesis called "The Chemistry of Frozen Milk and Cream." Baldwin was now head of Horn & Hardart Baking Company and was just the man Reverend Gray thought could assemble a syndicate of backers for me.

It wasn't long before Baldwin had brought together a group of about forty investors, black and white, who bought eighty-odd shares of stock at $250 a share—roughly twenty thousand dollars as start-up money for the corporate entity called Cloverlay, Inc., that would run my career.

That original group included Thatcher Longstreth, president of the Philadelphia Chamber of Commerce; Arthur Kaufman, a department store executive; Harold Wessel, partner in the accounting firm of Ernst & Ernst; Milton Clark, president of a building maintenance firm; Jack Kelly, contractor, former Olympic sculler, and brother of Princess Grace of Monaco; sports columnist Larry Merchant, who now does commentary for HBO fights; and lawyer Bruce Wright, who would handle Cloverlay's day-to-day business.

By the original agreement, which started on December 16, 1965, I was paid a salary of one hundred dollars a week, a sum that would increase as the purses I earned increased. From those purses I got to keep 50 percent off the top for the first three years of the deal.

The deal was structured so that if Cloverlay chose to exercise its options, it would be in business with me for six more years—two three-year option periods. If they did exercise those options, then my share of my purses went up to 55 percent and, in the final three years, to 60 percent of my purses, again that money coming off the top.

Separate and apart from me, Yank was to get 15 percent of my purses.

The provision to take my share "off the top" meant that Cloverlay, not me, got hit with the operating expenses. By that clause, I would not be subject to the creative bookkeeping by which some managers and promoters cut into a fighter's money, screwing him out of what is rightfully his.

Under this deal, Cloverlay's share would be 35 percent of my purses, that percentage decreasing to 30 percent and then 25 percent through the final two option periods. From these percentages the corporation had to meet its overhead and contribute to its corporate profits.

In order to avoid a huge tax bite, I did not get the lump sum of my purses after each bout. Instead Cloverlay gave me 50 percent of what was due, and paid out the rest as a weekly "salary." That approach let me escape the wolfish appetite of the graduated income tax rate schedule.

At the start, the Cloverlay people got me a job working as a salesman for a maintenance firm—an additional sixty dollars a week plus commissions. At that point, every little bit helped.

If you're wondering about the name Cloverlay . . . it combined the word "cloverleaf" for luck and "overlay" from a betting term that means good odds.

It was just the arrangement I'd been hoping for.

The first chance that my new backers got to see what their fighter could do came on January 17, 1966, when I fought big Mel Turnbow. Turnbow was considered a step up in class from the guys I'd been facing. As a sparring partner for Floyd Patterson, he'd once knocked Patterson down in successive sparring sessions.

That night, Bruce Wright, the lawyer for Cloverlay, was sitting with his wife and another couple in the bar of the Hotel Philadelphia, while four floors above the night's preliminary bouts were going on.

Just about the time that my fight was scheduled to happen, Wright began to rouse his party to head upstairs. At that moment, the ceiling shook and the dim clamor of cheers could be heard. Startled, Wright and the others made a mad dash for the stairwell. By the time he and his companions arrived in the auditorium, Turnbow was stretched out unconscious. In a neutral corner, I was grinning broadly at having knocked out the six-foot-three, 231-pound man in one minute and forty-one seconds of the first round.

The lesson was when Joe Frazier was fighting, don't be late . . . because Frazier worked as if he was doubleparked. From then on, Wright, and the folks from Cloverlay, learned to save that martini for after the fight.

There wasn't much of a crowd that night—621 customers paying $2,187. I got my $250 guarantee, and Cloverlay took $125 as its share. Yank's cut was $37.50. A slim payday. But with Cloverlay aboard, I felt things were bound to get better.

By now the local press was taking notice of "Smokin' Joe" Frazier, a name that had come from what Yank used to say in the dressing room before sending me out to fight:

"Go out there, goddammit, and make smoke come from those gloves. You can make smoke, boy. Just don't let up."

Smokin' Joe: It was a name that suited the aggressive, unrelenting way I worked an opponent, always moving forward, snorting and grunting as I came. If a freight train wore boxing gloves they could have called it Smokin' Joe as easily.

Even though the guys I fought early on were far from world-class, I fought them as though they had the abilty to ruin me. Wasn't no fooling around, or taunting or ridiculing them; I was dead serious when that bell rang, and went after them with—what's that expression—yeah, malice aforethought.

Wasn't no pity in my heart for them. If I hurt the guy, I wanted to put some more hurt on him and get him the hell out of there. The way I saw it, this guy was trying to mess up my future. Folks asked was I sorry about having to hurt these overmatched opponents? Yeah, sorry I couldn't get to them faster.

Like Dick Wipperman. On March 4, 1966, at Madison Square Garden, it took me five rounds to knock him out, which as these things go was a long night's work for me.

Maybe it was the prefight psych job Wipperman did that enabled him to last that long. One of my corner men had been in his dressing room before the match to watch his people tape Wipperman's hands, and he told me Wipperman was saying: "My name is Richard Wipperman. Richard for Richard the Lionhearted. And Wipperman, if you break it down, means whip a man. And that is what I'm going to do."

Some other night maybe. But not with Rubin's Billy Boy.

Exactly a month later, on April 4, Charley Polite went out in two rounds, with a broken jaw for which Cloverlay sent him an extra $250 to help him with his medical expenses.

"We are," said Dr. Baldwin, "a corporation with a heart."

That night, when I busted Polite's jaw, he did something that I'd never experienced. He flinched and then moaned—a straight-from-the-gut cry of pain that caused me, for a moment at least, to do something I ordinarily didn't do when I had a guy in trouble. I stepped back and looked in his eyes. I was so startled by his moaning that I hesitated, which was contrary to my take-no-prisoners approach.

By now I'd gotten my first serious national press mention when *Sports Illustrated,* scouting the up and coming heavyweights, wrote:

> *Frazier's forte is a strong left hook.*
>
> *"He's an excellent banger," says one Philadelphia trainer. "But."*
>
> *The but is his tendency to be a "one-arm banger," relying too much on the left and neglecting to develop the right.*
>
> *He is also a fierce competitor in the gym, a common failing among his home-town confederates that has given rise to the unflattering term, a "Philadelphia fighter," that is, one who leaves his fight at home. If this is true of Frazier, it has not been evident in his pro fights. He has won all seven by knockouts.*

Also mentioned in the article was Mathis, who by now had a five-and-oh record and was called by the magazine "the best news for reluctant dieters since Kate Smith."

I couldn't help but feel that Buster and I were on converging paths and that in the not-too-distant future would be tangling with one another again.

For now, though, I was fighting other men, and fighting them as regular as church bingo.

April 28	Don (Toro) Smith	Pittsburgh	KO 3
May 19	Chuck Leslie	Los Angeles	KO 3
May 26	Memphis Al Jones	Los Angeles	KO 1
July 25	Billy Daniels	Philadelphia	TKO 6

A year into my pro career, I was eleven and oh, all knockouts. Except for Daniels, an experienced veteran, most of the guys I'd whupped were picked as bodies for me to beat on. But even Daniels, who was supposed to be savvy enough to make a fight of it, was no challenge. I beat on him until the referee had the good sense to stop the bout.

Between what I was learning in these matches, and what Yank was giving me in the gym, I'd become a bona-fide fighter. Oh maybe there were some rough edges, still, that had to be smoothed. But there was no question in my mind, or Yank's, that the time had come to find out whether I could go with the big boys.

3

EMPTY POCKETS AIN'T MY FASHION

Every time I'd be in the same room with Oscar Bonavena, he'd tilt his chin up and start sniffing, his expression contemptuous, as if there was a foul scent in the room, as if Joe Frazier smelled like dogshit.

A weird guy.

Bonavena, who was from Buenos Aires, Argentina, was to be the first ranked fighter I would meet. He was a tough, experienced brawler, built like a bread van, with broad shoulders and a barrel chest. His movements in the ring were stiff, like Robby the Robot's. But crude though he was, he was strong and durable, with a chin that other fighters had hit without often upsetting Bonavena's equilibrium.

Zora Folley, a clever boxer, had knocked him down in the early minutes of their bout, yet Bonavena was fighting back at the end. And though often outslicked by Folley that night, and eventually beaten, Bonavena was never out of contention because of his punching power, stamina, and determination.

When I first met him, Bonavena acted like he did not know much English, but years later, when I'd run into him in Las Vegas, he knew enough *Ingles* to ask me: "Where's the pussy, Frazier?"

Bonavena didn't have any language problem on that score, so it didn't surprise me when still later Bonavena got into a big jam because of a woman. In the state of Nevada, there are legalized brothels. Bonavena not only managed to find one but also stole away with the girlfriend of the owner of the place. Some time later, he decided to return there, without the girl, and get her clothes to take back to Buenos Aires. Talk of foolhardy. Anyway, one thing led to another. Bonavena was shot and killed.

But that is getting way ahead of our story.

For in the autumn of 1966, Oscar Bonavena was alive and well, and sniffing the air like some police-trained German shepherd.

If it took a while to make the match, it was because Bonavena was cagey when it came to getting the *dinero*. When Teddy Brenner, the matchmaker for Madison Square Garden, went to Buenos Aires to sign him for fifteen thousand dollars against 30 percent of the net gate, Bonavena claimed to have a previous commitment for a fight at Luna Park, a sports facility. When Brenner told him he'd already cleared it with the Luna Park people, then Bonavena said, "Okay. I fight if you give me all television and radio rights in my country."

Brenner agreed to that, but the Garden screwed up that understanding when it sold the Argentinian rights over Bonavena's head to a network the fighter had no participation in.

"I do not fight," Bonavena said, just weeks before the September 16 match was to take place.

He wasn't fooling either.

"We're sorry," Brenner said, trying hard to appease him. "It is a terrible mistake."

"I am sorry, too," Bonavena said. "I am so sorry, I go home to Argentina."

"Can't we straighten it out?"

"No. I have a contract for four thousand dollars for the television in my country. That is what I want or I do not fight."

The Garden offered three thousand dollars.

"It is a nice number," said Bonavena. "Now I fight."

With a record of 23–2, Bonavena had more than twice as many fights as I did. That experience counted for plenty with some experts, who predicted Bonavena would beat me because of it.

For my Cloverlay backers the skepticism of a few so-called experts was nothing. They were convinced, no less than I was, that Joe Frazier was indestructible—and a future champion. While these men had invested their own money to help assure that future, it wasn't the expectation of getting stinking rich that had prompted them to lay out that two hundred fifty bucks.

It was for the excitement of being up-close-and-personal to a fighter who figured to be in the thick of the heavyweight action over the next few years. As a Cloverlay investor, you got privileges that the paying customer didn't. For that $250, a Cloverlay man could stop by the dressing room before the fight, and say hello. Afterward, there was the victory party at which he could pose for a photo with the warrior he'd backed with his money.

The pleasure was not unlike what folks get from being at tailgate parties before the big NFL game, or from being part of a rotisserie baseball league—a kind of boys-only excitement that being around sports gives the average man. For the Bonavena fight, as for future fights, many of the Cloverlay backers chartered a railroad car for the ride up to New York from Philadelphia.

Imagine all that clamor—the bar-car drinks and the boasts of what their guy would do to the shaggy-haired Argentinian. And then early into the second round, boom, a right hand by Bonavena and their man Frazier was on his butt in the middle of the ring at Madison Square Garden, with 9,063 maniacs screaming in English and Spanish. Yeah, if Bonavena's one-two sobered the Cloverlay guys up in a hurry, guess what it did to me.

I'll tell you this. The knockdown wasn't what boxing people call a "flash knockdown"—a knockdown that results from being hit while off balance and finds the fighter jumping right to his feet, clear-eyed and with a sheepish expression. Uh uh. Bonavena hurt me with that right hand, hurt me like I hadn't been hurt since Georgie Boy had sledgehammered me that first day in the PAL gym. I'd walked into Bonavena's right like an innocent who'd strayed into the war zone.

And when I hit the canvas it was as though I'd been awakened abruptly from a deep sleep. I was aware of my surroundings, and conscious of being in big damn trouble, as I got to my feet at the count of five and the referee, Mark Conn, gave me the mandatory eight count.

The challenge became to survive the round. But when Bonavena knocked me down a second time, pushing me more than punching me this time, it added to the pressure I was under. I was this close, now, to being beaten for the first time as a professional. Why? Because by the New York state rules we were boxing under, if a fighter knocked his opponent down three times in any round, the bout was automatically stopped.

With more than a minute left in the round, I did what I had to. I grabbed Bonavena and drew him into a clinch. He couldn't push me away quickly enough, desperate-crazy as he was to land that punch that would put me on the canvas a third and final time. But I had enough survivor's instincts to stall him while the lights came back on in my head.

Bonavena shoved and shouldered me, he pushed and pulled, and he swung wildly with both hands. But I stayed close to him, trying to smother his punching room. And when I could, I grabbed his arms and held him until the referee broke the clinch. By the end of the round I was clear-headed and fighting back.

You can guess what Yank told me between rounds—in his usual earthy way of speaking.

Well, I got my hands out of my butt and began banging away at Bonavena. But this guy was a hard-headed son of a bitch and it felt like I was punching concrete. Where other opponents had had the good sense to crumble when I hit them, Bonavena stood and took my punches without showing much affect.

It didn't take me long to realize this would be a real dogfight, and not the usual kick-butt-and-let's-party. Bonavena not only stood up to punches better than the men I'd been fighting, but he kept me from working at close quarters, where I was most effective. Whenever I'd get near enough to throw the left hook, he'd either entangle me in a clinch or push me backward with theatrically extended arms, as if he was showing off his massive biceps.

Back in the corner, Yank told me: "Don't let him straighten out those arms."

Easier said than done. At 225 pounds, Bonavena had about twenty pounds on me, and his strength was equal to mine. To beat him, I realized, I was going to have to outwork him. Punches in bunches—that was the only way to overcome those early knockdowns and re-establish myself with the three men scoring the fight.

It was hard work. Bonavena knew how to use those big arms of his to obstruct some but not all of the punches I threw. So I just kept at him, banging him wherever and whenever. It was a saloon brawl, with punches landing north and south of the waistline, and the referee acting as if it was all entirely by the Marquis of Queensbury.

Nothing fancy went down on this night. Neither of us was built for slick boxing. My game is, and always would be, punch and then punch some more, forever moving forward. Bonavena cooperated by being Bonavena. He stood there in his flat feet and sumo wrestler's stance, and was as mobile as a stanchion. That meant I didn't have to chase him. We fought.

When the final bell rang, after ten rounds, the night's work came down to what Conn and the two judges had to say. Conn's scorecard had it six rounds to four, my favor. (These days referees no longer score fights, but back then they did.) But one of the two judges, Nick Gamboli, scored the bout five rounds apiece, with Bonavena ahead on points, due to the two knockdowns, eight points to five. That meant the decision came down to the other judge, Joe Eppy. Eppy voted five rounds for Frazier, four for Bonavena, and one round even. By a split decision, I'd won my twelfth fight and had remained undefeated.

But while it was my biggest payday to date—a purse of five thousand dollars—it was a hard day's work . . . and something of a disappointment. In what amounted to my first big-fight exposure, I'd wanted to shine like a gem, and hadn't. I'd won, but had struggled to get through those ten rounds, providing ammo for critics who contended I was a lopsided fighter—all left hook—and so predictable as to be beatable by a shrewd boxer-puncher.

While the critics weren't entirely wrong—I was a fighter who relied heavily on the left hook, maybe too heavily by conventional wisdom— they missed what made me a whole lot more than met their critical eyes. An opponent might know what was coming when he fought Joe Frazier, but it didn't mean he'd be able to handle it, any more than hurricane warnings guarantee safe passage for anybody in the eye of that storm.

Before I fought Bonavena, there were investors in Cloverlay, and sometimes the occasional sportswriter, who would push for me to fight Ali for the title. As early as my fifth fight, that first-round kayo of Mel Turnbow, some of the investors began whispering into Yank's ear, "Ali . . . Ali . . . Ali."

Yank told them that in due time I'd whip Clay, but Yank Durham would say when that time was. Until then, the chief asset of Cloverlay, Inc., would be out there learning his business so that when he stepped into the ring with Clay, or whoever else might be champion, he'd come out of the fight the winner.

On the ride back to Philadelphia after the Bonavena fight, I urged Yank to make my next match against the veteran Eddie Machen.

Machen was that type of fighter—slick boxer, tricky and tactical—that the experts were sure I'd have trouble with. Machen had gone twelve rounds against that heavyhanded slugger, Sonny Liston, in 1960, only two years before Liston had knocked out Floyd Patterson to win the heavyweight title. Five years later, in 1965, Machen lost a fifteen-round decision to Ernie Terrell for the WBA heavyweight title. In sixty-one fights, only one man, Ingemar Johansson, had knocked out Machen.

Machen had experience, and against very talented fighters. I was determined to fight opponents I could learn from. I was in a hurry to get to the top, where the money and the glory were, and figured serious competition would get me there quicker and overcome whatever reservations the critics had about Smokin' Joe.

Yank's judgment—that it was too soon to fight Clay—bugged me, even though I understood that he just wanted to be safe rather than sorry. In my heart I felt what I'd felt watching Clay beat Liston for the title—that I could beat this loudmouth sucker. But then again, that sort of confidence was what enabled a fighter like me to operate the way I did, accepting punches to land my own.

The Bonavena fight might not have been a bust-out success to win over the boxing establishment, but that was no reason to grow cautious.

Yank agreed, even though he was criticized by the press now for, quote unquote, "moving his fighter too fast."

Two months later, on November 21, 1966, I was in Los Angeles, looking across the ring at Eddie Machen. Machen was a counterpuncher, with more moves than Allied Vans—slide moves to avoid getting hit, a robot jab that he brought up from the floor, and sucker shots that he fired with his hands down when he came bouncing off the ropes.

He was good, real good, but against the pressure I applied he wilted. Still, he caught me with some serious shots—a few late in the fight when

I thought I had him on the verge of a knockout. I took his best punches and came back at him with a nonstop attack that forced the referee to halt the bout in the tenth and final round.

Machen? He told newsmen afterward: "Frazier needs polishing, but he's awful good. The boy has no defense, but the way he stays on top of you, he don't need one."

With the victory over Machen, the damage done to my reputation by the close call with Bonavena was partially repaired. And with each fight that followed in 1967—knockouts over Doug Jones in six rounds in February, over Jefferson Davis in five rounds in April, and a ten-round decision over George (Scrapiron) Johnson in May—the attention being paid to Smokin' Joe, and the money, intensified.

Even Clay took notice, whoofing in public about fighting me, even as he was preparing to defend his title against Zora Folley in March 1967 at Madison Square Garden.

I decided to go up to New York to watch him work out. Clay spotted me and called me over. We made small talk a while, and then Clay began kidding me about the suspenders I was wearing beneath my sports jacket.

"Look at this guy," he said. "He's behind the fashion, wearing suspenders."

"They're good for holding your pants up," I told him. "Ain't much fashion if your trousers are drooping."

"No, Joe Frazier. You're a step behind the times. Just like you'll be if you ever get crazy enough to fight me."

"Then *you're* gonna need a pair of these," I said, tugging at my suspenders. " 'Cause when I get through with you, you sure as hell gonna need something to hold you up."

"Don't even dream that, Joe Frazier. It's a sin against truth."

"The truth hurts, Clay. And I'm the truth."

"Clay? I ain't no Clay. Aint you heard, Joe Frazier? Muhammad Ali is the champion of the world. Float like a butterfly and sting like a bee."

Ali was the name he took in 1964 when he announced that had converted to the Black Muslim faith.

"Okay, Butterfly," I told him. "Say goodbye to the Butterfly catcher."

It was good-natured kidding, and I was smiling as I left the Garden.

A week or so later, on March 22, Clay knocked out Zora Folley in seven rounds to retain the heavyweight championship. It was his ninth successful title defense in three years. Who could have guessed at the time that it would be some three-and-a-half years before the Louisville Lip, as sportswriters called him, would fight again?

What happened to cause this? Well, in 1966, the draft-exempt status Clay had been given after flunking the army's mental exam—"I never said I was the smartest; I said I was the greatest"—was changed to 1A. Civilians listed as 1A were in the first rank to be drafted. In other words, if you were 1A, Jack, you were going. Soon after, Ali was made a Muslim "minister" in order to claim a clerical exemption.

That led to the circumstances of April 28, 1967, in Houston, Texas. There, a little more than a month after beating Folley, Clay declined to take the step forward that would have made him a soldier in Uncle Sam's army. He told newsmen: "I ain't got no quarrel with those Viet Congs."

For his refusal to be inducted, he was convicted of draft evasion, fined ten thousand dollars, and sentenced to five years in prison, pending appeal.

"What can you give me, America?" he said, after the WBA stripped him of his title. "You want me to go fight a war against people I don't know nothing about. You want me to go get some freedom for other people when my own people don't have freedom at home?"

It sounded like a bunch of bullshit to me—words to justify his actions. Me, I was married with children, which made me ineligible for the draft. But if I'd been single, like Ali, I'd have had no problem serving this country if that draft board had called me. In fact, I tried to join the military when I was fourteen, but wasn't accepted. Ours is a great country, and worth defending. What Clay did was to make himself out as a man of conscience instead of the draft dodger he was.

A lot of people bought the man's jive, and pretty soon had him as a political cause—a kind of revolutionary figure. What a bunch of baloney that was. As I got to know Clay, I saw that all his political and racial mumbo jumbo was a smoke screen. Clay pretended to be out there doing battle for black folks, but in fact he didn't care about nothing but ole Cassius.

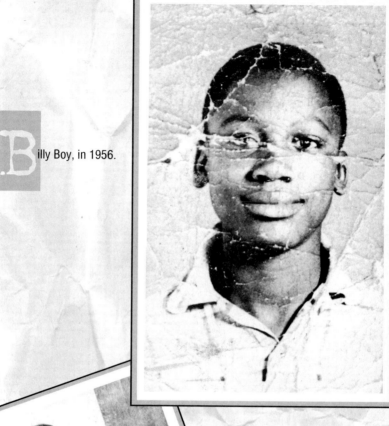

Billy Boy, in 1956.

My daddy, Rubin Frazier, at home in Laurel Bay, South Carolina, 1963.

My momma, Dolly Frazier.

When Buster Mathis broke a knuckle, I took his place at the 1964 Olympic Games. Despite a broken thumb, I beat Hans Huber to become the first African-American Olympic Heavyweight Champion.

Calling Florence from Tokyo with the good news that I'm bringing home Olympic Gold.

Already into my pro career, here's a familiar pose—this one's after my eleventh-straight knockout, against Billy Daniels on July 25, 1966. *Courtesy United Press.*

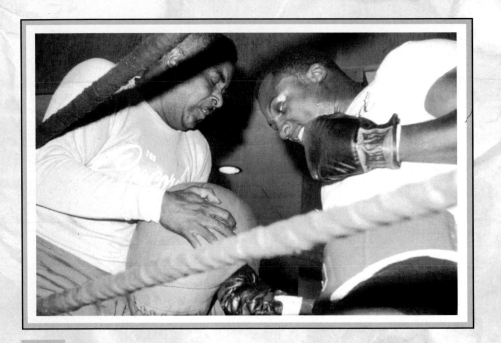

Hitting the medicine ball with Yank Durham in September 1966, as we prepare for the Bonavena fight. *Courtesy Associated Press.*

Me with the men who helped me put food on the table during my early professional days, including some of the Cloverlay investors, 1967.

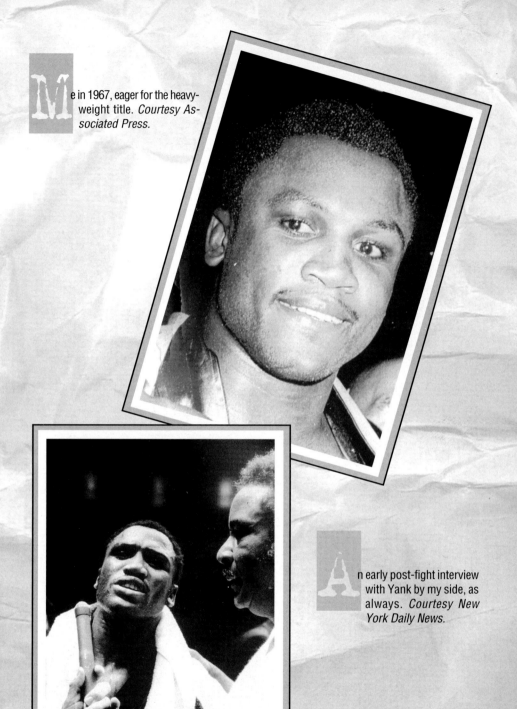

Me in 1967, eager for the heavyweight title. *Courtesy Associated Press.*

An early post-fight interview with Yank by my side, as always. *Courtesy New York Daily News.*

Post-fight congratulations from George Chuvalo, July 19, 1967, after I TKO'd him in four rounds. *Courtesy George Kalinsky.*

Training on the heavy bag for the vacant New York heavyweight title fight against Buster Mathis, 1968. *Courtesy George Kalinsky.*

Working up a sweat on the speed bag at the Concord, where I trained for many of my fights. *Courtesy George Kalinsky.*

An important part of training for any fight—relaxation and publicity photographs. *Courtesy George Kalinsky.*

Florence, Jacquelyn, Weatta, me, and Marvis on the Concord training camp playground in 1968.

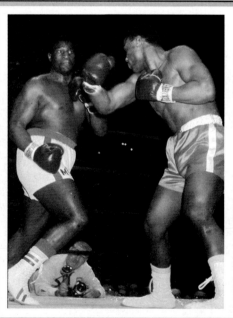

The Buster Mathis fight, on March 4, 1968. After a slow start, I knocked Mathis out in round eleven to win the New York heavyweight title. *Courtesy George Kalinsky.*

oncentration is an important part of a boxer's prefight regimen. Here I am in my Philadelphia gym preparing for the 1968 Bonavena fight. *Courtesy Big Book of Boxing.*

scar Bonavena enduring the ritualistic prebout exam, as I look on. In front of my hometown fans at the Philadelphia Spectrum, Bonavena toughed it out for fifteen rounds before I was declared the winner. *Courtesy Wide World Photo.*

After I TKO'd Jerry Quarry in seven rounds in 1969, my next bout was with Jimmy Ellis. Here's Ellis and me sharing a laugh at the prefight press conference.

Knocking out Jimmy Ellis on February 16, 1970, to win the undisputed world heavyweight title. *Courtesy George Kalinsky.*

This is one of the best known photographs of me and Clay, taken after one of my workouts for the Fight of the Century. Clay's hamming it up—what else is new?—outside my gym in Philly. *Courtesy George Kalinsky.*

Chatting with the Brown Bomber, Joe Louis, who showed up for the Frazier-Clay I prefight medical exam. *Courtesy Wide World Photo.*

With the ink still wet, the contracts worth $2.5 million are displayed. True to form, the Butterfly plays it up for the press. Yank is standing over my right shoulder, next to Howard Cosell. *Courtesy George Kalinksy.*

The photo shoot of me and Clay with Madison Square Garden photographer, George Kalinsky, during which I unintentionally scared him in the ring. *Courtesy George Kalinsky.*

THE FIGHT

The Fight of the Century was the biggest worldwide media event of the year, and our purses—$2.5 million each—were the highest ever seen. Our earnings set the precedent for athletes in all sports. Here's one of the countless promotional pieces that was sent out from Madison Square Garden. *Courtesy George Kalinsky.*

Posing for a publicity shot to hype the Bob Foster bout in Michigan on November 18, 1970. I knocked him out in two rounds.

Left to right) Archie Moore, Bob Foster, and I take time out to attend a benefit dinner in 1970. *Courtesy New York Daily News.*

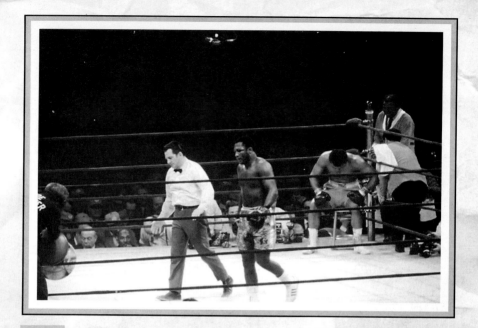

The Fight of the Century, March 8, 1971. For all his prefight talk, the Butterfly isn't looking too good in his corner. *Courtesy George Kalinsky.*

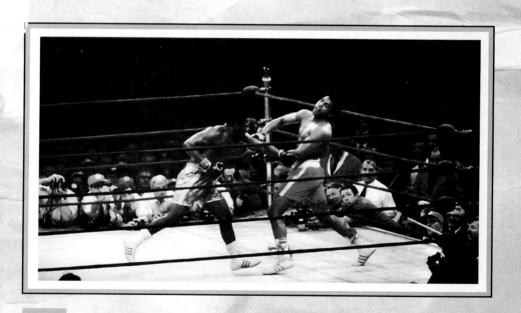

The Punch of the Century. Clay gets a feel of my left. *Courtesy George Kalinsky.*

Moments later, Clay hits the canvas. Round fifteen. Somehow Clay was able to get to his feet, but the fight was almost over, and The Fight was mine.

The Heavyweight Champion of the World exits the ring with bodyguard Ed Harrell (left), having shown the world who really is "the greatest." *Courtesy New York Daily News.*

Whatever. By refusing to be inducted into the armed forces, the man had brought helter-skelter to the heavyweight division. After the WBA stripped him of his title, the New York State Athletic Commission did the same. Clay was banned and his title was vacated.

The WBA then came up with a plan for a heavyweight elimination tournament to find the successor to Clay as champion: Their top eight ranked boxers were chosen to fight it out.

They were Floyd Patterson of Marlboro, New York; Jimmy Ellis of Louisville, Kentucky; Thad Spencer of San Francisco, California; Oscar Bonavena of Argentina; Ernie Terrell of Chicago, Illinois; Karl Mildenberger of Germany; Jerry Quarry of Bellflower, California; and me, Joe Frazier, of Philadelphia, Pennsylvania.

The only problem with the WBA's scheme was that Mr. Yancey (Yank) Durham wasn't buying it.

"Screw their tournament," he said. "I don't need them, they need me. Let them fight it out and I'll fight the winner."

Yank was gambling on the public's recognizing me as the real deal in the heavyweight division, now that Clay was out of the picture. While there was money to be made in the WBA tournament—escalating purses that for a finalist would amount to $175,000—once a WBA champion was crowned, there'd be only one big-money fight out there: that WBA champion against Smokin' Joe Frazier.

At least that was the way Yank saw it, and that was the way Yank talked it to Cloverlay's board of directors. On May 10, 1967, the board voted unanimously to back Yank's play, and then told the press of its decision, saying that not only was the money not enough but it refused to give the tournament's promoter, a group called Sports Action, the ancillary rights for two years to its chief asset should he emerge as champion.

In the meantime, Madison Square Garden had offered me fifty thousand dollars to fight George Chuvalo that July. Chuvalo was a fighter with a reputation for taking punches without showing any visible effect. The Human Shock Absorber of the heavyweight division.

Over the years he had fought the best men in the division—fighters like Clay, Terrell, Patterson, Bonavena, Folley, Mike DeJohn, and Doug Jones. And while most of them had beaten Chuvalo, in sixty-two bouts none of them had been able to knock the twenty-nine-year-old Canadian down or knock him out. Trying to knock down Chuvalo, it was said, was like trying to knock down Canada's Parliament Building in Ottawa. It just couldn't be done.

Well, the night I fought Chuvalo I put a crimp in the reputation he had for being indestructible. From the opening bell, I began tattooing that big-jawed face with left hooks. Almost immediately, small cuts opened under Chuvalo's left eye and under his right eye.

By the second round, the swelling around Chuvalo's eyes grew worse and his face was smeared with blood. But give him credit, Chuvalo hung in there. In the third round, in a kind of last-ditch effort, he went toe to toe and landed a few good licks, rousing the crowd of 13,984 paying customers.

By now, though, the cuts and bruises were turning purple. Chuvalo looked bad enough to prompt Dr. Edwin Campbell, the New York State Athletic Commission physician, to examine him between the third and fourth rounds. Campbell let the fight go on, but it wouldn't last long.

At the start of the fourth round, I walked out and hit Chuvalo with a left to his already-closed right eye. Suddenly he turned his back to me and groped his way to his corner, like a man feeling his way through a pitch-black room.

It turned out a blood vessel leading to his eyelid had erupted. "My eyeball felt like a grapefruit," Chuvalo would say afterward. "The pain was excruciating. I thought my eye was going to come out."

The referee, Johnny Colan, stopped the fight.

Days later, Chuvalo, complaining of pain and double vision, ended up in a Toronto hospital to have surgery for a bone fracture under his right eye.

The victory did nothing to jeopardize my standing with the boxing public. But it did aggravate the WBA enough so that I was dropped to the number-nine spot in the rankings . . . from the number-two spot I had occupied. That put me just to the rear of the eight-man pack that had agreed to take part in the WBA's elimination tournament: Bonavena, Ellis, Leotis Martin, Mildenberger, Patterson, Quarry, Spencer, and Terrell.

A transparent move, right?

But it did not faze me. For one thing, it was so clearly a politically inspired demotion that even a grade-schooler could see what the WBA was up to. Besides, I wasn't without those who felt I deserved better. The response of the New York State Athletic Commission chairman, Edwin B. Dooley, was to declare Joe Frazier the commission's top-ranking heavyweight contender.

It would be Dooley and his commission who would make the next move to challenge the WBA's claims on choosing a successor to Clay as champion.

It happened after I scored knockouts over Tony Doyle in two rounds in October and over Marion Connors in three rounds in December. That was when I signed to fight my old nemesis, Buster Mathis, on March 4, 1968—the main event of a doubleheader that would inaugurate the newest Madison Square Garden, a forty-three-million-dollar circular building on West Thirty-third Street and Seventh Avenue.

Dooley agreed to sanction the fight as a title bout, the winner to be recognized in New York as heavyweight champion of the world. In time, five other states—Pennsylvania, Texas, Illinois, Maine, and Massachusetts—announced they too would recognize the winner as champion.

For me the circle had closed. The man who had twice beaten me as an amateur was within my gunsights again, and I couldn't wait to get at him.

While Buster had turned pro at roughly the same time I did, he hadn't made nearly the impact. Although he was undefeated as a professional—twenty-three and oh, seventeen wins by knockout—Mathis hadn't fought the quality of competition I'd been in with. His opponents included people like Tom Swift, Everett Copeland, Charlie Chase, and a Waban Thomas, names that did not exactly ring bells in the boxing hall of fame.

As I jokingly told a reporter: "Mathis? Oh, yeah. He's the one who fights those guys that get carried in on crutches."

In actual fact one opponent of Mathis did fall down in anticipation of punches, then asked Buster for his autograph after the bout. Mathis' defense of his reputation was to point to a knockout he scored over a Gerrie De Bruyn, who had battled ninth-ranked Eduardo Corletti to a split-decision loss. Talk of roundabout ways of establishing your credentials.

Where Yank and Cloverlay had moved me smartly through the ranks—and gained wide public recognition for me—Mathis' people had struggled to get their man taken seriously. There were still questions about whether Buster could really fight.

Mathis' Peers Management was run by a couple of newcomers to boxing, Jimmy Iselin, twenty-five, and Mike Martin, twenty-six, both sons of wealthy and successful fathers. Iselin's old man, Philip, was the president of the Korell Company, and Martin's father, Townsend, was an officer of Bessemer Securities Corporation. Both older men were major stockholders in the New York Jets football team and in a race track.

The younger Iselin and Martin, like a lot of guys with money, thought that they could walk onto the fight scene and, presto, find magic with their fighter. But give them this. The boys gave it a grand shot, with an approach that was a lot more promotional-minded than Cloverlay's. Iselin and Martin had had thousands of key chains, lighters, and buttons made up to hand out to newsmen and other opinion-makers. These trinkets all had Mathis' name and likeness on them and the words: "Next heavyweight champ."

In all, the Peers boys would sink about $150,000 into Mathis, going first class in their operation. On the grounds of their fighter's Rhinebeck, New York, training camp, they converted a barn into a gym for Mathis, and then waited for him to blow out the competition. Well, after seven fights, Buster was looking so dismal that Iselin and Martin went out and hired Cus D'Amato to train their guy.

D'Amato had been manager/trainer of two past world champions, Floyd Patterson and light heavyweight titleholder Jose Torres. With those, and other fighters of his, D'Amato insisted on being more than a boxing tactician. He wanted to be involved in molding the fighter's mind and, some said, in making him beholden to Cus D'Amato for how that fighter saw the world.

D'Amato had his share of critics, who saw that Svengali approach as phoney baloney. Eventually, Mathis, who'd lived with Cus in a neat seven-room clapboard house on the Rhinebeck site, was among the detractors.

He told newsmen: "In many ways, Cus hurt me. I just wasn't going any place with him. He was a hard person to get along with. I hated to work for him.

"He tried to brainwash me. He tried to make me be exactly the way he wanted. He wore hats. So I had to wear hats. He was always around. I felt like I had had no freedom. If I wanted to watch TV, there was Cus deciding what to watch. If I wanted to go out, Cus wanted to know where."

Even though D'Amato had helped Mathis slim down from 300 pounds to 244 pounds, and even though he had sharpened his technical skills, the Peers boys felt that D'Amato's cautious nature was keeping their fighter from developing.

"D'Amato personally refuses to be a loser, so he holds a fighter back," Iselin said.

By that they meant D'Amato wouldn't risk Mathis against the kind of stiff competition that tests a fighter and makes him grow.

After D'Amato had worked with Mathis for eighteen months, Peers fired him. It was June 1967. Not much would be heard from D'Amato until nineteen years later, when he resurfaced with a new young heavyweight, a kid named Michael Gerard Tyson.

After Peers canned D'Amato, it replaced him with Joe Fariello, who'd once worked as a boxer and trainer under D'Amato. (Fariello would go on to train Buster's son, Buster Mathis Junior, for a fight against Mike Tyson in 1995.)

"D'Amato belittled Buster," said Iselin. "He didn't treat him with respect. A fighter without pride is nothing. Joe Fariello's changed that."

Well, all of that sounded like excuses being made beforehand for Mathis. Which was okay with me. I figured he'd need a whole ton of excuses when I got through with him. So why not let him get in practice now?

The idea that this fight would be for the title that Clay had held seemed to offend a lot of people, plenty of them black. As fight night approached, all these radical black cats were camping out by the Garden, picketing the fight. Those scamboogahs wanted the heavyweight division to stand still because Cassius didn't want to wear the olive-green fatigues for Uncle Sam.

On TV, you'd see them—the playwright Leroi Jones, Lincoln Lynch of the United Black Front, Floyd McKissick, national chairman of the Congress of Racial Equality. All of them pissing and moaning about poor Clay and holding news conferences to denounce the fight.

Well, that was their right and privilege. I didn't give a damn, though, what they said. Clay was not on my radar screen any more. The Butterfly had flown off, leaving the field open to the rest of us.

For me, this was what I'd been fighting for—a chance for the big money and the prizes. Those black radicals could say this and that—it didn't matter. I'd fought for this opportunity. I'd punched and got punched. And with my body, and blood, I'd paid the price.

Now it was time to collect on the hard work. For fighting Mathis, I was to make $175,000—a far cry from how it was when I'd started out.

That things had gone well in those three years I'd been a pro . . . that was obvious enough from the accounting ledgers at the Cloverlay office. After three two-for-one and one eight-for-one stock splits as dividends, an original $250 Cloverlay share now went for $7,200. The number of shareholders had grown to five hundred.

And face it: I was living better. No longer was I at Aunt Evelyn's place; with Florence and the kids, I'd moved into a four-bedroom semi-detached split-level home on Ogontz Avenue in West Oak Lane, a nice section of Philadelphia. I now drove a plum-purple 396 Turbo Jet Sports Impala and wore more stylish clothes, including a size forty-six burgundy-red suit that was a particular favorite and several that were tailored in the mod style that was in fashion then—doublebreasted, eight-buttoned, near-thigh-length jackets and ten-inch vents on the side, with bell-bottomed trousers. And come Christmas, I didn't have to depend on strangers to provide for my wife and children.

Yeah, the days of selling tickets to make my purse—those days were well behind me. The Lord had blessed me, putting me in this position, and I would pay no mind to naysayers and doomsayers and Clay apologists of any color. Screw 'em. My mind was on Mathis.

A few weeks before the fight, just to mess with *his* mind, Yank sent Mathis a wooden toy figurine of a devil. The object had a button you pressed that ejected a tiny placard with this message: Go to hell.

When Buster got it, he figured it was from me, showed it to a reporter, saying: "Joe, he have a simple sense of humor. Imagine him giving me this thing. He's liable to get me mad. But you can tell him this for me. I got a nice gift for him"—the clenched fist rising predictably.

When Buster's words, and gesture, were relayed to me, I told the reporter: "Buster say that? Shoot. He don't know no better. All this talk, you can be sure of only one thing. Once the bell ring, he gonna run like a thief."

Well, fight night came and, after the cofeature saw Nino Benvenuti regain his middleweight title from Emile Griffith, there was a knock at the dressing-room door, and the man was saying, "Frazier. Main event. You're on."

The Garden was rockin' as I walked down the aisle toward the ring. A crowd of 18,096 had paid $658,503, and among them was D'Amato, sitting up there in the cheap seats with a pair of binoculars. Me, I couldn't wait to get through those ropes and give my fat friend Buster the ass-whupping that would set him straight on who the better man was.

Mathis' best rounds were early. He was on his toes, moving well while firing off quick left jabs and snappy combinations. The referee, Arthur Mercante, had Mathis winning five of the first six rounds, and one of the other judges, Jack Gordon, gave him four of those first six rounds. Only judge Tony Castellano had me ahead at that point in the fight.

But this wasn't the amateur game, with its short fights and sissy scoring. This was the pros. Me and Buster were in there for the long haul, and I knew I was going to break him down sooner or later.

From the beginning I was raking his body with the hook. And while it didn't appear to affect his agility and stamina through those early rounds, I was sure that that old boxing cliché—kill the body and the head goes too—would take hold.

Nice as Mathis was as a human being, as a fighter I always suspected he was operating with, as they say, a defective ticker—no heart. I know that's kind of a rough thing to say, but boxing is a world of harsh truths and inevitable consequences. And that's what I believed that night in 1968, and nothing would change my mind after Mathis and I fought.

See, his size fooled people. They looked at how big he was and figured—whoa, this guy is an assassin. But he didn't have that mean thing in his heart. The guy was just so nice. I'm a good fellow too, but the bell rings, I come to kill Momma, no doubt about it. And I could feel the lack of that instinct in him. He didn't throw punches like a vicious guy. When a guy is grunting at you, he wants to kill you. What do dogs do before the bite you? *Rrrrhhhhh.* He was not that kind of guy. Buster was a great guy, a sweet guy. And seemed like he'd be just as happy if he drove a mail truck the rest of his life.

Truth is, from the sixth round on, as the fight was removed to a confined space, Buster was dead meat. All that hippety-hop stick-and-move of Buster's ground down, while my attack didn't. As the air came out of Buster, and he could no longer dance away from me, he showed me he had no appetite for the slam-bam kind of fight I was bringing. Suddenly, he was hiding his head behind his gloves, crouching as if to hide his $243^1/2$ pounds from harm. It was the body language of a scaredy-cat and it jacked my spirits up. Blood to sharks.

"Work, Buster, work," I teased him, as I slammed left hooks off his body and head.

I had him. We both knew it. It was just a question of time. Well, the eleventh round, it turned out, was when it finally happened. A right to the chin, a left to his temple. For a moment, Buster seemed frozen in space, like a tall tree just before it falls.

Then he toppled over, flopping backward through the ropes and onto the canvas that was stained with blood streaming from his nose. Mathis lay on his back for several seconds, his eyes rolling around in his head, his belly heaving, his mouth wide open and gasping for air.

By the count of eight, he was staring glassy-eyed at the ringside customers below him.

At nine, he slowly arose. He was staggering as he reached his feet, and held himself bent over the upper rope.

And that sorry sight was enough to prompt Mercante to stop the fight.

Hooo-boy: I was beside myself with joy. Yank charged into the ring like a big rhino and embraced me.

"Cocksucker, we done it," he said.

And damned if we hadn't. Heavyweight champion.

Of course, the writers afterward made sure to diminish the moment by asking did I really feel like the champion.

"What was that supposed to be out there?" I quipped.

But I understood the deal . . . understood that the ghost of Cassius Clay was in that building.

It's what the Butterfly had said would happen when he'd flown the coop. Yeah, he'd told the press he'd come back and mess with the game.

"There I'll be, wearing a sheet," he said, "and whispering, 'Ali-iiii, Ali-iiii.' I'll be the ghost that haunts boxing, and people will say Ali is the real champ and anyone else is a fake."

Well, I was no goddamn fake. That much I knew.

And I was hoping some day to have the chance to prove it personally to the loudmouth from Louisville.

4

THE LOUISVILLE LIP

For seven weeks, there was just me, Smokin' Joe, as heavyweight champion.

Then, on April 27, 1968, the WBA tournament was concluded, with Jimmy Ellis winning the title in a fifteen-round split decision over a tough white boy, Jerry Quarry. Now there were two men claiming to be *the* best heavyweight in the world. Not to mention the haunting man, Clay, who kept insisting that the title really belonged to him.

Yeah, Clay was here, he was there, he was everywhere, insisting the boxing organizations had done him wrong in taking his title. There was nothing I could do about the Butterfly's situation. The draft-dodging business was beyond my expertise. But if Clay could get free of all that, I had a lip buttoner in the form of my left hook to shut the boy up.

Until then, I had to go about my business, hoping Yank could persuade Ellis to fight me. I didn't much like the idea of another pretender to the throne.

But it quickly became clear that Ellis was in no hurry to meet Joe Frazier. What's it they say? Discretion is the better part of valor. In other words, Ellis and his manager, Angelo Dundee, knew that if Ellis got in the ring with me, their chance to exploit that WBA title would be blown lickety-split.

Dundee, who had trained Clay, among many other champions, was nobody's fool. A world title is negotiable, a ticket to make lots of

63

money. Champions can and do demand to be paid big bucks. So Angelo did what loads of boxing men before him had—he milked the title.

Why fight Smokin' Joe, who hits like a mule-kick, snorting and grunting and making you fight to the point of exhaustion? There were lots easier ways to make a living and stretch the value of that WBA title.

Like Floyd Patterson. That was a stroll in the park, compared to having me get on your ass. Ellis fought him in his first title defense, winning a fifteen-round decision in Stockholm, Sweden, where Patterson was a hero.

In the meantime, Yank hadn't any other alternative but to keep me busy—fight whoever was out there that the public would pay to see. Keep busy, make money. The business that I was in was—you punch me, I punch you. And for that, the man gives us cash dollars.

Manuel Ramos was a rarity, a Mexican heavyweight. He was six foot three, with a reputation for taking a good punch. Ramos, the son of a civil service clerk, had never been knocked down or, it was said, sustained a cut.

His record—20–6–2 with eighteen knockouts—was deceptive. All of his losses had occurred early in his career, when he'd come up from Mexico City to fight in Los Angeles. Since 1966, though, he had won fifteen straight bouts, twelve of them by knockout. And that streak was not against tomato cans. Ramos had beaten Machen, Terrell, and James J. Woody.

Machen, who was knocked down by Ramos, said of him: "I was hitting him to death, but he's a strong guy, a tough guy, he's got a lot of heart, he come to fight, man. And he's got a good chin. Don't sell him short, he comes to fight."

The Ramos fight was set for June 24 at Madison Square Garden. My deal was a guarantee of $120,000 against 40 percent of the net gate and ancillary rights, including television.

Unlike Buster Mathis, Ramos was no runner. The big guy dug his heels in and let the shit fly. Early into the first round, he hit me with a right hand that was like an electrical charge. It sent a jolt through my bones and buckled my knees. The man was a serious puncher.

And so we got to it, two guys standing in the trenches playing hit-me. It was my kind of fight; a no-frills punchout. We just stood there and whaled, each of us believing his punch would break the other man down.

For about two minutes, Ramos was whacking with conviction. He caught me two or three shots to the head and had me thinking: "Whew, this is some mean stuff." But by the end of that first round he was slowing down and I wasn't. I nailed him four, five hooks in a row, pinning him in a corner of the ring and leaving him groggy as the bell ending that first round sounded.

Between rounds, Yank told me: "Goddammit, get closer and stay down lower."

The idea was to take away Ramos' punching room.

Like Machen said, Ramos had come to fight. But after that hellacious first round, there wasn't as much fight left in him. I did what I had to, hitting him whenever and wherever. Ramos tried to fight back. But I could see by the look in his eye that the heat I was bringing was too much for him.

I knocked him down with a right early into the second round. Ramos took the mandatory count of eight, and got up looking like a Halloween mask. His right eye was swollen and beginning to close, he had a cut on his left cheek and egg-sized lumps on his forehead. Late in the round, I knocked him backward onto the seat of his trunks. He got up again, but just as the bell rang he signaled the referee, Arthur Mercante, that he no longer wanted to continue. Ramos didn't realize the round was over and didn't care. Enough was enough.

It was a strong showing: Smokin' Joe being Smokin' Joe. But even after so convincing a demolition job, it wasn't enough to persuade some folks that they'd seen the real champion that night. No, the haunting man still was on their mind. Like Arthur Daley, *The New York Times* sports columnist, who wrote:

> *By knocking out Ramos, the busy bee from Philadelphia strengthened his hold as a partial champion. Unless Cassius Clay can escape from his private war with the draft board and can soon meet Frazier, he might find Joe too tough to take a few years from now.*
>
> *It still is my conviction, though, that the swift Clay would jab Frazier dizzy and prevent him from getting inside to wreak havoc. It's also my conviction that Cassius would be able to throw enough rights on that exposed chin to bring down the prize investment of the Cloverlay Syndicate that keeps collecting stock dividends on the interregnum champion.*

Well, that's what they paid the Arthur Daleys for—to say what was on their mind. But it didn't mean much to me. Every joker with a typewriter had an opinion. And hadn't guys like him said that Cassius Clay was a bum before the Butterfly whupped Sonny Liston?

Now it was my turn to be taken for granted.

I could handle it, even when Clay complicated the situation. And of course he *had* to say something. Wherever he went, Clay talked up Clay.

Sometimes he would act like he was Christ on the cross—claiming he was in the jam he was in because of his religious beliefs: "If I have to go to jail, I'll study to become a topnotch minister—no phones to bother me—and stay in shape, if the food's good.

"It may seem gloomy now 'cause I can't fight now, but when I come out it'll be bigger than Jack Johnson, Dempsey, Louis, and Marciano. Can't you hear them now? 'Can he still fight? Has he still got it? Did he lose his legs?' Ooh, it'll be big."

Other times, he played it for laughs, as when he recited a poem about what would happen to me if I ever got into the same ring with him.

> *The referee wears a worried frown*
> *Cause he can't start counting 'til Frazier comes down.*
> *Who would have thought when they came to the fight*
> *They'd witness the flight*
> *Of the first colored satellite?*

And once he even pretended that he wanted to rumble outside a radio station in Philadelphia, where we'd just finished bumrapping one another over the airwaves.

When I stepped out onto the street, Clay was waiting for me, as though he was going to ambush me. I took it for playacting, even when he threw a long, looping right that landed on my shoulder. It was a jive punch, and from his expression I recognized he just wanted to create a scene. When I feinted like I was going to give him all he could handle, folks who weren't quite sure whether this was for real or not broke it up.

And that was that, except for Yank telling the news guys: "If Clay gets a license to fight, we'll fight him. Until then, we're willing to use him as a sparring partner—and we'll pay him."

In those days, Clay was living in Cherry Hill, New Jersey, across the bridge from Philadelphia. So he was around a lot. And whenever we'd meet and there was no crowd nearby, he'd tell me: "Just keep whuppin' those guys in the ring and I'll keep fighting Uncle Sam. And one day we'll make a lot of money together."

Word was that for all the lecture appearances and his stint as an actor in an Off-Broadway musical *Buck White* Clay made it to the gym often enough to keep in good shape. He also ran frequently in Fairmont Park. In fact, one time we bumped into each other while I was out doing roadwork.

Clay being Clay, he put his hands up and started jiving. He liked to do that with guys who were possible future opponents. He wanted to measure them to see if he could hit them. When I pushed his hands away, he said: "You really think you can whup me?"

"I'll whip Momma she try to take my title."

"I think you mean that, Frazier."

"You doggone right I do."

"Well, let's get it on right here," he said, flicking his left at me.

I blocked his left, then walked away, telling him: "I ain't fighting you now, Clay. I don't want to waste it in private. I want the whole world to see what I'm gonna do to you and in a ring, not here."

In those days, we were on a friendly basis—rivals who could talk to each other in a reasonable way. That was mostly when there were no crowds, microphones, or cameras. Once Clay had an audience, he was like the comedian who opened the refrigerator and, seeing the light go on, had to do ten minutes of his best material.

That was goddamn Clay—a nonstop self-promoter. The sucker had fifty-seven varieties of bullshit—and he needed it all. With a legal bill reported to be up around $280,000, Clay was hustling the buck on the lecture circuit, talking up the Black Muslims and his favorite subject, himself.

The rumors of his coming back to box again wouldn't quit. Everywhere you went there'd be this whisper, and that. Clay was going to fight in Salt Lake City. Clay was going to fight Bob Foster. No, Floyd Patterson. No, Eduardo Corletti, an Argentinian who lived in Rome and frequently fought in London. Clay was going to . . . going to . . . going to.

All that got tired after a while. There was nobody I wanted to fight more than Clay. But until he got his situation straight, I had to concentrate on the live bodies out there, and the hell with the Butterfly.

In December 1968 in Philadelphia, I fought a return match with Bonavena and beat him again, by unanimous decision, in a fight that was easier than the first time. Easier but not easy. Bonavena was a guy I couldn't crack. He had a style that for me was like oil and water.

It's that way in boxing. Certain guys who don't figure to be a big problem end up being hard to solve. Ken Norton was like that for Clay. Michael Spinks was like that for Larry Holmes. And Bonavena was like that for me. In two fights, a total of twenty-five rounds, I couldn't put his big butt on the canvas.

Strange, because other guys who didn't have the punch I possessed—namely Zora Folley and Jimmy Ellis—*had* knocked Bonavena down.

It ticked me off that I couldn't dispose of Bonavena, because I didn't like the guy. That arrogant air of his, and that habit of sniffing— I'd go into the ring with more rage than I did against most opponents. Deep down I thought Bonavena was a racist, and that when he made faces as if the air was foul, he was saying—you niggers all stink.

Yet in the ring I tried to keep those personal feelings in check. I wanted to maintain my cool . . . because you can throw your punches out of whack by being angry. After weeks and months of preparation, why get crazy and wild now? It was not the professional way. You don't get emotional in training camp. And a fight is no different than a workout. Just get the job done.

The job paid me $105,000 plus a graduating percentage of ancillary income. Bonavena's purse was $75,000 plus expenses, and South American ancillary income.

Dave Zyglewicz was next, in April 1969—for 40 percent of whatever the gate would be at the Houston Coliseum. Zyglewicz was a white guy from upstate New York, who had read an ad in *The Ring* magazine, placed there by a Houston fight manager :

YOUNG BOXERS WANTED

I want boys from 18 to 23 years old that weigh around two hundred pounds and six feet tall who want to become scientific boxers and make a lot of money. It's all free. If accepted I will send you a ticket, take care of you on arrival and get you a job so you can train after hours. I have three of the finest trainers in the world and one of the finest equipped free gymnasiums and I supply all training clothes and equipment free. Give weight, height, age and nationality. No experience is necessary.

—Hugh S. Benbow, manager of Cleveland Williams, hardest hitting heavyweight contender in the world.

SEND PICTURES TO A & B GYM, 110¹/₂ TRAVIS STREET, HOUSTON, TEXAS.

At the time he picked up that copy of *Ring*, Zyglewicz was finishing up a hitch in the Navy. When he was mustered out, he notified Benbow, who sent him bus fare to Houston. Five years and twenty-nine fights later, as a 10–1 underdog, he now had a shot at the heavyweight title and that bundle of money that Benbow had promised—20 percent of the night's gate proceeds. It was a story that seemed to be out of a movie script.

Only this time there was no Hollywood ending. Before a crowd of ten thousand Zyglewicz came out at the opening bell with bombs-away abandon, but sobered up once I began hitting him. I knocked him down twice in the opening round. The second time he hit the deck, he received what sounded like moral support from the referee, Jimmy Webb. Webb, a light-heavyweight contender in the early 1940s, administered the knockdown count like this: ". . . Seven, get up. Eight, get up. Nine, get up."

But Ziggy, as they called him, wasn't getting up on this night, not with what I'd laid on him. It was the second-fastest knockout in heavyweight-title history—thirty-six seconds of the first round. A forty-thousand-dollar quickie of payday for me.

The press made the fight out to be a farce and wondered out loud whether Smokin' Joe was ducking the serious contenders to fight dogmeat. Ducking, hell. Get me Ellis. Get me the Butterfly. But there was nothing doin' with either of those guys. Address unknown.

So we shut the critics up by signing to fight Jerry Quarry, at Madison Square Garden on June 23, 1969. My guarantee would be $205,000 and 20 percent of the door.

Quarry was a skilled counterpuncher, with quick hands, a decent punch, and a good head for tactics. The fight the experts projected was the boxer versus the brawler—Quarry using the jab to keep me at bay and spearing me every chance he got with right hands delivered over my attempts to reach him with my left. That was the match that on paper figured to happen as long as Quarry could keep me at a distance.

But through twenty-three fights so far, nobody had been able to prevent me from fighting my fight. I was the irresistible force, as well as the unmovable object.

Yet Quarry was no slouch as a fighter, and had an appeal that made the public snap up tickets, even the hundred-dollar ringside seats that were the highest-priced tickets ever for an indoor heavyweight title match. Why not? He was a good-looking Irish kid, with a nice smile and an engaging boy-next-door manner.

But Quarry hadn't had the kind of *Leave It to Beaver* upbringing you might have figured. He'd been raised to be a fighter by his father, Jack, a rough sort of man who had the word HARD tattooed on his left fist and LUCK on his right. Old Man Quarry had been a club fighter in his youth. And when the fighting part of his life was done, he'd bolted from the Texas dust bowl and went looking for a better life.

The first home of his that Jerry could remember was a tent in Utah that his parents and the five children shared. From there they headed for the promise that California held for so many poor folks. And like so many poor folks, like the Fraziers of Beaufort, South Carolina, what work they found was in the fields for wages that barely supported a family.

With Pappa Jack training him, Quarry had his first fight when he was only five years old, and as a schoolboy won Junior Golden Glove titles from 1955 through 1958. While shuttling between thirty different elementary and high schools in California, quick-tempered Jerry broke his right hand punching a baseball umpire and later needed twelve stitches to close the bloody gash he got when someone smashed a pool cue over his head.

That pool cue didn't knock any sense into Quarry's head, if what he was saying in the weeks leading up to our fight was any indication. The noise coming out of Quarry's training camp was full of fist-waving bravado, Quarry making as though he was going to put aside tactical considerations and go toe to toe with me.

"I'm ready for anything Joe Frazier can hand out," he told newsmen.

I didn't know whether he was just blowing smoke, or meant to be that brave on fight night. It didn't add up, though. In the past, Quarry had been criticized for being overly cautious in the ring. And in boxing, as in life, a leopard doesn't often change spots.

But before a Garden crowd of 16,570, that chalk-Irish fellow did what he threatened: He took me on at my own game. Jerry Quarry really did want a war, and he didn't have to look far to get one. For three minutes of that opening round, we stood in the center of the ring and threw head-rattling shots at one another.

Forget stick and move. This was a night for blood lust. The crowd was roaring as Quarry traded bombs with me. Whatever made him fight this kind of fight, he sure as hell wasn't pretending. He hit me with big, noisy punches, and kept coming. And coming hard. Two rights of his slammed off my head, and hurt. But not enough to keep me from firing back.

Truth is, even though he was getting the better of these first-round exchanges, I felt exhilarated. A punchout nose-to-nose, without having to chase the scamboogah—I was in my element. For me there was nothing like the feeling of letting it rip and seeing which man would break.

Whatever might be happening now, in this opening round, didn't concern me. Wasn't anybody, I felt, who could stand up to fifteen rounds of pure and unadulterated Smokin' Joe. Yeah, Quarry was there to fight and was giving me hell, but it was early, and easy now.

By round two, Quarry still wanted to rumble. I couldn't figure why he'd choose to challenge a puncher like me dead-on. Whatever his thinking, Quarry came out firing again in the second round, as if he'd decided this night would be his ultimate test of will, and courage. So be it. I lowered my head and took him on. I felt the sting of his hooks to my liver and spleen, but made him wince with the blows I returned to his body.

As the rounds unfolded, Jerry Quarry would come undone. Not all at once. He was determined to fight to the last. But the signs that he was headed for trouble were there to see. Where early on he'd held his right hand protectively against his cheek, the better to ward off my left hook, now he began to drop the hand so that his elbow and forearm might obstruct the shots I hit him in the body with.

And where earlier I'd had all I could do to fend off his furious assault, now I was smiling through my mouthpiece, mocking him as he hit me with punches that had nothing on them. Or I was telling him, "You through? 'Cause it's my turn now."

And I took my turn, believe me. Hit the sucker north and south— all over. Late in the third round, I landed a left hook that opened an inch-long cut beneath his right eye, on the cheekbone. At the end of the round, Dr. A. Harry Kleiman of the State Athletic Commission's medical staff examined the wound, and, in response to Quarry's plea to let the fight continue, waved Quarry back to action.

But the action got more and more one-sided, and the cuts and bruises on Quarry's face got more scary. Both eyes were swollen and closing. Quarry, though, wouldn't quit trying. He'd made up his mind to take the hard road. But when Dr. Kleiman got another look after the eighth round, he signaled the referee, Arthur Mercante, that Quarry had had enough.

As Mercante waved an end to the fight, Quarry protested, stomping about the ring, tears mixing with the blood on his right cheek.

Quarry was not the first opponent who'd dreamed big and crashed. I'd busted other guys' bones, shattered their careers and sent them into deep depression. Boxing is a hard business . . . and a sometimes cruel and unforgiving one. After big Mathis had lost to me, his management had added insult to injury by telling reporters that they intended to take down all the pictures of Buster from the wall of the gym he trained in.

"He's going to have to wash dishes if he wants to be fed, and help clean the gym and his room," Iselin said. "He will either respond as Joe Louis after being knocked out by Max Schmeling, and become a great fighter, or go the other way."

For me, though, the dream that had kept me pummeling that burlap sack, back in Beaufort, South Carolina, was well on its way to being fulfilled. Say "Smokin' Joe," and people knew you meant the fighter. I was no longer a face in the crowd—I was the face that excited the crowd.

I was a champion, with the earning power to live beyond even what that stocky Carolina farmboy in overalls could have imagined. What did Billy Boy know of trust funds and stock splits and treasury bills and annuities? For me they'd become the stuff of everyday business.

With my cut of the gate, I'd earned four hundred thousand dollars for knocking out Quarry. I had a house; money in a time savings account, at $4^1/_2$ percent interest, at the Provident National Bank in Philadelphia; trust funds for the children; Cadillacs and Chevies and a twenty-five-hundred-dollar, twelve-hundred-cc motorcycle that had made the Cloverlay folks jittery when I bought it and absolutely nuts when I crashed the sucker in Philadelphia and then a second time down in Beaufort.

Bruce Wright and his lieutenants tried to persuade me to retire the motorcycle, but I liked my hawg too much to play that. I say you have to go all the way, whatever you do. Besides, Cloverlay was doing damn fine with me. By the time I fought Mathis, one of those $250 original shares was worth fourteen thousand dollars, and potential new stockholders were elbowing one another to buy in. Among the big-name folks who had become stockholders were Pete Retzlaff, the Philadelphia Eagle end, ex–heavyweight-contender Dan Bucceroni, and the sportscaster Les Keiter.

A taste of this good life made me hungry for more. You get one car, you want two. So you work harder. You get a new house, you look around for nice things to put in there. So you work harder. You beat Mathis for the title, and you want that goddamn crown of Ellis' too.

No sooner had Mercante stopped the Quarry fight than my mind was running to the next obstacle, that scamboogah Ellis, sitting there at ringside next to Angelo Dundee. Only by whupping Ellis would that nasty phrase "partial champion" that the press liked to use, when it mentioned me, disappear. Looking down at Ellis I shook my still-gloved left hand at him and told him: "I got more of this for you."

"We got you, sucker," Dundee shouted back, with a grin.

"Any time, baby," I told them. "Any time."

Whether Ellis really wanted to risk his WBA title against me, who could tell? Earlier in the year, a match between us had almost been made. A date was agreed upon, and the percentages each fighter would get were all but settled. But at the last minute Ellis, who would have gotten 32 percent of bout revenues, compared to my $27^1/_2$ percent, backed out, claiming that fighting at Madison Square Garden—where I'd fought so often before—gave me a kind of homecourt advantage.

It sounded pretty lame. To me it didn't matter where I had to fight a guy or what time of day they wanted to turn the lights on to show it. Get the money, sign that contract, and let's get to work.

With Ellis, though, it was always something. Before he decided he couldn't fight me at the Garden, he'd used as an excuse the nose that Patterson busted when the two of them fought. That nose was the longest-running excuse I'd ever heard. Every time we'd approach Ellis' people about getting it on between us, the goddamn nose was still too tender to take up negotiations. A Guinness Book of Records nose it was.

You had to wonder about this guy Ellis. After he'd beaten Patterson in a disputed decision, Ellis kept signing for fights that came undone— three fights canceled for one reason or another. Coincidence? Or was the guy afraid that even a Henry Cooper or Gregorio Peralta—two of the jokers he had been scheduled to fight—might get lucky and defeat him, blowing a payday with me that got more lucrative every time I beat up a Ramos, Bonavena, Zyglewicz, or Quarry.

Well, after the excitement of the Quarry match, the public's eagerness for Frazier versus Ellis, and its box-office potential, must have been obvious even to Ellis. This time, as negotiations started up again, there were no excuses or bogus reasons from the Ellis side to blow off the showdown to unify the heavyweight title. In late December, right before New Year 1970, Ellis and I arrived in New York to sign for a February 16, 1970, fight at the Garden. Each of us would be guaranteed $150,000 against 30 percent of bout revenues, including ancillary rights.

Once we signed the contracts, the Garden had us pose separately for publicity photos. At one point, the photographer splashed a little water on Ellis so he would appear to be sweating.

"Hey, Ellis," I called over. "You better look good now, 'cause I'm going to make you look bad."

"Man, you better not even think that."

But it's exactly what I thought.

Jimmy Ellis' careeer had been a strange one. He'd started out as a middleweight who got beat more than scrambled eggs. Holley Mims beat him. Henry Hank beat him. And in one year alone, 1964, Ruben (Hurricane) Carter, Don Fullmer, and George Benton all whupped him. It was at that point that Ellis, on the verge of retiring, decided to write to Angelo Dundee and ask the veteran trainer to become involved in his career. At the bottom of the letter, Ellis signed his name and added a single word that summarized how lowdown he'd sunk: H-E-L-P!

Angelo Dundee was not the Hollywood image of a trainer—you know, the tough-talking loner with a lifetime cigar. Angelo was a small man—five feet seven and a half inches—who was outgoing and upbeat, a man who joked and mixed easily with others, including fighters.

He'd worked as a trainer or manager or both with champions like Willie Pastrano, Carmen Basilio, Luis Rodriguez, Ultiminio (Sugar) Ramos, Jose Napoles, Ralph Dupas, and of course Clay.

Dundee had a reputation for being able to think on his feet during fights. When Clay fought in England against Henry Cooper in 1963, a left hook floored the Butterfly at the end of the fourth round. Clay was on his feet but dazed when the bell rang. Between rounds, however, Dundee made an issue of Clay's gloves being split. The maneuver bought time—new gloves had to be found—and allowed Clay to clear his head. He knocked out Cooper in the next round.

The next year, when Clay went for the title against Liston, he came back to the corner after the fourth round in a panic. His eyes were burning from the liniment Liston's corner was using. With his vision impaired, Clay wanted to quit. "Cut the gloves off," he told Dundee. "I can't see."

Dundee was convinced that the condition was temporary, and refused. "This is the big one, Daddy," he shouted. "Jab and keep circling until your eyes clear."

When the bell sounded for the fifth round, Dundee lifted his fighter off the stool and pushed him across the ring. By the seventh round, the bout was over. Liston was on his stool, complaining of an injured shoulder, and Clay was the new world champion.

Dundee got Ellis' letter and agreed to work with him. Soon after, Ellis had his tonsils removed and his body began to fill out. As he grew into a heavyweight, Dundee had him spar regularly with Clay—as much for the press to notice him, he said, as to have Ellis absorb the moves the Butterfly could show him.

Ellis became a boxer-puncher. He had a quick and powerful right hand, and yet in most of his fights he fought so cautiously that the right hand was a state secret. Dundee called him "a beautiful boxer but deadly dull and also deadly efficient."

It was a mistake, though, to disregard his power. In March 1967, Johnny Persol, a light-heavyweight fighter Madison Square Garden had high hopes for, walked into that right and was knocked out in the first round.

The victory opened the door for Ellis in that WBA tournament. And he took advantage, beating Bonavena in a preliminary round and then Quarry for the WBA championship.

Ellis had come full circle. Where once he had been better known for being Ali's sparring partner than a legitimate contender, now he was WBA champion, victor in twelve straight bouts and part-time employer of Clay, who'd gotten one hundred dollars a day to spar with Ellis earlier in that summer of 1969.

Ellis told newsmen that Clay had been sharper than he had expected him to be, given his inactivity as a fighter.

"I thought he was as fast as ever, though he did tire more easily," Ellis said of Clay.

Whatever. The ring work seemed to inspire Clay, who soon after showed up in Philadelphia to heckle me on a radio talk show, calling me flat-footed, slow, and without class.

By now the Butterfly's case was on appeal to the U.S. Supreme Court, and it seemed he had nothing better to do than mess around with Joe Frazier. At first I'd ignored the jiveass sucker, letting him talk his shit, figuring that it was building interest in the fight between us, if it ever happened.

But the more Clay talked, the more personal he made it. And truth is, I was getting tired of it. Clay might be a big deal to the media and to folks who bought his martyr act. But to me Clay was like a big spoiled kid who needed to have attention, and would do anything to get it.

I didn't dig his coming into my city, and acting high-hat on me. While he was dodging the draft, and talking about it on the lecture circuit to pay his bills, I was earning my upkeep by getting down with the Bonavenas and Quarrys. I had fought my way up from nothing. I'd earned my way with hard work, work that was owed respect. But this scamboogah thought nothing of talking about me as if I was some head-scratching dumb nigger.

Talking about me being flatfooted and ugly.

So I told him: "Show up at the PAL gym and we'll have it out. We'll see who the real champ is."

Well, when Clay showed up, so did about a thousand civilians . . . for a gym that seated maybe fifty or sixty spectators. The police arrived and, realizing the fire hazard, told Clay and me to take our little show to Fairmont Park.

"I came here to rumble," Clay hollered. "If Joe Frazier don't follow me, I want it known he backed down."

Clay, who, like me, had been in boxing clothes, got back into street clothes, climbed into a red convertible, and departed.

I told friends of mine: "He came here to run me out of my hometown. If I don't take him on, he'll try to run me out of my own house next."

By the time Clay got to Fairmont Park, the crowd had increased and so had Clay's bullshit.

"He wants to show he can whup me," Clay shouted. "He says he's the champ. Let him prove it here in the ghetto where the colored folks can see it."

Well, Clay and those two thousand curious folks waited, but by then Yank had heard about what me and the Butterfly were planning and had hurried to the gym to head it off.

"Cocksucker, you crazy or what?" he hollered. "A street fight in Fairmont Park? You fight the bum when the time and money are right." And that was that.

When Clay realized I wasn't showing up, he got crazier than his usual jiveass self.

"Here I am," he shouted to the crowd. "I haven't had a fight in three years, I'm twenty-five pounds overweight, and Joe Frazier won't show up. What kind of champ can he be?"

"A smart one," Yank told newsmen when they relayed the question. "He wants Clay to get paid when Clay gets his butt whipped. No sense the man taking a beating for free. Joe is thoughtful that way."

For now, though, Clay was on hold, and the man he'd raised up in the gym, brother Ellis, was the target.

The Frazier–Ellis fight got a lot of hype. The New York and Philadelphia columnists were all over it, which was no surprise. Those were hard-core boxing cities. But this time around, interest ran beyond the usual suspects. There were 512 requests from press, radio, and TV guys all across the country, and overseas, for credentials for the fight. The Garden's public-relations director, John F. X. Condon, said those requests were the most ever for a fight at the Garden. Among those who had been cleared to cover the bout was a reporter from *Izvestia,* the official newspaper of the Russian government. That was unusual for those times because the Russians rarely covered free-world sports events, unless the event had a negative twist that the Commies could take political advantage of. Or if the event was simply important enough, as this fight was.

Some of the writers looked beyond Frazier versus Ellis and wondered whether the Butterfly would ever be there to fight the winner.

The question was in the back of my mind—I wanted to give the boy Clay a serious buttwhupping—but I wasn't looking past Ellis. I'd learned early on not to take any fighter for granted. In my second bout as a pro, a supposed nonentity, Mike Bruce, had put me on my ass. Bonavena had abused me when I'd gotten sloppy. Machen shook me up when I figured I had the scamboogah ready to fall over and play dead.

Make a mistake in my business, and it could cost you millions of dollars. Yet the way I fought provoked risk: I was constantly taking chances to get close enough to the other guy to put some short-armed hurt on him. And more than that—to stay at him like a dog on a bone. No letup. As Marvelous Marvin Hagler would later say: Destruct and Destroy.

I liked what the fella from *Sports Illustrated,* Mark Kram, would say about the way I fought in his preview of the Ellis fight:

> *His [Frazier's] best weapon, the one that is just as crippling as his bearlike swipes, is his rhythm—that pace is directed by a music that he alone hears. It is intimidating and, if you are not of a proper professional mind, the starkness of it alone can be defeating. He is a special fighter, one who makes us all feel better for being in his presence, a producer who will try to give us—for $100 as it is now, or $3.50 as it was not so long ago—the best of what he has, and this in itself is something we so seldom see anywhere.*

To be a fighter that, like the Energizer bunny, just kept going and going and going was no simple deal. It took a certain outlook. You had to train like a demon so your body would respond. But fighting was body and mind both. You had to have that focus that nothing—not success or newfound wealth—could alter. We are really talking about pride.

You look around this past decade, you see so many instances of heavyweights without that pride. Riddick Bowe wins the title, then lets himself put on forty or fifty pounds and, though he sheds some of the weight, shows up for his first title defense in lesser condition. And he loses.

Tyson gets so cocky he doesn't bother to train for a fight in Tokyo with the urgency he did on the way up. And he loses.

The man who beats him, Buster Douglas, sleek and sharp as could be against Tyson, comes into the ring for his first title defense looking like the Pillsbury Doughboy. And he loses.

That lack of pride, and stick-to-it, is like an epidemic with heavy-weights these days. Only Evander Holyfield has had the discipline to stay in shape and put out that big effort fight after fight. And though he'd made eighty, ninety million dollars by 1995, and didn't need to fight ever again, he couldn't give up the game.

And I know why. 'Cause Holyfield, like me, loved the competition, loved to test himself against bigger men and cut them down to size. Holyfield, like me, lived on heart in the ring. He never let up.

The boxing writers would talk about the glee I showed when I took apart a guy. Why not? I'd come into the fight game marked down as damaged merchandise, as too small to operate against the big guys. Well, let me tell you. There wasn't a feeling much better than seeing that look in the big guys' eyes when I'd unload on them. That look said—oh, shit, so this is what fighting this little son of a bitch is gonna be like.

Sure I smiled through that mouthpiece. It felt damn good to be a giant killer. I loved being under those bright lights, performing. It was what I was meant to do—what the Lord had in mind for me. There was nothing like the thrill of locking ass with another well-trained athlete.

But like I say, to fight the way I did meant living up to that Boy Scout motto: Be prepared. And you can't do that fight after fight unless you really care about your business. It's especially tough in winter. In summer, the air feels good when you get out there for roadwork early in the morning. But in the winter, that cold hits you in the face and your whole body tightens up. When I come back off the road, I have icicles in my hair.

Sometimes I think, hell, I don't need all this running. Then I get to thinking about Jimmy Ellis or whoever I'm fighting. I know that scamboogah is doing the same thing at the same time and that he has icicles in his hair and his legs hurt and his chest feels like it will explode, too. That makes me go on. I read where he runs five miles a day, so I run six and sometimes eight just to have an edge on him.

Then, back in my room I'll soak my head in rock salt and water to toughen my skin. It ain't no party to do that to yourself, but I'm willing to put up with whatever unpleasantness is necessary to get that edge.

And while I'm doing all this training, I never think about losing a fight. I think the other way around. I think about two years from now when I will have a million dollars and I'll retire undefeated.

For Ellis, I'd started training in Miami Beach. But the weather was so hot there that I began to worry that the tropical sun might harm me. See, I don't lollygag when I train. The sparring partners who were there—Charley Polite, Ken Norton, Ray Anderson, and Moeman Williams—knew that when we got in the ring I'd put serious licks on them. And that's how I was with the rest of the program—heavy bag, speed bag, skip rope, calisthenics, and roadwork. I went full-tilt at everything. Which was well and good except for the fact that the sun can be unforgiving on a man who's working like sixty mules.

Come fight night I didn't want to be drawn too fine. That was the risk of staying in Miami Beach. Sap my strength and Ellis might have a fighting chance. So in the dead of winter we moved camp to the Concord Hotel in Lake Kiamesha, New York. Better to freeze my butt and keep all of my godgiven strength than shortchange myself just to be warm and cozy. Yank was also watching out for me, too. He put the staff on alert when I had enough training, because I always wanted to do one more mile, one more round, one more day of working out.

The days wound down and finally it was time to drive Route 10 into the city, and put a whupping on goddamn Ellis. Two years of waiting for this sucker, of listening to the bullshit excuses. I couldn't wait to have at him.

At the weigh-in, I needled him, "You look a little flabby to me."

"You better worry about yourself, not me," Ellis said.

"Just make sure you're paid up on your Blue Cross."

I went in confident against Ellis, but the fight was even easier than I expected. Ellis' punches were pudding. Nothing. By the third round I was walking through them, cracking him with vicious shots and practically laughing at him when he tried to counter me.

"Sissy, you can't hit," I told him. "I'm taking everything you got, man, and you ain't hurtin' me."

He looked too beat-up, too discouraged to reply. Blood to the shark. I whipped it on him, hitting whatever he left exposed.

A round later, in the fourth, I bulled him into the ropes and hit him with one shot after another—one columnist counted eleven unanswered blows before Ellis had the good sense to fall, face first, onto the canvas.

He got up and tried to back me off by swinging wildly. Fat chance. I decked him again, this time with a left hook that I reached down to my shoetops for. The impact was like when you hit a baseball flush, and it soars off your bat like a rocket.

Ellis was so whupped from all the punches I'd hit him with that he hadn't the strength to get his hands up in time to defend himself against a punch that came from suburbia. It landed flush on the chin, and Ellis fell backward to the canvas. Instinctively, he brought his gloves up to protect his face. He seemed unaware that he was on his back.

Ellis slowly stirred. By the count of five, he was still on the floor when the bell ending the round sounded. The bell did not save Ellis. Under New York state rules, except for the final round the referee continues his count at the bell when a fighter is on the floor. And if that fighter does not get to his feet before the count reaches ten, then the fight is over.

Ellis barely beat the count, crawling to his knees and then struggling to his feet by nine. But he was in bad shape when he made it back to the corner. Dundee sponged his forehead and tried to talk to him. Nothing. Ellis was a zombie. Dundee pinched Ellis and poured ice down his trunks as a wake-up call. Still no response. When the bell rang for the fifth round, Ellis started to get up off his stool. But Dundee knew it was just a reflex response. He knew Ellis had nothing left. And he stopped the fight.

For most folks it was a pretty convincing victory—and evidence of a better-than-ever Smokin' Joe. In *The New York Times,* columnist Robert Lipsyte would write:

> He [Frazier] is no longer simply a shuffling, plodding, mechanical monster willing to absorb many punches until an opponent's arms are so tired they drop to expose his chin. His combination punching has become sharper. It has become a little harder to hit him.
>
> But when he does strike out, it is with a wide-eyed, smiling, joyful "Hripp" that sends shivers through the crowd an instant before the crunching sound of his glove against flesh.

That seemed to be the opinion of most of those who saw the fight.

But in Philadelphia, at a closed-circuit theater site, there was one man who was not so impressed. To the amusement of the crowd, Clay shadowboxed in the aisle of the movie house and shouted: "I want that Joe Frazier! I'm starting my comeback now!"

5

CLIPPING THE BUTTERFLY'S WINGS

When I first began knowing Clay, he wasn't a bad guy to be around.

We'd talk and joke the way friends do. Not that we were what you could call friends. There was always that edge there, as future rivals, that kept us from being real close. But we got on okay. It was easy enough to pass the time.

From the git-go, Clay saw me as a guy he might some day make big money with. Before I'd even turned pro, he'd say, "Work hard and I'll make you rich."

He was champion then, and loving every minute of it. The guy couldn't get enough of that spotlight.

Then came the problem with the Selective Service, and Clay's life got a lot more complicated. And difficult. The sucker couldn't be certain he'd ever fight again.

It was a time when people in high places turned their backs on him.

Me? I was there for the guy. The whole time Clay was stripped of his title, I never said a bad word about him, even though I didn't agree with what he'd done.

I kept him in the public eye . . . and went along with some of the stunts he'd think up to keep alive the notion of the two of us fighting one another some day.

I sure as hell didn't need to do that. I was getting all the media attention a fella could want by fighting regularly.

Sometimes the press would try to get me to badmouth Clay, or trash his religion. But I never played along with that. I'd tell them his religion was his business.

Meanwhile, Clay was trying to convert me to the Nation of Islam. Yeah. He invited me to the mosque in South Philly, but I was and still am a Baptist, and proud to be one. For me religion is about love. Love the Lord, praise the Lord. Respect one to the other and love each other.

The Muslims at that time were into the white-man-is-the-devil, and all kinds of angry hate talk. Sorry, I couldn't buy into that. Like Ali, his Muslim brothers would try their patter on me. Black this, brother. Black that. They'd tell me black is beautiful. Well, so is red; and so is white.

I was, and am, happy to be my color. My daddy and momma made me, and I love them for it.

And when I was in training, my religion was a comfort to me. I kept a Bible on the night table and read it in the morning, after road-work, or before I went to sleep. My favorite was the Book of Judges. Chapter Seven. It's about fighting. Gideon has to fight a battle, but God tells him, "Most of your men can't be counted on. Fight with just three hundred." And Gideon wins. It shows how there's a danger in a crowd. That's why you never see me travelin' with a lot of guys. Somebody will shirk his responsibility.

Sunday mornings in training camp, I liked to sit in my room and dial around the radio to catch the different preachers. Or I'd put a record on the turntable of Minister C. L. Franklin of Detroit—Aretha's daddy. That man could speak the Bible. He'd talk of Jacob rassling with the Angel. Or the wild man that met Jesus. It gave a fellow peace of mind to hear him tell it.

🥊   🥊   🥊

What Clay gave me, after a while, was an Excedrin headache. It seemed like the more successful I got, the more envious he became. When he was top dog, he didn't have no need to talk shit about Smokin' Joe. But soon as the sports page was full of Frazier Frazier Frazier, Clay got bent out of joint and started talking unkindly about me.

It made me want to fight the guy in the worst way. From the beginning, Clay had been my objective. He was the man—the one I wanted to beat. The Big One. Before every bout, Yank would tell me: "Every time you're fighting, you got to think you're in there with Clay."

When newsmen would ask me about Clay, I'd tell them: "I'd love to fight Clay, even at Leavenworth, if they jail him."

And soon after I whupped Ellis, there were rumblings that maybe the fight could happen. Word was that attorneys for Clay had gotten a promise from boxing officials in Toronto that they'd grant their man a license to box. The hitch was that Clay's five-year sentence was on appeal, and he was not allowed to leave the country while he was under five-thousand-dollar bail.

For a while, it was thought that a petition to permit Clay to go to Canada for twenty-four hours to fight might be approved by the court. It wasn't, but where earlier unsuccessful attempts to revive Clay's career left his supporters feeling as if the situation was hopeless, now there was a sense that the time might be right for Clay's return.

Part of that had to do with the war in Vietnam. As that conflict dragged on, public sentiment against it grew here; protests around the country became routine. All of which created a mood less hostile to Clay than when he'd refused induction three years earlier.

Earlier attempts to get Clay back in the ring had been shot down in Chicago, Louisville, Montreal, Detroit, Tampa, and Tulsa. Every time a fight featuring Clay—sometimes against me, sometimes against somebody else—was about to be made, the backlash would just make it too risky for politicians to approve.

In Tampa, when it looked as though Clay had the backing of the state's governor, Claude Kirk, to fight there, the local paper, the *Tampa Tribune,* opposed the match in an editorial. It noted that as late as May of 1969 Clay had said he was through with boxing "forever" because it was against the teachings of the Black Muslim religion.

"Now, Clay's religious scruples apparently have been overcome by the promise of a $300,000 guarantee for the Tampa fight," the editorial said. The governor scrambled away from Clay as though he was a toxic waste dump.

Clay's people kept trying, though, even seeking approval to use an Indian reservation to hold a fight involving him. That too failed.

But me and Yank, in contact with Clay's manager, Herbert Muhammad, were hearing that it was beginning to look like Clay might be able to get licensed in Georgia, where there was no state athletic commission. That left it to businessmen and politicians to grease each other and make a Clay comeback happen.

Meantime, *The Ring* magazine, which for the three years of Clay's exile had kept him as its champion, now revised its rankings and put me up top.

Clay was bumped down to the contenders' list.

It was a good time for me.

After beating Ellis, I got to take up my other pleasure, rock and roll. I headed out to Las Vegas, where "Joe Frazier and the Knockouts," a nine-piece combo, was booked into Caesars Palace, with me as the lead singer. I was singing oldies but goodies and some tunes written for me. Like:

> *Baby, my lovin' is like TNT.*
> *If you don't believe me, try me and see.*
> *Whatever ails you, my love can stop,*
> *'Cause my love, my love, is like a knockout drop.*

As that was happening, Cloverlay was putting half a million dollars of mine into 139 acres of land in Bucks County, Pennsylvania. A planned residential development would later be built there, and by the terms of the deal, my investment would bring serious dividends, quarterly, until 1999. It was like a slot machine having a thirty-year seizure of spilling money down the chute.

And there was money left over to move the Fraziers—Florence and I now had five children, including two more daughters, Jo-Netta and Natasha—into a new place: a seven-bedroom stone Colonial house on two and a half acres in the historical Lafayette Hill suburb of Philadelphia. It was the dream house that Billy Boy had imagined back in Beaufort—a $125,000 digs with a swimming pool, and recreation rooms that had pool tables, video and pinball machines, and an air hockey game. Not to mention a six-car garage that would hold a Cadillac limousine, a gold Cadillac Coupe DeVille, Florence's custom-made Chevy station wagon, a couple of older vehicles, a 1934 Chevrolet and a 1954 Corvette that I liked to tinker with, and a forty-seven-hundred-dollar Harley-Davidson motorcycle that I could run up to one hundred miles an hour on empty country roads.

The bad news was that while performing at Caesars, I'd fractured a bone in my leg while doing a split on stage. Believe that? Fighting the baaadest dudes around, nothing. Rocking the night away at Caesars, and I'm a casualty.

In August, that scamboogah Clay phoned me up. Clay was practically a neighbor now, living in a $92,000 home on Philadelphia's Main Line. Yeah. For a martyr he didn't seem to be doing too bad.

During his three years of exile, he'd scrambled a bit but found he could make a living—a thousand dollars a day for a week's work on a documentary about him, *A/K/A Cassius Clay;* ten thousand dollars and a percentage for his role in a computerized fight between Rocky Marciano and him; twenty-five hundred dollars a pop for working the college lecture circuit; and $225,000 from a publishing deal for his autobiography. Clay told me the house he was now living in had a color TV in every room, twelve telephones, and a swimming pool. It also had a new wife (his second) and three daughters.

What Clay wanted, it turned out, was to meet up with me so he could tape a conversation that he could use in his book. Since I had to be in New York the next day, and so did he, we agreed to ride up there, with the tape recorder rolling.

About noon the next day I drove by the pickup spot in my Coupe DeVille. Clay was waiting, and climbed into the front seat. We took off, making small talk for a while until Clay started mouthing off, as he usually did, about what would happen if the two of us ever locked ass.

I told him that when the day came I'd knock his light, bright, damn-near-white self out.

"You see, the kinda stuff I'm gonna put on you, man, you ain't had to dig yet," I said. "You ain't never seen this before. You understand?"

Clay said that with his jab it would be *Mission Impossible* for me to beat him. Nobody had been able to handle that jab.

I told him: "See, them other cats out there let you have your own way. They let you jump around the ring, and dance and all that . . . ."

"You couldn't stop me from jumping around the ring and dancing. What you gonna do?"

"I'd get right dead on you! Every time you breathe, you be breathing right down on my head."

Clay just couldn't seem to believe I really wanted to fight him—he was under the impression that I was scared, or ducking him.

"Listen," I told him. "I wish I had the power to get you a license, man. 'Cause there's nothing in this world that I want more than to give you a whupping."

He got all excited, picturing what an event it would be: Clay versus Frazier.

"I'm telling you," I said. "They ain't gonna see nothing in their life like this fight. 'Cause you ain't afraid of me, and I ain't afraid of you. Right?"

Well, Clay wasn't satisfied with what I was telling him—that for all his talk he was gonna get beat. He started telling me how he was a heavyweight Sugar Ray Robinson—ain't never been a heavyweight that could move and dance like him. How did a thick-legged nigger like me hope to keep up?

I told him I'd been up against race horses before, and once I started smokin' on them, they slowed down to a trot.

"I put quicksand under their feet," I said.

"I gotta admit you good," he said, "but I'm the fastest. Fastest in the history of the whole world."

"Maybe, maybe moving away. But I'm the fastest moving in."

Yackety yack: The boy had a motormouth. Telling me Mildenberger, Liston, Cooper, Chuvalo—none of them had been able to deal with his speed. Telling me I had no footwork. To hear him talk, I was slower than Buck and Jenny, the mules that used to work our ten acres back in Beaufort.

He could say whatever he wanted; he'd find out. When he was on his butt, and looking up at the ring lights, he'd know that talk don't whip Joe Frazier, it takes a real man to do that.

But Clay is like a little kid that just can't shut his mouth 'til you smack his ass. On he went. At one point, he recited a little poem he'd made up about the fight.

Joe's gonna come out smokin',
And I ain't gonna be jokin',
I'll be peckin' and pokin'
Pourin' water on his smokin'
This might shock and amaze ya,
But I'll retire Joe Fray-shuh.

I laughed. The cat had shit that didn't quit.

Later, as we neared New York, he got more serious. He was acting like a veteran fighter handing out the benefit of his experience to the new guy on the block, which I appreciated: tips on how to handle my money, on playing safe with the motorcycle, on how to dress so as to make a good impression—he recommended dark suits that made him, he said, look as dignified as a senator.

I left Senator Clay on West Fifty-second Street, not far from the old Madison Square Garden, where he'd beaten Zora Folley in his last fight. That seemed like an eternity now, with all that had happened in both our lives.

Until now, Clay's attorneys had kept him out of jail by laying one appeal after the other on the courts. Then on June 15, 1970—a month and a half before Clay and I rode up to New York—the Supreme Court ruled that "conscientious objector" status was not restricted to those who were motivated strictly by religious belief, but applied equally to those who refused to serve for moral and ethical reasons.

While that did not clear Clay—the appeal was still to be ruled on—it did give the men trying to make a fight for Clay a wedge against those opposed to him being licensed.

In Atlanta, LeRoy Johnson, a state senator; Sam Massell, the mayor of the city; and Robert Kassel, a lawyer, were pulling the strings that would overcome the politics that previously had prevented Clay's return to boxing. This time there would be no last-minute opposition to override their attempts.

The Butterfly was back, with Jerry Quarry the opponent in a fight that would take place on October 26, 1970, in a five-thousand-seat arena in Atlanta.

I might have gone to sit ringside if I hadn't been in training for a fight of my own—against Bob Foster on November 18 in Detroit. Instead, I would learn the result of the bout later than most Americans did. While those folks made it to closed-circuit sites, or just waited until the eleven-o'clock news, I was already asleep, keeping to my training routine.

In the morning I heard that Clay had stopped Quarry in three rounds. The boxing writers said that the Butterfly had moved well, and punched even better, opening a gaping cut over Quarry's left eye. The cut was "right to the bone," the referee, Tony Perez, said. A disturbing sight it must have been for Perez, who took one look and stopped the fight.

For me, it meant that Clay was back on my radar screen. Word was that he would take another fight—probably against that sniffing maniac Bonavena—and then be ready to get down with Smokin' Joe. Goddamn. I couldn't be happier.

For years, Clay had been the wind that whipped the fire in me. For as long as I'd been lacing on the gloves, I'd wanted to bust his ass and show the world that Frazier, not Clay, was the greatest. When I'd be out doing roadwork, I'd picture Clay out there ahead of me, and that would get me a second wind. In the gym, he was a part of my conscience and a reason to put out the best effort. Keep building, keep getting better . . . so on the night we rumbled, I'd be all I could be.

But that would wait until I took care of Foster, who, as light heavyweight champion of the world, was stepping up in class.

Bob Foster was a tall, thin fellow—six feet, three inches, and 175 pounds when he fought as a light heavyweight. He figured to be heavier against me—he told newsmen he'd been taking a food enricher called Results—but not to where folks would mistake him for a full-blown heavyweight.

As a light heavyweight Foster was known as a big puncher. From the time he won the title from Dick Tiger on a fourth-round knockout in May 1968, he had scored twelve straight knockouts, including four of them in title defenses.

But the skinny man's punch did not always translate when Foster got in there with legitimate heavyweights. Doug Jones had knocked him out in 1962, Ernie Terrell had knocked him out in 1964, and Zora Folley had beat him by decision in 1965.

And I didn't have trouble beating him either. One reporter described it like a rhinoceros stomping on a cobra. Fact is I hit him so hard in knocking him down twice in the second (and final) round that he sprained his ankle when he fell to the canvas and back in the dressing room he didn't remember he'd already fought me.

That's right. When Foster put back on his high-top boxing shoes, one of his handlers asked, "What are you doin', Bob?"

"Got to fight Frazier," Foster told him.

After the first knockdown, Foster was so shaky on his legs that I looked toward the referee, Tom Brisco, hoping he'd stop the fight. Instead he waved me on.

For the final knockdown, I hit Foster with a left hook to the body and then another left to the head. He went down as though yanked by a string. He fell into the ropes and then forward. He was out of it, but the poor guy didn't know it. Like a knee-jerk response, he tried to get to his knees before falling over to his right again. It was scary enough to bring Yank and a bunch of medical guys with stethoscopes rushing into the ring as the referee was finishing the count.

Yank was cradling Foster's head when Brisco told him, "Let the doctors take care of him."

"Shut up, you stupid son of a bitch," Yank snapped. "Why didn't you stop the fight? This man could be seriously hurt."

Three weeks later, after successfully suing the New York State Athletic Commission to have his license reinstated, Clay fought Bonavena at the Garden.

I watched it on a closed-circuit screen up at Monticello Raceway. And for a while there the pictures on that screen frightened me a lot more than any Dracula or Frankenstein flick ever did.

That was because Bonavena was not there just for the payday. He was giving Clay enough of a fight to raise the possibility that the goddamn Butterfly could lose . . . and blow our chance to make history.

Yeah. So I sat there, chewing on my fingernails and watching Clay struggle with Bonavena. In the fourth round, he tried to mess with Bonavena's mind by letting Bonavena hit him. Didn't work. If anybody seemed to be shaky, it was Clay. He began complaining to the referee about low blows from Bonavena, as if he had calculated that a deduction of a point or two from the other guy's score might matter.

Clay had predicted that he'd knock out Bonavena in the ninth round. Well, when round nine came he swung so wild on a left hook that he slipped to his knees and when he got to his feet he had a streak of white resin dust in his hair.

Put it this way: It wasn't Clay at his best. He was parceling out his fight, as if Bonavena was fatiguing him. Rather than being on his toes, and dancing, he was flat-footed and faking it. Clinch, make faces, catch his breath. That sucker was having an off-night, and it was making me nervous.

Late in the fifteen-round nontitle match, the Garden crowd began booing him for, I guess, not being the Clay of their dreams. There were even chants for Bonavena, whose nickname was Ringo:

Ring-go . . . (whistle, whistle) . . . Ring-go . . . (whistle, whistle). Ring-go.

Then came the surprise ending. Midway through the fifteenth and final round, Clay nailed Bonavena with a left hook. Bonavena went down sideways. When he got up, he was out on his feet. Clay knocked him down twice more. Three knockdowns in one round—the fight was over.

That finish would cover over what was really a so-so performance by Clay. But I only cared that he'd won, making him eligible to get what he had coming from me.

It figured Clay would make a big deal out of knocking out Bonavena, who'd gone the distance twice with me.

At two in the morning, when he arrived at the victory party downstairs at Toots Shor's, Clay spotted Yank and began jabbering: "Where is he? Where is Frazier? Ah, there is his trainer."

"This is his manager," Yank corrected.

"You tell him I'm ready for him now."

"And I'm ready for you," said Yank. "You will go in six."

Sounded right to me. The question was when-where-and-for-how-much.

The answer would take a while to develop as various parties bid to get the rights to promote the fight between Clay and me. There was Madison Square Garden. There was Sonny Werblin, the former owner of the Jets, who partnered up with TV's Johnny Carson. There was Fred Hofheinz of Houston, whose father was the man with the Astrodome. There was General Electric.

But in the end, it was a man who'd never been involved in boxing, Jerry Perenchio, who would put together the deal that would finally get Clay and me into the prize ring.

Perenchio was head of Chartwell Artists, a show-business-management firm in Beverly Hills that represented Marlon Brando, Richard Burton, Elizabeth Taylor, Jane Fonda, the Smothers Brothers, Glenn Campbell, Jose Feliciano, Sergio Mendes and Brazil '66, Andy Williams, and Nancy Wilson.

On December 15, the forty-year-old Perenchio was in London on business when he got a call from Frank Fried, a concert promoter he knew. Fried, who also owned the Aragon Ballroom in Chicago, happened to have met with Herbert Muhammad and learned that the rights to The Fight, as Frazier–Clay number one came to be known, were still available.

"How much would it take to get it?" Perenchio asked Fried on their transatlantic call.

"Five million."

"Let me get back to you."

Up to that point Hofheinz and the Garden, separately, had made the same bid: a $1.25-million guarantee against 35 percent of the total box-office gross for each fighter. That offer was still on the table, but Herbert and Yank were shooting for a flat guarantee at least double of what Hofheinz and the Garden were proposing. From his room at the Dorchester Hotel in London, Perenchio began running up a sixteen-thousand-dollar phone bill trying to find possible backers. His first seventy calls got zilch. Aristotle Onassis wasn't interested in coughing up the money. Nor was former network TV executive Jim Aubrey.

But back in Los Angeles Perenchio found a willing partner on his next call—Jack Kent Cooke. Cooke was a multimillionaire who owned the Los Angeles Lakers basketball team and the Los Angeles Kings hockey team as well as the building both teams played their home games in, the Forum in Inglewood, California. If that wasn't enough, Cooke also held 25 percent of the stock in the Washington Redskins football team. Cooke, a one-time door-to-door salesman from Canada, agreed to put up $4.5 million. The Garden came with five hundred thousand more, in return for having the fight staged in its building.

That led to an offer of $2.5 million each for Clay and me—the largest guarantees in boxing history. That $5 million exceeded the record live gate of the second Liston–Patterson bout, which grossed $4,747,000.

And for the first time in history an unbeaten former champion would face an unbeaten current champion.

On December 30, 1970, both of us signed in New York.

At the news conference that day to announce the March 8 bout, Perenchio stated that he expected the fight to gross between $20 million and $30 million, prompting Clay to stand up in mock protest and shout over to me: "They got us cheap. Only five million out of twenty to thirty. We've been taken."

Perenchio had not overlooked any revenue-making possibility. There would be posters, souvenir programs, books written, and a feature-length documentary about the fight, ready to go into the movie houses soon after the final bell. And he'd put in the contract that our gloves, trunks, and shoes became his property after the fight.

"Why not?" Perenchio said. "If a movie studio can auction off Judy Garland's shoes, Gary Cooper's belt, and Marilyn Monroe's dress, Muhammad's and Frazier's things should be worth something special. We get a little blood on the trunks, it makes them all the more valuable."

It looked as though he'd maximized his end of the deal. Yet many business sharpies felt that Perenchio, Cooke, and the Garden had overpaid. They insisted that the $5 million in guarantees plus operating expenses would require the fight to generate $9 million in revenues from all sources to break even. And that number, they said, was not reachable.

Perenchio disagreed. With ringside seats going for a record high of $150, the gate was scaled at $1.25 million. Another million dollars could be expected from foreign rights. That meant the closed-circuit take would have to be roughly $7 million for the fight to break even. The biggest closed-circuit fight previously had been the first Patterson–Liston bout, which had brought in $3.2 million.

But Perenchio was insisting that past standards did not apply to this match—that Ali–Frazier would be off the charts: "It's potentially the greatest single grosser in the history of the world. It's like *Gone With the Wind.*"

Perenchio was shooting for 2.5 million closed-circuit "buys" in 500 locations, compared to 563,000 customers at 253 locations for Patterson–Liston.

And ticket prices would be higher—as much as thirty dollars in some locations, where the average price for a closed-circuit ticket for Patterson–Liston had been six dollars. Perenchio wanted to change the traditional fifty–fifty split between promoter and exhibitor for a sixty-five–thirty-five division that favored him.

"What we have here," Perenchio told newsmen, "is the Mona Lisa. You expect us to sell it for chopped liver?"

Before the news conference broke up, Clay had dusted off a poem for the occasion, which went like this:

> *It's a good thing Frazier had a band to hire,*
> *When I hit him, he'll have to retire.*

Sticks and stones, it was time to break his bones.

The millions of dollars tied to the fight were just one indication of how big the fight was. The attention of the media was also of record-breaking proportions. The heaviest writers had come aboard to cover the fight—Norman Mailer for *Life* magazine, Budd Schulberg for *Playboy*, and William Saroyan for *True*.

Frank Sinatra would be ringside as a photographer working for *Life*—in fact, the photo from the fight that would run as the magazine's cover would be one shot by him.

In all, the Garden would approve 760 requests for credentials from media members all over the world, and would be forced to turn down 500 more. The fight would be shown all over the world on either satellite TV or at closed-circuit sites. South America, Europe, Africa, and the Far East—the joint would be jumping there as well as in the U.S., Canada, and the United Kingdom.

All that attention was made to order for the Louisville Lip.

He had the audience of a lifetime, and he used it to do his usual boasting—and more. This time around, it wasn't enough for Clay to jive about the outcome. ("After the first round with him is over, the people will rise from their seats and cry, 'Ali tricked us! He's *still* the greatest.' ") He needed to make this fight out to be some sort of political statement.

And that statement came at my expense. Clay projected himself as the second coming of Jack Johnson, a persecuted black man who was fighting the righteous fight. Yeah. The Cassius Clay of his dreams was an example to his black brothers. He'd stood up to the white establishment and here he was, in all his technicolor glory three and a half years later, unvanquished, ready to reclaim what that other guy was pretending was his—the heavyweight championship.

Making me . . . what?

Well, to hear it from Clay, I was a lame specimen of a black man, a kind of Stepin Fetchit in boxing trunks:

"If you got all the black people in this country to vote for the man they want to win, 90 percent of them would say me. Especially the young ones. Joe Frazier is no representative of the black people. Wait until you hear who they cheer when we get in that ring."

And: "I'm not just fightin' one man. I'm fightin' a lot of men, showin' 'em here is one man they couldn't conquer. My mission is to bring freedom to 30 million black people. I'll win because I've got a cause. Frazier has no cause. He's in it for the money alone."

And: "Frazier's no real champion. Nobody wants to talk to him. Oh, maybe Nixon will call him if he wins. I don't think he'll call me. But 98 percent of my people are for me. They identify with my struggle. Same one they're fighting every day in the streets. If I win, they win. I lose, they lose. Anybody black who thinks Frazier can whup me is an Uncle Tom. Everybody who's black wants me to keep winning."

And: "All those people from Georgia, they will say to Joe Frazier . . . 'Stop that nigger! You gonna be white tonight! Stop the draft-dodging nigger.' "

And: "Joe Frazier is too ugly to be champ. Joe Frazier is too dumb to be champ. The heavyweight champion should be smart and pretty like me. Ask Joe Frazier, 'How do you feel, champ?' He'll say, 'Duh, duh, duh.' "

It was mean-spirited talk—a cynical attempt by Clay to make me feel isolated from my own people. He thought that would weaken me when it came time to face him in that ring. Well, he was wrong. It didn't weaken me, it awakened me to what a cheap-shot son of a bitch he was.

It wasn't as if talking that garbage would jack up our end of the take. We had that two-point-five-million-dollar guarantee—and that was it. No percentages of the take, no upside. If nobody showed up on March 8 to watch us fight, we were still walking away with our pockets full.

But Clay—being the insecure phony he is—needed to feel superior to me. He knew he couldn't beat me physically so he tried to beat me with words. And that was his way—talk shit about me. Let's face it: Clay was smooth, and quick, with the mouth. Me, I'm not much of a talker. But that doesn't make me ignorant, or a goddamn Uncle Tom. Or a disgrace to my race.

But repeat the lie often enough, and people begin to think it's so. Particularly when you're a favorite of the press, like Clay was. Most of the writers let him slide, not calling him on the dirty little game he was playing.

There were a few who recognized Clay for what he was, like Dick Young of the *New York Daily News,* who wrote:

> *He has run out of white opponents, and now he feels the need to whitewash Joe Frazier. And so, for the next weeks, Muhammad Ali, in his charming and shrewd way, will paint Joe Frazier as the standardbearer of the white bigots, as the white man's lackey, the betrayer of his people, the Uncle Tom, the Oreo cookie.*
>
> *It is a cruel and unworthy thing he does.*

Or the syndicated columnist Jimmy Cannon, who got after the news guys who were Clay's accomplices in deblackening me:

> *They also assisted Ali as he denounced Frazier as an Uncle Tom. It is slanderous and cruel, but Ali's lie is still encouraged. They go along with Ali's line that Frazier is the white man's champion, and Ali alone represents the blacks.*
>
> *On occasion, I have found Frazier disagreeable and hostile to me. But this is an honest man who is not a racial opportunist. He doesn't need defending by me.*
>
> *He is black and just as proud of it as is Ali.*

Cruel and unworthy. Yeah. And in its way, sadistic, like pulling the wings off a dying insect. I mean, Clay knew the facts—knew the hard road I'd traveled. Knew the struggle a black man had, growing up in Beaufort, South Carolina. Knew that in saying what he did, he was playing me cheap and leaving Joe Frazier, and his children, open to ridicule—worse, he was encouraging it.

He didn't give a damn. Figured he could just talk his shit and walk away, as if it never happened. Like a three-year-old that makes a mess and scoots off before anybody can discover it.

He did that, and left me to deal with it. Left me to see on a cover of a magazine called *Black Sports* a blurb asking: "Is Joe Frazier a White Champion in a Black Skin?" by Bryant Gumbel, the editor of the magazine. The same Bryant Gumbel who went on to become the host of *The Today Show.*

He left me to try to explain to Marvis what to do about classmates at the Lafayette Consolidated School, who called his father a "Tom." Marvis, a fifth-grader, had to be restrained from going after one boy who'd said that word.

He left me to deal with death-threat phone calls to my home and, later, to the hotels I stayed in while training. "Joe Frazier, you beat Muhammad, we gonna kill you, you Tomming dog."

What a joke. If I did any Tomming, it was for Clay before his reinstatement. Whenever he phoned up and had an idea to create a little noise in public, I'd go along with it, figuring it'd help him. He had a family that he needed to provide for. The publicity that the two of us whipped up would keep his face before the public and, I thought, help in the different ventures he was fooling with—the lectures, and so on. While I might have been against his politics, I felt he deserved a chance to make a living.

Even before negotiations for The Fight began, I'd gone down to Washington, D.C., and met with representatives from one of the sport's governing bodies. Those boys wanted to know whether I had any problems with their recognizing Clay. Hell, no, I told them. Let him fight. When he finally gets around to me, I'm gonna make him wish he'd stayed retired.

Point is: Joe Frazier didn't turn his back on Cassius Clay when practically everyone else did. And for that the scamboogah insulted me in the way most calculated to hurt—by picturing me as a pawn of white folks, a shuffling woolly-headed nigger. To me that was not only a low blow—it was a perfect example of Clay's nature.

He couldn't stand that he was no longer king of the mountain. Smokin' Joe had come along and stolen some of his thunder. Where once he'd told me: "Keep at it, kid, and I'll make you rich," now it was me who was making him his biggest-ever payday. That was hard to take. So he set out to cut me down, and hurt me, the only way he knew how—with his lying, jiving mouth.

All that about his being the shining knight to black folks was a crock. All that was to turn people against me. People in the ghetto thought Clay would help them with their economic problems. But this man didn't care 'bout anything but Cassius.

Now if you're talkin' about makin' a whole lot of noise—of woofing on the TV: "I'm a bad nigger; I know Whitey don't like me but I don't care"—you tell me how that represents your black people. Or say you tell the newspapers: "I'm a pretty nigger." Does that make you a fine example to your people? Not the way I see it. If you're nice to folks, and go about your business, then you're doing something. You don't have to be plugged into a wall socket by the mouth to shine.

This guy Clay used his blackness to get his way. Plain and simple, he was a nigger when it was in his interest and when he could get folks fussing about him. Yeah. He'd go into the ghetto and create a stir. Block streets and bring the cops out. And after he caused a traffic jam, it was back to Sugar Hill, or Cherry Hill, or whatever hill the joker lived up on.

What did he know about hard times? Shooting his mouth off—he was an authority at that. But hard times? He never had to do real work growing up in Louisville. Spent his summers on a white millionaire's estate, training for the amateurs and occasionally scooping the leaves out of massah's swimming pool. And later as a pro, everything was greased for his success. He had a white man in the corner and those rich plantation people to fund him. A white lawyer kept him out of jail. And *he's* going to Uncle Tom me.

THEE Greatest, he called himself. Well, he wasn't The Greatest, and he certainly wasn't *THEE* Greatest. Whatever God you pray to, whatever direction you face when you go to your knees, there's only one *THEE*. But this scamboogah had the nerve to put himself above the Lord. Well, it became my mission to show him the error of foolish pride. Beat it into him.

He should have been listening to his momma instead of shooting his mouth off. 'Cause when his momma told him not to underestimate me, and Clay said, "Don't, worry, Momma. He's a bum," his momma replied, "Frazier's no bum."

Well, Clay got his first inkling that mother knows best a month or so after signing for The Fight. That's when John Condon of the Garden had both of us meet in Philadelphia so that George Kalinsky, the Garden photographer, could take publicity photos that would go out all over the world and help build interest in the fight.

By now, Cloverlay had bought a three-story building on North Broad Street, and converted what had been a bowling alley into a gym for me. That's where Clay and me met to do the shoot. Kalinsky, who knew and had photographed both of us before, did the standard posed shots, separately and together, and then proposed that he move about the ring with each of us, as if he were an opponent. Only instead of his fists being cocked it would be his camera. His idea was to create a photographic impression of what it would look like facing Clay or Frazier.

Well, he did it for three minutes with Clay, no problem. But once I started moving in on him, George got a bit nervous and cut short the routine. He was, he said, afraid. I hadn't touched his camera, but he told me I was menacing.

The next part was the best part. Kalinsky had Clay and me step into the ring together. Then he asked us to go through the motions of sparring. The idea was to simulate action. Well, as we tapped one another, and Clay mugged for the camera, I could feel a kind of rush in my veins. This pittypat stuff was not enough.

"Let's go at it now," I told Clay.

He wasn't sure I meant it. But when I whacked him a little harder, he realized what I was up to and fired back. That was when I let him have a shot to the stomach, a left hook that I laid on him nice and sweet. I buried it in the sucker, and for damn sure he noticed.

"Son of a bitch can really hit," Clay said, acting stunned.

And in the next instant he was pulling his trunks up to his chin—I don't quite know how he did that—and said, "That's it."

He didn't want any more of that.

Funny, in the years of his exile from boxing, whenever Clay ran into me, he would put his hands up and try to fool with me—you know, an open-hand fight. He made like it was just a goof, but I knew what he was trying to find out about me—get a sense of how strong Joe Frazier was, and how quick his reflexes.

But whenever he played that, I ignored him . . . until that afternoon in Philly. Then I gave him something to think on—the disheartening fact that when I hit him on March 8 it would rattle his bones.

And with that little nugget stored away, the Butterfly had flown the coop. So much for that "water on my smokin'."

Afterward, I asked Kalinsky: "You see the look on his face when I buried that hook in his belly?"

Let him talk. I'd do what I had to so I'd be ready. While Clay went down to Miami Beach to train, I stuck it out up north in the cold weather—at the Concord resort in the Catskills, and in Philadelphia. It was business as usual. The fact that the opponent was Clay changed nothing about my routine, except that the sparring partners we brought to camp were guys that could move on their feet, the way he could.

We knew what to expect from Clay, knew that he would stick and move, using his jab to break up my rhythm and then sneak the quick right hand over the jab to bust me up. If he could do that consistently, my face would swell up and there was the risk of being cut badly enough around my eyes that my vision would be impaired.

What Clay was counting on was a Joe Frazier who was easy to hit and incapable of slipping past his jab. But I hadn't any doubt I could elude the jab and get close enough to punch the hell out of bigmouth Clay. Our strategy was to pound his body early enough, and hard enough, to take the bounce out of those legs. Once he came down off his toes, he would have to fight in the trenches. And that was my kind of fight. I might get hit plenty, but so would he.

While Clay was as slick a heavyweight as there'd ever been, he wasn't no damn phantom. He could be hit. What's more he had a habit of preserving that pretty face of his by leaning back from punches, and that played into our strategy. See, fighters are taught never to lean back from punches, the way he did, because it leaves their head exposed and vulnerable. But Clay was not the ordinary fighter. He could break the rule and get away with it because he was so damn quick.

That was okay with me. I'd let him keep that pretty face early in the fight, and concentrate on hitting his body. And the body would be there. When he leaned back to avoid getting hit in the puss, he'd be offering up his body. You couldn't lean back without making yourself more vulnerable downstairs, and I'd be downstairs waiting for the sucker.

What I would do was pound his kidneys and spleen. I figured on him snatching his pretty head back through the first four rounds. Then his body would get to aching and he'd start pulling it back. But he couldn't do that without his head getting in harm's way. Once his head became a ready target, I'd be there popshotting it. But strategy would not be enough. I would have to be strong and unrelenting and in top condition to whup Clay. And on that count, I gotta admit I was worried. For one thing, it was freezing cold at the Concord, and I couldn't get comfortable. At times the temperatures dropped well below freezing, and that bone-chilling cold seemed to overpower the heating system at the hotel. The room was never warm enough for me. It got so bad we finally just checked out of the place and headed back to Philadelphia.

Bad as it was, the cold was not as troubling as another problem I was having. The hard workouts that in the past I'd handle without a problem were suddenly a drain on me. Four, five weeks out from the fight, I felt run-down, fatigued.

My family physician, Dr. J. Finton Speller, examined me and said I was suffering from high blood pressure. The blood pressure was a problem of long standing—the doctor had kept an eye on it over the years. At this point, he felt it was probably the pressure of the upcoming fight, in combination with the hard training that was elevating the blood-pressure problem. Maybe it wasn't the ideal setup—to be fighting the biggest fight of my life with a body that was under siege. But there was no way I was going to postpone the fight.

I'd waited all my life for this chance. So I did what I had to. After every workout, I'd slip off to Dr. Speller's office and get shot up with vitamin E and vitamin C to keep my energy up.

That helped take care of the body. Meanwhile, Yank was working on my mind.

"Joe, goddamn, I'm telling you if you can get past this guy, your way in life is paved forever," he said.

"Don't you worry," I told him. "I got this monkey. He ain't going nowhere but down."

"You beat this clown, you'll be treated like royalty. You'll have the best of everything. The world will remember you whipped Clay's ass."

"Bet on it. They gonna remember it."

Meanwhile, the promotion was cranking. The twenty-thousand-odd tickets to the live event at the Garden had been sold out hours after going on sale in late January. Ticket scalpers were getting seven hundred dollars a ticket.

A total of thirty-five nations had signed on to get the fight on satellite TV—and they ranged from Canada and England to Nicaragua, Nigeria, Rumania, Yugoslavia, and the Crown Colony of Hong Kong. Perenchio and Cooke had sold the rights only when their price was met. When France and Australia wouldn't cough up what Perenchio and Cooke were asking, they were shut out.

Three hundred sixty-nine theaters and arenas throughout the U.S. and Canada would carry the closed-circuit telecast, charging prices from ten dollars to thirty-five dollars. The high-end price led some black organizations to complain that the cost would keep fans of Clay's from seeing him fight. A few of these black radicals picketed the Cloverlay gym, and sometimes would bitch to Yank about the closed-circuit price. These cats even wondered why the fight hadn't been given to black promoters, and provisions made for some of the money to be funneled back into the black community.

Yank told them straight-out: "What do I care how much money go here and how much go there? I got two-and-a-half million dollars each for the fighters, and nobody has ever given me nothing. No white group has ever given me nothing. No black group has ever given me nothing. I worked for everything I got. I worked on the railroad; I worked as a stevedore; I worked with fighters. I had a number of fighters who were fighting, and this is the only fighter I ever had that be successful, so I ain't giving up nothing. I think it's right for the fighter I'm working with, and that's all I'm interested in."

Every day the Cloverlay gym would fill up with reporters, and radio and TV people, and down in Miami Beach it was the same for Clay. Stories appeared in every newspaper, including a Countdown to the Fight series in the *Philadelphia Daily News.*

Clay was still trashing me as a Tom, and finding an audience for it. *Jet* magazine referred to me as "the unheralded white-created champion for the primary enrichment of two white businessmen: Jack Kent Cooke and Jerry Perenchio." What horseshit. As if Clay was going to put his two-point-five into the black community.

But Clay had lots of folks bamboozled. Some of them would show up at the Broad Street gym, and after the workouts try to heckle us. I didn't stick around; I'd head straight for the showers. As the fight drew near, I was in no mood to talk with these turkeys. But Yank didn't mind taking them on.

"When I fight Clay," Yank would tell them, "I'm going to get him somewhere in the middle rounds."

"You ain't fighting him, man," one of them would shout. "Frazier is."

"And why you call him Clay?" another asked. "He Ali."

"His name is Cassius Clay to me," said Yank.

"What you got against the boy's religion?"

"Not a thing. He can pray to a hole in the ground for all I care."

"Yo, man. You gonna make money on this?"

"If not, it's time to get me a new job."

He'd get them going with the patter. Yank was quick on his feet, and wasn't shy about expressing what he felt, whether those fans of Clay liked it or not.

Me, I was concentrating on the job ahead, and didn't care much about scoring any points with the public. That was Clay's game. He had a mouth big enough to take care of boxing fans *and* the media.

When the press asked Clay if he was ready for me, he promised, "If Joe Frazier whips Muhammed, I am gonna get on my hands and my knees in Madison Square Garden right in the ring and crawl all the way to his corner, look up at him, and say, 'You are the greatest. You are the true champion of the world.'" Not a bad picture, huh?

Not that I didn't try to do my bit for the promotion. When the Garden's John Condon asked me to talk to a newsman, I'd usually go along with it. What the hell. It was part of doing business as a fighter. I may not have been as eager or as talkative as the Louisville Lip, but I was willing to do my share for the guys putting up the money. That was only fair.

But there came a time several weeks before the fight when I wasn't in the mood to talk to newsmen, or anybody. Even Yank. Word got out that Joe Frazier had suddenly gone silent. And pretty soon Condon was knocking at my door, asking what the problem was.

"I just don't want to see anybody," I told him.

"Nobody?" he asked.

"No. I just want to be alone, John."

Condon caught my low-down mood and became concerned.

"You all right?" he asked. "You're not sick, are you?"

"I'm okay. Just sad. See, my dog got killed this morning. He was run over . . . right outside the house, right out in front. A six-year-old white German shepherd. We called him Prince. No two people ever came to love each other so fast as a dog and a man can come to love each other. That dog would guard the house, and morning when I'd do roadwork, he'd run with me. I'm just having a hard time about it."

For three or four days, I kept to myself, trying to get over the hurt I felt. After a while, I got back into the routine, and talking became easier.

By then, because of the death threats from Clay supporters, I felt like a jailbird. Wherever I went, even when I did roadwork in the early morning, I was surrounded by Philadelphia police.

On the day we broke camp and headed to New York, five Philadelphia cops rode up there with us—Jim Turner, Tony Fulwood, Ed Harrell, Tom Payne, and Ralph Taylor. Once we got through the Lincoln Tunnel, a contingent from the New York Police Department joined us.

A week earlier, there had been an anonymous letter threatening to kill me if I beat Clay. A phone call followed, making the same point. Was it Black Muslims trying to shake my confidence or just the odd lunatic acting out some twisted idea of support for Clay? I didn't know. Or care. I was too far into my prefight gameface to worry about such things. Give me Clay. Nothing was going to move me off the objective. I was ready to go to war.

In New York, as we checked in to the City Squire Hotel at Seventh Avenue and Fifty-second Street, a bomb threat was phoned in. The police searched the hotel but found nothing. But security around me, and Yank, was increased. As the clock wound down to fight night, there were now eight detectives guarding us.

To reduce the chance of an incident, and to get away from fans and relatives, Yank and I checked into the Pierre hotel nearby.

In Philadelphia, where Marvis and his sisters would hear the bout on radio, they also had police guarding them. Florence, who was coming to New York to watch the fight, had also hired a nurse and a babysitter for the children.

Meanwhile, Clay was shacked up at the Garden, in an apartment that had been improvised for him there. The reason for this unusual setup was to limit his exposure to the public.

The night before the match, I was relaxing, watching a crime show called *The Naked City* on the TV. The phone rang. When I picked up, there was Clay on the other end of the line.

"Joe Frazier, you ready?" he asked.

"I'm ready, brother," I told him.

"I'm ready too, Joe Frazier. And you can't beat me. 'Cause I am the greatest."

"You know what?" I told him. "You preach that you're one of God's men. Well we'll see whose corner the Lord will be in."

"You sure you're not scared, Joe Frazier?"

"Scared of what I'm going to do to you."

"Ain't nothing you *can* do. 'Cause I'll be pecking and poking and pouring water on your smokin'. Bye, Joe Frazier. See you tomorrow night."

"I'll be there. Don't be late."

🥊   🥊   🥊

Talk about a night being electric.

Hoo-boy, March 8, 1971, was it. The Garden was high-voltage, with 20,455 ticket-buying customers shoehorned into the building.

The great fighters of the past—Joe Louis, Dempsey, Sugar Ray Robinson, Willie Pep, James J. Braddock, Gene Tunney—had been introduced, and now, as I headed down the aisle toward the ring, that hum of excitement turned up in volume.

"Make room, make room," Yank was shouting over the crowd's roar, in that deep rumble of a voice.

I was behind him, my head bobbing as I touched his shoulders with my gloves. Around me fans leaned in to shout, "Go get him, Joe." "Kill that mutha, Joe." Under my green-and-gold brocade robe, on which the names of my five children were printed, I was flexing my shoulders, eager to get this thing going.

The fans were with me, shouting *Fray-sher, Fray-sher, Fray-sher.*

Another roar: Clay was moving toward the ring now.

The crowd chanted, *Ah-lee, Ah-lee, Ah-lee . . .*

Clay glided along the ropes, playing to the crowd. When he got to the corner of the ring where I stood, he brushed up against me and said, "Chump."

I just glared at him, and watched him dance away. Was nothing he could do that could unsettle me now. My time was here. This was real. Me and damn Clay in the four-squares.

Then the ring announcer, Johnny Addie, in a tuxedo and blue shirt, was saying: "Ladies and gentlemen. In this corner, wearing red trunks and weighing 215 pounds, from Cherry Hill, New Jersey, the return of the champ . . . Muhammad Ali."

Cheers, and more chants of *Ah-lee . . . Ah-lee . . . Ah-lee . . .*

"And in this corner," Addie said, "wearing green-and-gold trunks, weighing 205 ½ pounds, from Philadelphia, the heavyweight champion of the world . . . Joe Frazier."

The crowd erupted with *Fray-sher . . . Fray-sher . . . Fray-sher.*

The bell gonged several times—a signal that it was time to remove our robes and move to center ring, where the referee, Arthur Mercante, stood, waiting to give us final instructions.

Whatever Mercante said I never heard. That was 'cause Clay was jabbering away at me, with that bug-eyed nutball look of his. I didn't hear any of what Clay said either. I was just staring at him, letting the anger inside me fester.

Where most fights were strictly business, Clay was another story. With that trash mouth of his, the scamboogah had made this personal. As he babbled on, I looked at him and told him: "I'm gonna kill you."

Back in the corner, Yank said: "Get on his ass. Work him 'til he don't want no more."

The crowd was on its feet. Ringside was full of celebrity faces— Senator Hubert Humphrey, Ed Sullivan, Diahann Carroll and David Frost, Alan King, Joe Namath, Diana Ross, Aretha Franklin, George Raft, Bing Crosby, Ted Kennedy, Pat O'Brien, New York City mayor John Lindsay, Count Basie, George Plimpton, and Burt Lancaster. I didn't see any of them, or think of any of the 300 million fans who were watching on satellite TV and closed-circuit. My focus was on the jiveass sucker in red velvet trunks.

The bell rang, and I moved toward him.

I landed the first punch. My strategy was to stay in close, taking his head apart with hooks and straight right hands. With me at five foot eleven and Clay at six foot three, my plan was to whack at his body to make him come down to my height when he covered up. For most of the first two rounds, I was an elusive target, slipping and sliding in and out. This early he figured to look good, and I was putting the pressure on him.

But I knew what I knew: that if I stayed after him, he would slow down. As Yank always said, "Kill the body and the head will die." Once I started banging left hooks off his body and head, and anywhere else I could—ribs, biceps, shoulders—well, then he would be forced to fight my fight. And that smug expression of his would fade like grease before a spot remover.

Yeah. I wasn't worried that he was hitting me with the jab because I was forcing him to jab so that he would be vulnerable to my left hook. Toward the end of the second round, I gave all those Clay fans a sneak preview of what was to come when I slammed a left hook against the side of his face. A good shot, and it hurt Clay, who threw his arms around me as if I was a treasured possession.

It stopped me from punching, while it gave him the opportunity to mug for the crowd that no, the punch didn't hurt. At the bell ending the round, he waved his glove at me to make the point again. Then, between rounds, he refused to sit on his stool, standing nonchalantly in his corner as his handlers attended to him.

Go ahead. Let him prance and posture. The sucker was whistling in the dark. I hadn't yet begun. In the third round, I blocked Clay's uppercuts and continued digging into his body. Clay landed some good shots, but they weren't as strong as the announcers made them seem. To listen to them, I wasn't even in the ring. Clay's shots got called, but when I'd land one on him, all the guy would say was, "Oh, Ali took that really well."

I sent a powerful message in the fourth round when I nailed him on the jaw with a left, and saw by the look on his face that it shook him. This time when he tried to tie me up, I pushed free and pounded away at his ribs. Pretty soon, he was no Fred Astaire. The dancing stopped, but Smokin' Joe didn't.

I kept after him. But even as I pounded him, he was acting like he was still in command, talking his stuff while blood trickled from his nose.

"Don't you know I'm God?" Clay yelled out after I landed a few good shots on him, pinning him against the ropes.

"God, you in the wrong place tonight. I'm kicking ass and taking names."

Mercante tried to hush us up. But this Clay was a talking machine. No way this fight would be waged in silence.

But for all his talk, and for all the playacting he did for the crowd, he was no longer the fighter that razzle-dazzled folks in those first couple of rounds. Now he was down off his toes, and had taken to leaning up against the ropes and jiving. Sometimes he shook his head to the crowd to discount the damage of my punches. Sometimes he looked toward the ringside press and told them, "Nooooo connnnnteessssst." Sometimes he threw these pittypat punches against my gloves, or against my forehead as though testing for termites, joke punches, as if he was goofing on me.

But the joke was on him. I was fighting in earnest, and he was just trying to disguise the fact that he was stalling—that he couldn't do what he used to and dance for fifteen rounds. Not that he *couldn't*. I wouldn't let him. I was pounding the body and the head, and making those nimble legs of his say whoaaa, what's happening here.

All the while, he kept jabbering away, ignoring Mercante's warning to keep it buttoned.

"I'm gonna kill you, nigger," he said.

"Yeah, that's what you got to do," I told him. "'Cause I ain't goin' nowhere."

And I didn't. I worked his body, beating it like a tomtom. And to rub it in, I lowered my hands and slipped his punches, laughing in his face when I did. When the bell ended the fifth round, I cuffed him across the top of his head.

As he usually did, Clay had predicted the outcome of the bout in advance. In fact, he had wanted to read the prediction in the ring just before the match started, but the commission had refused to permit that. So he'd written his prediction in his chicken scrawl on a piece of paper and read it in his dressing room while closed-circuit cameras recorded it and then showed it minutes before the bout started.

That closed-circuit audience—which included my mother watching in Charleston, South Carolina—heard him say, "Flash. I predict first of all that all the Frazier fans and boxing experts will be shocked at how easy I will beat Joe Frazier, who will look like a amateur boxer compared to Muhammad Ali, and they will admit I was the real champion all the time."

"Frazier falls in six."

Well, by round six, Clay was no longer standing in his corner between rounds—he was back on his trusty stool, getting the minute's rest he needed. Me? I was looking across the ring at him, knowing this was the round he'd called, and eager to make a liar of him.

When the bell rang, I sprang off my stool like a sprinter to meet him in center ring.

"Come on, sucker," I shouted. "This is the round. Let's go."

Bobbing and weaving under the right-hand leads Clay fired at me, I maneuvered him to a corner of the ring and began whacking the left off his ribs before taking it upstairs. Bingo. I hurt him with a left hook to the jaw. He sagged into the ropes, like a wilted flower, while the crowd, sensing he was in big trouble, roared. People stood on their feet, throwing punches right along with me. I fired away, scoring repeatedly with big thudding punches, trying to finish the sucker. But he took what I dished out and somehow managed to survive the round.

Back in my corner, I asked Yank, "What's holding him up?"

"Don't worry," he said. "Keep beating on his ass, and he'll fall."

But Clay showed heart and fought back. I was relentless in round seven, slipping and sliding, making Clay miss his shots. I kept at him in the eighth, taking away his timing and catching him before he could hold me. In the ninth round, he suddenly mustered an attack that revived his supporters and had me looking all of a sudden like a tired fighter. With right hands, he nailed me repeatedly. I was bleeding now from the mouth, and my face had begun to lump up. Clay hit me with a series of rights to the head, but I refused to acknowledge their effect and just kept wacking at him, as if he hadn't showed me shit.

Toward the end of the round, Clay landed a combination that made me redirect my steps. The crowd which booed him earlier for laying on the ropes now came alive, as if another Clay miracle was about to occur. I stunned him twice; he fired back and missed. I was hitting him three punches to one and was scoring heavily. I nailed him with a hard right hand, he missed four punches, then I landed eight unanswered punches. For a guy that boxing experts said had no right hand, Clay knew otherwise. I trapped Clay in the corner for almost the entire round. When he tried to come out, I put him back in there with devastating hooks that threw him off balance. At the end of the round I flagged him and he flagged me.

Back and forth we went. In the tenth, he opened his big mouth to shout down to the ringside press: "He's out," but the real story was that Clay was so tired that all he could do was just stand there, taking my punches.

A round later, Clay looked as if he could use an oxygen mask when I began using his head for batting practice. Left hook, left hook, left hook. Clay backed to the ropes and waved me to follow him. Okay, Butterfly. You asked for it.

I nailed him with another left that sent him reeling into the ropes. His face got exaggeratedly big-eyed. He was really hurt, and tried to find the ropes to get his balance. I staggered him again with a left hook and caught him with some right uppercuts. At the end of the round he walked rubber-legged to his corner, bringing Dundee and another handler, Chickie Ferrara, rushing through the ropes like firemen responding to a four-alarm blaze. Back in the corner, Dundee slapped Clay's legs and shouted at him, trying to revive him, as the ring physician, Dr. A. Harry Kleiman, looked into Clay's eyes to make sure he was conscious enough to continue.

Apparently he was because when the bell rang for round twelve, he rose up off that stool and walked toward me, throwing punches. Some of them hit me—I didn't care. I was crazy to get at him, knowing he was running on empty, knowing the hurt I put on him. The shots Clay got hit with were like wrecking balls that would take down a cement building. I was enjoying it and having a ball getting the job done. But the guy surprised me: He stood and traded with me. And what he was throwing wasn't pittypat.

But my adrenaline made me feel no pain. I didn't just want to beat this guy; I wanted to knock him out. I kept moving forward, letting the punches fly. Hit me, I hit you. I don't give a damn. I come to destroy you, Clay.

But wouldn't you know it, in the thirteenth round the Butterfly got wings again. Don't ask me how. As bad as I wanted to leave him a battered heap on the canvas, he found it in him to get up on his toes and move about the ring. Dancing and shooting the jab at me. And when those dancing legs got tired, he just lay on me like a sack of mush, waiting for Mercante to break us up.

The fourteenth round. As two tired men, we fought, Clay trying to keep me at bay with that jab of his, while I kept stepping in on him, landing punches, trying to get one more industrial-strength hook on target. The times I got within range, Clay would try to lay on me and bury me in a clinch. I kept pushing him off, looking for a chance to land the big one.

That chance came in the fifteenth and final round. By now there were more folks chanting *Joe . . . Joe . . . Joe . . .* than there were singing out Clay's Muslim name. Yeah, maybe I'd walked into the arena a supporting player, but over fourteen rounds I'd proven I wasn't fodder for no Cassius Clay fairy tale. And that point was about to be made as forcefully as a tired ole country boy could.

Clay came out aggressively for that final round, as if he knew he needed a knockout to win. He opened up with a left and right, and threw the same combination a second time. Then as he maneuvered to find an opening, I threw a left hook that he caught on his right forearm. It was a punch meant to "locate"—to get a bead on him for the next punch.

As he stepped toward me, I dipped down and let fly another left, leaving my feet to throw a looping shot that landed against the right side of his face and sent Clay onto the seat of his trunks. Boom, and there it was—Mr. Him on his butt, his legs kicking up into the air—the very picture of a beaten man.

Tell you the truth, though, it was not a killer shot. But it landed right on the button, on a very worn-out man. And the roar it set off was like from the belly of a beast. The crowd—those twenty-thousand-odd souls—were up off their chairs, crazy with anticipation. In Philadelphia, around their little box radio, the Frazier kids leaped to their feet, and began jumping up and down. Were they about to hear the unthinkable—Clay knocked out?

The way he went down, I thought so. But Clay showed big heart as he climbed up off the canvas by the count of four, and took the mandatory eight from Mercante. By now the right side of his face was swollen, and he looked unsteady on his feet. I pursued him, but there wasn't much left in my tank either. Hard as I tried, I just couldn't get across the finisher.

I cracked two lefts off his jaw, and then a right to his chin and a left to the body. Clay folded his arms around me, but I pushed him away and fired two more lefts that drove him into the ropes. When the final bell sounded, the crowd noise was so deafening neither of us heard the clang clang clang. Mercante had to throw himself between us to get the message across that our evening's work was done.

With that, I raised my hands in victory, thanked the Lord, and with a bloody mouth told Clay, "I kicked your ass."

The fight was over.

The Fight was history.

As an eerie hush settled over the building, Johnny Addie read the official scorecards.

"Referee Arthur Mercante scores eight rounds for Frazier, six rounds for Ali, one round even."

Boos, cheers.

"Judge Artie Aidala scores nine rounds for Frazier, six rounds for Ali."

I turned toward Yank, who embraced me and said, "You done it, Joe. You done it." My brother Tommy jumped into the ring and started yelling to Clay, "Crawl! Get down on your knees and crawl to Joe Frazier!"

The crowd noise drowned out Addie's announcement of Judge Bill Recht's scoring—eleven rounds Frazier, four for Ali.

I thought I'd won the fight 12–3, but it didn't *really* matter.

The unanimous decision left me winner and still champion and Clay beaten for the first time in his career. But this time I was a champion without reservations and qualifications. U-n-d-i-s-p-u-t-e-d heavyweight champion.

Hear that? Undisputed champion.

I was twenty-seven years old, and there would never be another night like it in my life.

$\quad \text{\Large \texthv} \quad \text{\Large \texthv} \quad \text{\Large \texthv}$

The front page of the next day's *Philadelphia Daily News* headlined: JOE'S THE GREATEST, with a photo of Clay lying on his back and me turning to go to the neutral corner.

That knockdown landed in newspapers all over the world.

It was in the minutes after the fight ended, and the adrenaline bottomed out, that the realities of the night's work set in. One second you're jumping up and down in ecstacy, so full of joy that you feel like you could float into orbit. The next moment you're sitting back in the dressing room and all the gremlins come out—there's nothing but pain.

Hoo-boy, I was spent.

By now, Clay had been helped into his trousers, as he lay there limp as a wet noodle, and then driven by limo to Flowers Fifth Avenue Hospital to have x-rays on that swollen jaw.

Me? I sat there like a zombie while folks patted me on the back and congratulated me. Then I was up on my feet, headed to a large area set up in a corridor of the Garden, where the press sat waiting.

While one of my guys held an ice pack to my face, I answered questions through my puffed lips.

Then it was back to the dressing room, now crowded with friends and relatives who fussed about me.

My brother Tommy hugged and kissed me and said, "You're the greatest."

Florence had an even bigger hug and a question: "Are you okay?" I told her no problem, but that was a damn lie.

But the fight had taken a toll on me. My blood pressure was dangerously high. It wasn't Clay's punches so much as the effort I'd put in with a body that was not one hundred percent to begin with. I was drained, ten to fifteen pounds lighter than when I walked into that ring. Fifteen hard rounds and, unfortunately, there was nothing to fall back on.

I felt too exhausted to go running back to Philadelphia the next day. Instead I stayed for a few days in my room at the hotel and waited for my body to recover.

It didn't. I couldn't urinate. I couldn't stand up and walk. I couldn't eat or drink. My eyes were puffed and sensitive to light. We kept the shades drawn and the doors closed, and it also helped to stick my head in a sink filled with ice water.

It seemed like my body had shut down from exhaustion.

I sat in the room and prayed I'd get back to my old self.

Whatever it is, Lord, help me.

Yank was there with me, and so were my sisters Martha, Rebecca, and Flossie and a few business guys. Florence had gone back home to be with the kids.

Somewhere in there, Dr. Campbell, the commission doctor, came by the room. A plan was proposed to move me to a hospital up in the Catskills, away from the big-city press. We didn't want headlines that would make it sound like Clay had beaten me so badly I had to be hospitalized.

Call me suspicious. Call me paranoid. But I had a bad feeling about going up to the Catskills—that the forces that had wanted Clay to be champion would do me in there. And damn Clay somehow would end up with the title I'd won fair and square.

Uh uh. Said no to the Catskills and instead headed back to Philadelphia, where I was put into St. Luke's Hospital there.

Dr. James Giuffre had them set me down in the recovery room, where I lay on a bed of ice. I stayed like that all night. Was it a dream that a spirit took my hand in the wee hours and told me I'd be okay? To this day I can recall His presence, His touch on my hand. But the security guard the next morning assured me there had been no visitors.

Whatever. I was now in good hands. There was really no way to keep my stay at St. Luke's a secret. So Dr. Giuffre, who was director of St. Luke's as well as a friend of mine, told the media that I was being treated for high blood pressure and athlete's kidney.

Wouldn't you know that that scamboogah Clay would use my medical problem as a reason to say that it proved the judges' scoring had been incorrect and that he had really beaten me. What a weasel.

Actually, all it proved was that I needed a rest after The Fight, while Clay had rested during it.

I stayed in a private room at St. Luke's for several weeks. But once things began to stabilize, and the fear of a stroke occurring vanished, I began to lead two lives. Daytimes I was a hospital patient. Come nighttime, I would lace up my shoes, tell the nurse, "See you later," and slide out the back door and party.

I had a backdoor key so when I'd come back later I wouldn't have to go through hospital security. And nobody would know my business.

It was while I was in St. Luke's that I had time to play back that night of March 8, and let what I had done sink in. What a wild night it had been, the excitement so overpowering that tragically two spectators at the Garden had died of heart attacks during the fight.

For me, it had been redemption for all the nasty racial garbage Clay had spewed in the weeks and months leading up to the fight.

It was nasty stuff he said. And you want to know something? First time he called me an Uncle Tom, I didn't even know what that was. I thought it was someone who peeped in windows. No matter. I had spoiled the Butterfly's coming-out party. Me. The "other guy" in this drama. Yeah. Lots of people had expected Joe Frazier to roll over and play dead for the loudmouth. But surprise surprise, I kicked his butt.

Like Yank had said—beating Clay changed my life.

It put me at the center of an event that succeeded in every way— and would be remembered for as long as boxing fans existed. Frazier–Clay number one, The Fight, was now up there with Dempsey–Tunney, Louis–Conn, Marciano–Walcott, Graziano–Zale, Robinson–LaMotta, and Pep–Saddler as one of the sport's great matches. In fact, our matchup is considered the greatest fight of all time.

The press raved about what a thrilling, competitive fight it had been. And the business that The Fight did far exceeded the revenues generated by any previous bout in the sport's history. The Fight of the Century was the biggest worldwide media event of the year, and I'm proud that our purses of $2.5 million each set the precedent for professional athletes in all sports.

The live gate of $1,342,951 from a crowd of 20,455 was a record for an indoor bout. The closed-circuit take was $16.5 million—more than four times any previous fight return. With a gross of about $20 million, Perenchio and Cooke would end up with a pretax profit of $1.5 million.

The arrangement that the promoters had was a sixty–forty split, in Cooke's favor for putting up the dough. That meant that after taxes Cooke would clear $450,000, or ten cents on the dollar for his $4.5 million investment. Perenchio? He would clear $300,000 as his share. Together, their $750,000 after-tax profit equaled what I would clear for taking all those punches.

But then again, I could say what no other man could:

I whupped Cassius Marcellus Clay.

6

"Daddy, Quit Playing Around"

To the victors go the spoils.

When I got out of St. Luke's, I got a call from the Garden's John Condon, who suggested I come up to New York. Turned out there was a guy up there who'd won big money betting on me against Clay, and this fellow wanted to show his appreciation.

The guy was in the diamond business. What he did was give Florence and me matching diamond-studded rings, each of them with nineteen diamonds and each of the rings worth ten thousand dollars.

Yeah. Yank was right. By beating Clay my way in life was paved. The kindness of the diamond man would be repeated wherever I went. For the rest of my life, there would be deals, discounts, gifts, and favors for the man who had clipped the Butterfly's wings.

The first time I went home after the fight the city of Philadelphia hosted "Joe Frazier Day" with a parade and all the hoopla. Even good old Beaufort County had a parade for me and a giant billboard reading WELCOME JOE FRAZIER.

And everywhere I went, there were now people that wanted to say hello, shake my hand, get an autograph. Then, as now, I appreciated the attention. There are athletes today that won't sign an autograph unless they're paid to do it. And then they act like the fan's not even standing there—they won't look that individual in the eye, and add a kind word or smile.

We're living in a generation of spoiled-rotten sports heroes. Me? Over the years there have been times I was paid to sign my autograph, sure. But when I'm out in public, and asked for my signature, I sign, and happily, for nothing. In fact, these days, I always carry business cards that have a color photo of me, which, when asked to, I autograph.

I'm grateful for the way my life turned out, and feel an obligation to people who are fans. It doesn't take an awful lot to return the good feelings fans brought to me and to make those people feel good about themselves. A few words. A joke. I take that obligation seriously enough that when Marvis, ten years old at the time, scared away a fan of mine it became a point of contention between us.

It happened a month or so after I beat Clay. I had gone with Marvis and his sisters to Disneyland. On what was supposed to be a day with their daddy, their time with me ended up being shared with hundreds of fans who asked me to sign autographs and pose for pictures.

For Marvis, whose daddy was often away from home for months at a time, it seemed an unfair intrusion. Late in the day, as I signed what I thought was the last autograph, a little boy shyly approached.

"No no, get out of here," Marvis shouted at the boy, frightening him so badly that the youngster ran off.

"Marvis," I said, anger in my voice, "you go catch that little boy and bring him back. These are people that pay your daddy's salary. You never get too big for people."

Marvis ran after the child and fetched him back.

"Now you apologize," I told Marvis.

"I'm sorry," Marvis mumbled to the little boy.

"I can't hear you," I told him, fixing him with a look.

"I'm sorry," he said, in a clear and distinct voice.

Then I turned to the little boy and asked him what his name was.

In the weeks, and months, that followed, for the first time in years I was not consumed with boxing. I felt free to lay back a bit and have me some fun. Hang out with Florence and the kids. Hit the road with my musical group in the States and in Europe. Do a guest spot on Dean

Martin's TV show. Run down to Beaufort in my custom-made Lincoln and go see my momma.

We laughed, Momma and me, about what had happened the morning after I'd knocked Clay on his ass.

Seems like all of a sudden Dolly Frazier was a V-I-P.

Folks that for decades wouldn't so much as look at her when they passed her on the street now wanted to be her best friend. Yeah, the morning after Frazier–Clay, her yard was full of people, including ole Trask, whose fields she had worked in for all those years.

Trask invited her into his car to look at properties he owned around Beaufort County, figuring, I guess, her Billy Boy would be moving her to a fancier address.

But we didn't talk much about that. It was The Fight that was Topic One of our conversation. Momma told me how crowded it had been at the closed-circuit arena in Charleston, where she'd gone to see the bout.

"There were a lot of people there," she said. "So many you could hardly stand up in the place. And there were plenty of them around me that put their money on Clay, and were tellin' me Clay was gonna whup my boy.

"I told them, 'I raised up that boy on corn bread, beans, rice, and plenty of fish. He got strength. He gonna win. Hush up with that.'

"Then when you knocked him down, and his legs went straight up in the air, I sang out, 'Amen to that. Praise the Lord.' But I tell you, son, you had me worried, all those licks in the head he was fetchin' you."

"Momma, no way he was gonna beat me. He'd have to shoot me first."

Trask was right about one thing. Momma was gonna be moving on. I'd heard about an old plantation near Yemassee (population seven hundred), nineteen miles from Laurel Bay, that sat on 368 acres. The Brewton Plantation went back to 1732, when a Miles Brewton had gotten a royal grant to the place from King George II of England. Other owners followed, including Charles Pinckney, who was a signer of the Constitution.

Whenever ownership changed hands the house slaves and field slaves were included in the bill of sale. Those that did stoop labor worked in rice paddies that they were obliged to share with water moccasins.

During the Civil War the place was said to be owned by a white man named Frazier, who might have been the master of my ancestors, who had been slaves in this part of the country.

In any case, the plantation was torched during the Civil War, but afterward its owner rebuilt the main house. Sight unseen, I bought it on the advice of lawyers and money managers.

The real-estate agent had told me the place needed some work, but the night I drove over there I damn near cried. The land was overgrown, fences were down, the ponds were all choked up, and the big house was a mess. Some parts of the fields had turned to swamp, which meant you'd better think twice or that swamp would be having your tractor for lunch.

But as I looked the place over, I got to thinking—what the hell: I've worked land lots worse than this. Let's get the job done.

Over the next two, three weeks, I set about to fix this place proper for Momma and my new farming business. Worked from six in the morning 'til it got dark. Cleanin' up, burnin' down, fixin' and repairin'. The planation came with four homes, a four-car garage, three or four ponds, a six-horse stable. So it took a lot of work . . . and a good piece of money to get it right.

When Brewton Plantation was ready for Momma's move, I told her I wanted to burn the old Laurel Bay place down. It was a kind of gesture— a way of burning away all the hardships and troubles we'd known. But Momma wouldn't hear of it. She said that that little raggedy house was Rubin's place—he'd built it himself and, even if it some day crumbled apart and fell to the ground, she'd leave it right there.

"It reminds me of your daddy," she said. "So we're keeping it."

Yes, Ma'am. No arguing with that lady.

I had heard that shortly after I earned $2.5 million for whupping Clay, she had gone into the fields to pick tomatoes for twenty-five cents a bucket. When I tried to persuade her she didn't need to work anymore, she paid me no mind again. She'd hardly settled into the plantation— along with other kin I'd had move in, like my sisters Rebecca and Flossie— when she was out there putting in a backyard bean patch and looking after her goats, chickens, and pigs.

"I'm gonna keep working long as I got my health, boy," she told me in no uncertain terms.

Yes, Ma'am.

While in Beaufort, I was invited to address the South Carolina legislature by Governor John C. West.

That day, when I stepped into the State House wearing a conservative gray suit, a yellow shirt, and a striped tie, the legislators gave me a standing ovation that went on and on.

Soon after, I stepped toward the microphone and said:

"Today, as I stand before you, I will not deny that I am a proud and happy man . . . and yet somewhat sad, and a little hurt to know that I am one of the very few black citizen guests to address this General Assembly in almost a century. . . .

"With South Carolina being so big and beautiful and of course having so many wonderful black citizens, there must have been more black men or black women also deserving of this honor.

"As I stand here and look around this chamber, I can see that South Carolina has come a long way since I left Beaufort eleven years ago.

"I remember working on the farm when I was a boy. I'd say, 'Good morning, boss,' and he'd say, 'To the mule.' At noon, I'd say, 'Lunch time, boss,' and he'd say, 'One o'clock.' And in the evening, I'd say, 'Good night, boss,' and he'd say, 'In the mornin'.' "

There was laughter now. When it stopped, I took note of the state's three black representatives, and said:

"I am proud to see the few black faces that have been duly elected to this legislature and it gives me great pleasure to know that finally white and black citizens are working together for the betterment of its people.

"But ladies and gentlemen, I am here today not as an orator or as a statesman, but as a young man whose boyhood dream was realized when I won the heavyweight championship of the world.

"You can do anything you want to do if you really put your heart and soul and mind into it. When I started boxing, I had two jobs, a wife, a couple of kids, and I had to train. But if you put your right foot in front of you and the left behind, somebody will give you a hand.

"We must save our people, and when I say 'our people,' I mean white and black. We need to quit thinking who's living next door, who's driving a big car, who's my little daughter going to play with, who is she going to sit next to in school. We don't have time for that."

When I finished, there was another big ovation. Then it was on to a luncheon as the state's guests at a nearby restaurant. Speeches followed, full of nice words for Smokin' Joe. But the speech I liked best was in the form of a poem written by Marvis, which was recited by my daughter Jacquelyn:

> *Fly like a butterfly, sting like a bee,*
> *Joe Frazier is the only one who can beat*
> > *Muhammad Ali.*

Short but sweet.

It was a helluva day for a high-school dropout, who'd left Beaufort County, South Carolina, poor and unknown and had come back a boxing hero.

All that was missing was my daddy. Lord, how I wished he could have been there to see what his Billy Boy had amounted to. And more: to enjoy what success in the ring now enabled the Fraziers to have.

He'd have liked Brewton Plantation, with its gated entrance opening to a long driveway lined with tall oak trees, dripping in Spanish moss. And he'd have gotten a kick out of sticking his fishing pole in one of the ponds, and seeing if he could catch one of the black bass that were swimming about in there, coexisting as best as they could with the rare alligator or two that called the plantation home.

For that matter, Daddy would have had a swell time up north, in the Lafayette house, rassling with his five grandchildren on broadloom carpeting or splashing about with them in a swimming pool that was shaped like, what else, a boxing glove.

Sadly, it couldn't be. But it set me to thinking about family and friends that were still alive and well.

Some of them, like my old pal Dickie Murray, were far off—in his case in Vietnam, where as an infantry sergeant he was earning medals for bravery. It was only when he got back that I'd learn he'd made seven thousand dollars betting on The Fight, never once letting on to other GIs that he knew me.

"Woulda been ten thousand dollars, but one of them sumbitches had the misfortune to go and get his ass killed," Dickie told me when he finally got back.

But if some of those close to me were dead, or some just far from home, there were plenty others I could share my good fortune with. That summer, I called for the first Frazier family reunion—a six-day celebration at the plantation that brought out two thousand people.

We opened the big metal gates with a sign at the entrance that displayed doves and the name "Frazier." Then we fired up the barbecue pits, and put out endless platters of ribs, chicken—we even barbecued venison. There were snap beans and butter beans and corn and cucumbers from Momma's garden. Plenty of food, plenty of drink. Relatives came from as near as Washington, D.C., and as far as California, from my side of the family and from Florence's. Some of them I'd never met before. It was a grand time.

Right after I'd beaten Clay, Yank and Bruce Wright urged me to retire. Their thinking was why not retire young, and undefeated, and live in comfort? Why take the sort of punishment that my style guaranteed? For them it seemed a hard way to make a living. For me it was doing what came naturally.

No, I wasn't ready to put the gloves in mothballs. It wasn't just a job to me. It was my pleasure and passion. I felt that boxing was what the Lord had always had in mind for me.

Fact is by the summer I was eager to be fighting again. But as it was explained to me, another bout in '71 just was not practical. With all the money I'd made from the Clay fight, and what the tax man stood to take if I fought again, it'd be like fighting for nothing.

But that couldn't keep me from getting back in the gym and working out.

And that went a long way to killing the rumors that Clay and his people put out that I was lame and decrepit, a ghost of the mighty Frazier because of the damage he had done me in our fight.

Meanwhile, Clay had that dark cloud removed from over his pointy head. On June 28, 1971, the United States Supreme Court overturned his conviction. That meant the now Second Greatest was free to fight, whenever and wherever he pleased.

It wouldn't be me he'd tangle with. Not right away. Yank was in no hurry to make the return match. And neither was I. Not after the trash he had talked going into the March 8 fight.

Had he taken his defeat like a man, well, then I might have seen fit to give the guy a rematch sooner than later. But he'd gone weasel on me again. And rather than owning up to the asswhupping I'd put on him, he was now making as though he'd been the victim of a bum decision. Blaming the loss on the white establishment and all that crap.

Clay said, "Joe Frazier is ugly, he don't talk good, he's got no footwork. All he does it take punches. He's not recognized when he walks the streets. . . . In Japan they treated me like a president. All the things I stand for, all the things I went through . . . being a Muslim, staying out of the Army, being deprived of my right to work for almost four years . . . and to go fifteen hard rounds and send him to the hospital is why people still regard me as the champion. He says he's satisfied. Sure he's satisfied, with a crumb. Man been in a meathouse all his life, he's thankful to get a crumb. White folks . . . give a nigger a crumb and expect him to be thankful."

When I heard that, I got steamed. I told the press: "He keeps forgetting I won the fight. In what country is he dreaming I'm not the champion? Why does he have to talk hatred and separation? Why can't people live together? He's fooling himself. People who believe him are crazy, just like him. I'm not trying to make them come over to me. I'm not going to twist their elbow or beg 'em to like me. The night of the fight, his fans just said, 'Well, we lost.' And walked out. And Clay didn't say nothing either. I just think he's a bad loser—in everything."

Yank wanted me to ease back into action for my first fight since Clay. That was, traditionally, what fighters did after a demanding match. You didn't take on Godzilla after you whupped King Kong. You looked for some breathing room. Besides, Yank probably wanted to assure himself that I wasn't showing any ill affects from the fight with Clay, and that down the road I'd be up to fighting stiffer opposition. He was being cautious, the way managers often are, and, like all champions, I had the right to an easy opponent once in a while. Clay had fought a patsy named Brian London when he held the title. Joe Louis had gone through so many opponents that the quality of them declined to where those guys were referred to as "the bum of the month." Then there was Pete Rademacher, an amateur champion who, turning pro, became the opponent for Floyd Patterson and his heavyweight title in 1957.

So that's how Terry Daniels became my next opponent.

The fight was made for January 15, 1972, in New Orleans, with me being guaranteed two hundred thousand dollars.

Daniels? He was not your typical heavyweight contender, which is to say poor and from the ghetto. No, Daniels was a twenty-five-year-old prelaw student at Southern Methodist University, who came from a well-to-do Willoughby, Ohio, family. Daddy was a successful business-man, and son Terry a hotshot high-school athlete.

At SMU he had made the freshman football team as a defensive back, but a knee injury made him look to boxing for his sport. After fighting amateur some, he'd turned professional, as a lark, and before he knew it he was fighting some serious people. In three years as a profes-sional, Daniels had compiled a record of 29–4–1, with his biggest vic-tory coming over Manuel Ramos. His losses had been to Floyd Patterson, Tony Doyle, Jack O'Halloran, and Floyd Casey.

The bout had been scheduled in the same city and on the night before Super Bowl VI—the Miami Dolphins against the Dallas Cow-boys. The fight would be shown nationally on home television, meaning it would be free and meaning that more people would end up watching it than saw Frazier–Clay.

For New Orleans it was the first heavyweight title bout since 1892, when Gentleman Jim Corbett had stopped John L. Sullivan in the twenty-first round of the first title match ever fought using gloves. Before that, boxing had been a bare-knuckle sport.

Whatever. Most of the press was skeptical about the fight because of Daniels' size—he weighed 191 pounds, whereas I came in at 215½ pounds—and because of what they glimpsed of his skills while the both of us trained at the Monteleone Hotel.

"Is Daniels better than your sparring partners?" one newsman asked.

"A little," I said.

But that didn't mean I was gonna fool with the boy. Boxing his-tory was full of examples of longshot nobodies landing that one punch that turned them into overnight successes. I wasn't about to let Terry Daniels make his reputation at my expense.

In four rounds, I knocked him down four times before the referee, Herman Dutreix, stopped the fight.

"They needed a math major for a referee, he had to count so much," Daniels joked afterward.

A nice kid he was, and he'd gotten paid for his troubles—thirty-five thousand dollars. That would cover the cost of a few law books.

Afterward, Daniels came by the dressing room with two paper cups of beer. He gave me one, and we tapped our cups together and toasted one another.

"Anytime you're in my vicinity," he said, "my house is yours."

Where Terry Daniels was a fine and refined sort of guy, Ron Stander was more rough and tumble.

Stander, my next opponent, was called the "Bluffs Butcher," which was a takeoff on his hometown, Council Bluffs, Iowa, where he'd been a star fullback for the local high-school team.

We signed to fight across the Missouri River in Omaha, Nebraska, on May 26, with the promoters guaranteeing me $150,000 from the home TV money and 40 percent of the live gate.

Half of whatever ended up in my hands was going to a fund for sickle-cell anemia, a blood disease that occurs mostly in blacks and that Yank's four-year-old son, Mark, was suffering from.

Stander was known as a beer-guzzling, knockabout character—a kind of midwestern Tony Galento. He said things like, "How much beer do I drink? I lose count after a case." Or: "Have I ever been knocked down? Yeah. By the police with a nightstick."

Fighting me, he would weigh 218 pounds, but his training habits were so slack, and his beer drinking so enthusiastic, that he had gone into the ring weighing as much as 247 pounds.

As a fighter, he had a record of twenty-three victories, one loss and one draw, although his opponents were mostly no-name guys he had fought in the friendly confines of midwestern arenas, where judges were inclined to be charitable to the local boy on their scorecards. Places like Sioux Falls, Waterloo, Omaha, and Elgin, Nebraska.

I hadn't seen Stander fight, but Yank described him as a crude, brawling sort, who was susceptible to being cut. He had had sixty-odd stitches, it was said, most of them from gashes opened up during his bouts, some from police nightsticks, and a few from a plate of spaghetti that his wife, Darlene, supposedly had thrown at him.

Those reports seemed true enough—at least the part about his cutting easy. When I got out to Omaha and met the scamboogah, I could see he had scars over both eyes and under his chin. I never asked him about the dish of pasta.

At least one of Stander's victories had been over a recognized fighter, Earnie Shavers, and the draw had been with Manuel Ramos, but that result even his wife, Darlene, questioned.

"I thought he lost to Manuel Ramos the first time, when he got a draw," she said.

She was not crazy about his boxing career.

"He's a little boy at heart," she told reporters. "Boxing made him an instant hero around here. He was an excellent husband until he turned pro. Then his whole lookout on life changed. Now we have nothing in the bank. No hospitalization. And we're two months behind on the mortgage. You can't raise two kids on fantasy."

The reality, as she described it to the news guys, was that Stander's biggest purse, until he fought me, had been three thousand dollars. And for that, she said, he left too much of himself in the ring.

"Ron gets hurt every time he goes in the ring because he's never been in shape," she said. "How do I know Ron gets hurt? Because after a lot of fights he doesn't know what he is doing and doesn't remember what happened. God only gave you one brain, and you shouldn't abuse it."

That was the gamble a man took coming into this game. You put up your body, and nerve, against another man on the chance it could get you onto Easy Street. For most fighters, it didn't turn out that way. For most fighters, boxing was a losing investment.

And even for the ones who were luckier, like me, there were minuses to go with the pluses. Few of us got off scot-free. Me, for a while now I was aware of a developing cataract in my left eye. In fact, my eye trouble started right after the Olympics in 1964. In case you're wondering, when the light-focusing transparent lens that sits behind the pupil becomes clouded, you have a cataract. My eye specialist, Dr. Myron Yanoff, had told me that boxing would increase the damage and quicken the eye's deterioration. I had told him: "Blind and poor is no fun." He understood what I meant—that with the money boxing provided my family and me, I would be in a better position to get and pay for the attention that the eye eventually would need.

There were times, particularly on the championship level, when the prefight examination did not require me to look at an eye chart. A doctor simply shined a light on your eyes and examined them. Doing that he wasn't going to uncover any cataract damage.

But on those occasions when I had had to read that chart, I simply changed hands when the doctor said, "Cover your other eye." In other words, the good eye read the letters the doctor pointed to, and the bad eye just got covered with a different hand. Changing hands created the illusion I was changing eyes. So far it had gotten me by.

But once the cataract problem started, minor though it was for a while, we knew that we wouldn't be going back to California, where they were more stringent in their prefight examinations than elsewhere. That had an effect on the rematch with Clay, whenever I got ready to fight it. See, the deal we'd made with Perenchio and Cooke for the first Frazier–Clay match called for us to fight the rematch out there, in California, for a guarantee of only $750,000 for each fighter, plus 50 percent of the profit. Well, after the kind of show Clay and I put on at the Garden, the money didn't seem nearly enough. And given their strict examinations, California was not a place I wanted to fight in.

When newsmen asked Yank about California as site of the rematch, he would tell them there was no chance of our fighting there and say it was for "personal reasons."

Anyway. That was still a way off. For now, there was Stander to worry about. And in truth, I wasn't too worried, particularly the way Stander's handlers were talking. At the rules meeting before the bout, they made a point of telling the referee, Zack Clayton, that Stander cut easily and not to get shaken up by it and stop the fight before Stander had a chance to get his licks in. In their own way, they were saying they figured their guy was going to bleed.

Well, they were right. In front of ten thousand people, most of whom had come across the Missouri River from Council Bluffs, Stander tried to muscle with me, in the first round hitting me with good body shots, even knocking me off balance at one point. But that was about it for Stander, as those fans wearing hats that said, "Who in the hell is Joe Frazier?" began to find out that who I was was not only the better man but still another guy who could make their hero's blood run.

First round—Stander bled from the nose, even though he was holding his arms high to protect his face.

Second round—he was cut along the side of his nose, as I hit him with hooks, uppercuts, everything but the ring stool. He took the punches without going down.

Third round—he was still standing under my assault, but had begun to bleed from above the right eye.

Fourth round—he went back to his corner with his face puffed and bleeding and a cut now under the right eye. And from the way the blood poured from his nose, my guess was that I'd broken it.

He had taken a lot of punishment and hadn't gone down. But he looked a mess and it wasn't likely that it was going to get any better for him the way I was going. As one of his handlers said, "He ran out of skin." So when Stander came back to his stool, his corner said enough, and that was it. Fight over.

As Darlene put it: "You don't enter a Volkswagen at Indy unless you know a helluva shortcut." At least they'd catch up on the mortgage. Stander would earn $42,631.

Afterward, the newsmen naturally wanted to know whether, with these victories over two relatively obscure fighters, we now had Clay within our sights.

Well, we did and we didn't.

I was open to fighting Clay so long as I got a minimum guarantee of $3.5 million and the other guy got less. There weren't gonna be equal shares *this* time around.

By now, Jack Kent Cooke held the rights to the rematch, with Perenchio no longer actively in the picture. Whatever arrangements they had made were between the two of them. All Yank and I knew was that Cooke was the man to deal with.

He seemed willing to renegotiate the money on the deal, and by May we'd heard he was prepared to up his offer to $2.7 million. That wasn't three-point-five, but it sure sounded like a starting place for discussions. Yet through the summer and into the fall, nothing came together.

Cooke had been quoted as saying that he felt a rematch could gross $30 million, and when Yank huddled with him he told Cooke that this time around the fighters should share in the profits.

"I said to Mr. Cooke, 'I want 30 percent,' " Yank told me later. "I asked him if any promoter is entitled to as much as the athlete. He said that's a matter of opinion."

Some folks thought that since Cooke had my John Henry on the dotted line he could do pretty much as Jack Kent Cooke wanted to. But I didn't necessarily go along with that view. As I told one reporter: "Cooke got that contract, but Cooke don't have that championship."

At one point Bob Arum, an attorney for Ali, claimed to have a British group interested in buying up Cooke's rights for $8 million—$3 million each for the fighters and $2 million for Cooke.

But the Brits and their deal soon disappeared, in what became a pattern. It was always one thing or another to screw things up and keep the rematch from getting made. And every time Clay opened his big mouth, it made me want to keep his ass on hold.

Seemed like wherever I was, there was always someone relaying what Clay had said, and wanting me to comment on it. And I got bored, and tired, of playing that because what he said continued to be that insulting and sometimes racially based bullshit that he'd talked before I'd whupped his ass.

After a while, Yank and Cloverlay looked beyond Clay, who had fought and beaten Jimmy Ellis and Buster Mathis after losing to me. They began to zero in on a young undefeated contender named George Foreman.

Alex Valdez, a theatrical agent who'd booked the European leg of the tour I'd made with my musical group, became point man in the negotiations that led to a company called National Sports Limited offering me an $850,000 guarantee against 42 percent of bout revenues, and Foreman $375,000 against 20 percent of revenues.

National Sports Limited was owned and financed mostly by the Jamaican government, which was how and why Frazier–Foreman ended up in Kingston, Jamaica, for January 22, 1973.

The money for our guarantees was provided by a loan from the Bank of Nova Scotia Jamaica, Ltd., and was expected to be repaid by the closed-circuit proceeds as well as whatever the anticipated crowd of forty thousand would contribute.

Foreman was a big fellow—six foot three and 217$\frac{1}{2}$ pounds—who came out of Houston's Fifth Ward. Fifth Ward was a nasty ghetto on whose streets ole rambunctious Foreman had drunk quanities of cheap wine, mugged people, and seemed headed for the jailhouse. But George, who, like me, was a high-school dropout, had seen a TV ad in which Johnny Unitas, the Baltimore Colts quarterback, urged young drifters like him to change their lives by joining the Job Corps.

Foreman signed on and was sent first to Grants Pass, Oregon, and then to Pleasanton, California. In Pleasanton he continued his habit of beating up the other boys there on a regular basis, and was on the brink of being drummed out of the corps and sent to a nearby state prison when a Job Corps counselor invited him to try boxing.

Charles (Doc) Broadus, a former Air Force sergeant who ran the gym at the Pleasanton facility, would tell folks about the phone call he got that led to his meeting up with big bad Foreman: "Somebody said, 'There's a young man here trying to beat up everybody.' I go over there and find this sixteen-year-old kid, George Foreman, had taken the door off the hinges, beat up on a kid and thrown him out the window."

The five-foot-four Broadus, who was a martial arts expert, walked over to Foreman and said, " 'Why don't you pick on somebody your own size!' That stopped him. He looked at me sort of odd. I told him, 'Come on, big fella. Let's walk and talk.' I told him, 'You big enough and ugly enough to be a fighter. Come on down to the gym.' "

Foreman joined the corps boxing team and suddenly had a new way to channel that anger and aggression. One thing led to another, and Foreman followed me as Olympic heavyweight champion at the next games, which were in Mexico City in 1968.

Turning pro in 1969, he won thirty-seven straight bouts, thirty-four of them by knockouts. But where I'd fought recognized tough guys early on—Bonavena, Machen, Doug Jones—Foreman had beaten up mostly tomato cans, with only Gregorio Peralta and a well-worn George Chuvalo being considered worthy opponents.

As a result of his feeble opposition, that record was regarded as a masterwork of deception by lots of boxing insiders, including quite a few of the boys in the press. Their sentiments were pretty much represented by what Barney Nagler of the *Daily Racing Form* wrote: "Only Foreman's record in numbers is formidable; he is not."

But you know by now my feeling about taking an opponent for granted—that way lies trouble. So I prepared, training at the Playboy Club Hotel at Great Gorge in McAfee, New Jersey, and then the final two weeks in Kingston. I did assume, though, that I would handle George's size and strength the way I had with other big, tough guys I had fought. Why not? I'd been doing it as an amateur, and a professional, for more than a decade. I did not see Foreman as being special. Big, strong, young, and ambitious—yes, all of that. But beatable just the same.

Yet in those final two weeks, I was worried by how I was feeling. The Jamaican heat—temperatures hovering in the nineties, and sometimes worse—had a bad effect on me. My energy just wasn't there. When I worked out, it felt like there was a burden over me, like voodoo or a spell, I just couldn't get right.

I ran the streets, and I could hardly breathe the air. It smelled like somebody died. Yank knew I wasn't tiptop. He told me to work hard, and then rest as much as I could. Yet as many hours as I lay in bed, I still felt faint, tired. Why should I be tired? I wondered.

To try to get me right, Yank had different foods packed in ice and flown down from Philadelphia. But even eating those lobsters and steaks didn't revive me the way he hoped. Still, I figured that come fight night, the adrenaline would kick in and for fifteen rounds or less I would find what I needed to do the job. What the hell, I always had before. So why not against Foreman?

I had added incentive because Marvis, who was twelve now, had come down to Kingston to see the fight.

Well, Foreman, it turned out, had incentive, too. You don't go 37–0 without thinking and dreaming of what it would be like if *you* were the boss of bosses.

"Frazier ain't different from anybody else," Foreman told reporters. "I'm going to knock him stone cold."

In that optimism, he was like a whole lot of others—the Bonavenas, Quarrys, and Ziggys—who figured their lives could change with a big night against me. Like them, Foreman came into the ring with a plan—the basic strategy for fighting Joe Frazier. You know how that goes: Keep

Joe Frazier from fighting at close quarters and you had a real shot at beating him. Trouble was nobody really had been able to do that. One after another, I eventually worked my way inside their reach and beat them down piece by piece.

Until Foreman.

Foreman had a plan and the muscle to carry it out. He was strong. Uncommonly strong. He was able to keep me arm's length just by pushing me backward; he just straight-out shoved me back on my heels, and kept me pinned there with a pistonlike jab.

That left me out there as a target for George's fully extended uppercuts. It was like a deer caught in a motorist's headlights; there's nothing to do but wait for the impact.

And that night I didn't have to wait long. Early into the first round, Foreman hit me with a left to the body, and right to the chin. Down I went, and when I got up my legs were jelly. With another right, Foreman knocked me down a second time.

By now, Marvis was screaming from ringside, "Daddy, quit playing around." He was used to his daddy making other men fall, and couldn't believe what he was seeing.

Neither could Willie (the Worm) Monroe. Monroe was another of Yank's fighters, and he was scheduled to box after the main event—what is called the "walk-out bout." Well, Willie heard the roar of the crowd and he strolled out from the dressing room just in time to see me getting to my feet from the second knockdown—and he went running back inside.

"I didn't want to get my mind messed up," he told people. "I didn't want to see no more. I couldn't believe my eyes."

Just before the bell ending the first round, Foreman knocked me down a third time. With no three-knockdown rule in effect, the fight would continue.

By now poor Marvis knew his daddy was like other men, subject to going down if hit right. It was a reality lesson I'd just as soon he didn't have to learn this early in his life.

In two rounds totaling four minutes and thirty-five seconds, I would be knocked to the canvas six times. Unwisely, I kept jumping right up rather than gathering my wits before rising—up and down like a yo-yo, they said in the papers. I have to take them at their word; truth is, I can't remember the details of what happened to me, although I had a pretty fair idea afterward of the big picture. For the first time in my career I'd gotten my ass kicked.

I can remember at one point late in the fight, Foreman turning to my corner and shouting something. According to one reporter, he was telling Yank: "Stop it or I'm going to kill him."

The fight was stopped.

It was a shock to everybody—to Marvis, to the Worm, to the crowd that stood at ringside after, staring up into the ring, as if trying to decipher what they had just seen.

And sure as hell it was a stunner to me.

But one man's pain is another man's pleasure. At ringside, a Jamaican fella standing near Marvis was grinning as he crooned: "Smokin' Joe won't smoke no more."

"Shut up," Marvis told him. "Leave my daddy alone."

I'd been knocked down before, but Foreman was the only guy who'd really hurt me. If you're champion of the world, you don't make plans for getting your butt whupped. When it happens, it comes as a shock. Like: What the hell happened?

By the time I got back to the dressing room, I felt disappointed, and embarrassed. My brother Tommy was there, tears in his eyes. "My brother," he said, hugging me while sobbing. But I wasn't looking for sympathy.

I sat there for a bit, feeling particularly bad for Marvis. Looking into his eyes, I told him: "I'm sorry, son. I let you down."

"Don't worry about it," he said. "I love you, Pop."

I tried to smile, but now tears came to my eyes.

To Yank, I said: "Back to the drawing board."

"That's okay," Yank said. "We'll come back."

Later, after I showered and dressed, I sat there staring at my shoetops as Yank dealt with the last reporter.

"What happened?" he was saying, sounding a bit annoyed. "He got hit. Didn't we all see the same fight? He got hit and he fell down. What happened to Marciano when he got hit? What happened to Joe Louis? He fell down. It's no mystery."

And yet it *was* a mystery, because I couldn't accept that this was how the fight was meant to come out. In my head, it should have been what it had always been before—another night of glory for Smokin' Joe.

No fighter will buy the notion, in defeat, that the better man won. I was convinced that if not for dumb mistakes of mine it'd have been business as usual, with me explaining to reporters how I beat this young fella Foreman. But that's how you think when you're a fighter. You can't let a loss mess with your mind—can't because beneath the aggression you bring to the ring you gotta have the confidence to execute. Without that, you're just a target, a casualty waiting to happen, a loser.

But even after I'd explained things to myself, I was still left with a hollow feeling. What the hell. I'd walked into the ring the undisputed heavyweight champion of the world—the keys to the kingdom were mine. But I'd left that ring in Jamaica as just another guy knocking at the door.

What happens next?

I really hadn't a clue. It had been a long time since I was just a contender.

7

Vision to Conquer

As champion, you carry an air of invincibility.

When you crush opponents, one after the other, the way I did, folks see you as bigger than life. When you lose, though, they feel as though they'd been fooled, suckered into thinking so highly of you. That's why folks jump off that bandwagon quick as can be, and then throw stones at it. They don't want to be associated with opinions that now seem so mistaken. Where once they heralded you as king of the mountain, now they want to make you low boy on the totem pole.

That's what I was faced with in the weeks, and months, after Foreman beat me. Suddenly, there were all these theories about what had gone wrong with Joe Frazier. Some in the media said that my style was an invitation to disaster—that I fought with my face. By that, they meant that I readily accepted punishment in order to get close enough to opponents to brutalize them. It was a style, they insisted, that was bound to diminish a man fight by fight, like water dripping on a rock and slowly eroding it.

Others said that I was obsessed with Clay, and having beaten him, I'd lost the spark, the interest that made me the unrelenting aggressor I'd been.

And still others bought into the propaganda Clay was putting out—that he had punished me so badly that I would never be the same fighter again.

Know what? There may have been a bit of truth to each of these theories, or maybe none whatsoever. Looking back even now, I can't rightly say. Because the Joe Frazier who lived and breathed back then, in 1973, just didn't allow himself to entertain negative thoughts. Once you start down that road, you might as well find another line of work.

No real fighter wants to accept a defeat as stone reality. From the second the other man's hand is raised, your loser is finding a way to make the fight fit his image of invincibility. I'd been beaten, yeah. But I now believed it wouldn't have happened if I'd only been myself. That was the truth that I took away from watching the film of the Kingston bout. As I told reporters:

"I fought a dumb fight. I can't blame George for hitting me. If I stand in front of my son, Marvis, and do the things I did that night, he's gonna clobber me too.

"What things? First, I was pulling back instead of staying in and smothering his punches. Then, I came straight at him, instead of coming in from the sides. And I came in with my hands down, like I was saying, 'C'mon and hit me.' My other fights, I always kept my hands higher and my body lower so I could take those shots. I just wasn't thinking clearly.

"Finally, when I got hit with a wicked shot, my old hot head took over. Instead of stepping back and clearing my head I went after him. I got hit and hit and hit."

That was the world according to Smokin' Joe. Now the trick was to get Foreman back into the ring and prove that he'd caught me on an off night. That didn't seem like it would be a problem. The contract we'd signed called for a rematch if Foreman beat me.

But Foreman, it turned out, was bugged about certain problems his manager, Dick Sadler, had gotten him into. In 1971, Sadler had made a deal with Barbra Streisand's manager, Marty Erlichman, and persuaded a reluctant Foreman to go along with it. The deal gave Erlichman one-half of all ancillary rights Foreman earned for the next ten years in return for five hundred thousand dollars, parceled out over the ten years.

In 1971, that five hundred thousand dollars was real money for Sadler and Foreman. But on the night he whupped me, the world opened up to George Foreman, and suddenly the Erlichman deal was not that financially sound—like millions of dollars' worth of not-so-sound. It led Foreman to dismiss Sadler as his manager while keeping him on as trainer. And soon after, Foreman was conferring with lawyers about undoing the

Erlichman deal, which by now was complicated by Erlichman's having assigned his agreement to a Philadelphia group headed by an attorney named David L. Miller.

In that foul mood, Foreman decided the hell with the rematch, and charted a new course. He signed to fight a no-name opponent, Jose (King) Roman, in Tokyo on September 1, 1973. Well, when we threatened to sue George to enforce the rematch clause of our contract, Foreman promised to give me a shot after he beat this guy Roman.

In the meantime, I spent more time around the house and resumed my training routine. Folks that ran into me around the city seemed genuinely puzzled by the outcome of the Foreman match. "What happened down there in Jamaica?" they'd ask. I wasn't into talking about what was past. I'd just say, "I'll be back." Or, "I'll get him next time." Even Marvis asked what was wrong with me that night. "Was nothing wrong," I told him. "I was weak. I couldn't get it right."

Eventually, I signed to fight Joe Bugner at Earls Court in London on July 2. Bugner, a former circus strongman, had gone the twelve-round distance while losing to Clay in February, even after suffering a cut eyebrow in the first round. At the time it was considered a pretty fair accomplishment, less so when Ken Norton, a former sparring partner of mine, broke Clay's jaw and won a twelve-round decision from the Butterfly in March.

While the Bugner fight didn't get much play in the States, in London it was a big deal. When we arrived there, Mickey Duff, the matchmaker, told us: "When we announced this fight, so many ticket orders came in that the people at the promotional office couldn't open the front door because the postman had dropped the mail through a drop in the door and it was so heavy you couldn't push the door open."

Bugner, a Hungarian-born British citizen, was a boxer type who'd been booed often for his lack of aggression. But after going the distance against Clay, he'd acquired a halo. The Brits were ready to knight him if he could only beat me.

Bugner was six foot four, blond, and good-looking when the fight started. By the end of twelve rounds, he was bloody, his right eye was swollen, and his momma would have had a hard time recognizing him. I knocked him down once, in the tenth round, and kept on his butt for the whole twelve rounds.

The way the British score, the winner of a round gets five points and the loser four and three-quarters. The referee, Harry Gibbs, was the only official, and he scored the fight 59¼ points for me to 58½ for Bugner.

The victory gave me a jolt of confidence. I felt ready to go for the title again. In September, when Foreman knocked out Roman in one round, I figured I'd get my shot at him. But a boxing promise is like Confederate money—worthless and out of date. On the flight back from Tokyo, Foreman decided to renege on our agreement. Soon after came word that Foreman would fight Ken Norton in Caracas, Venezuela, in March of 1974.

It left me out in the cold, and feeling real disappointed. But more shattering than that was the news I was about to get.

𝆓   𝆓   𝆓

My family and I had gone down to South Carolina to spend time with Momma, and while I was there a phone call came that hit me like a sledgehammer.

Yank had suffered a stroke and was in the intensive care unit of Temple University Hospital, and the outlook was not good. He was in a coma, and breathing only with the aid of a respirator.

I rode my motorcycle to Charleston, then boarded a flight to Philadelphia. Over the next two days, I was at the hospital night and day. Hoping. And praying. But Yank never did come out of the coma. He was only fifty-two years old.

It was a hurtful time. Me and Yank had been more than a business proposition. We were like father and son, and sometimes like brothers. While we took care of the boxing, we always managed to have a few laughs as well. With that big booming voice that sportswriters likened to Senator Everett Dirksen's, and the way he had of expressing himself, he'd crack me up. And all those years we'd done things the same way we'd started out, no contract but just a handshake agreement. Unlike so many of the scamboogahs in boxing these days, Yank was 100 percent loyal and trustworthy to his fighter. The man was always looking out for me.

Yank was the boss in the corner, but outside the gym and arena, he was fun-loving and easy to be with. When Marvis had come to London for the Bugner fight, the boy wanted to get into the card games my sparring partners and I played. As his daddy I said no, figuring he was just a kid. But Yank understood how Marvis wanted to feel part of that adult world, and said, "All right, cocksucker, let him play. Let him have some fun." The way he said it made sense, and I waved Marvis into the game, where he proceeded to lose the twenty-five dollars I'd given him.

At Yank's funeral I couldn't help feeling sad, and a bit angry. Yank had had a running problem with high blood pressure, and wasn't as regular in taking the medicine the doctors gave him as he should have been. I'd remind him regularly, "You taking that damn medicine?" He'd go, yeah, yeah, in that tone of voice that I knew meant he was slacking off. *Dammit, Yank,* I thought, as I sat there in the funeral parlor, *I told you take that medicine.*

I missed Yank that day, I still miss him. He left us way too soon.

Yank had brought Eddie Futch into our camp around the time of the fight with Quarry in 1969. And Eddie has been with us since. He came out of Detroit, where as a young man he had been a basketball star, good enough to play against semipro teams like the Savoy Big Five of Chicago. But when Eddie got married at the age of seventeen, he had to give up basketball and go to work as a waiter at the Hotel Wolverine, where he regularly served breakfast to Hank Greenberg, the great slugger for the Detroit Tigers for fifteen bucks a week and tips.

Through a friend, he became interested in boxing, not intending to do more than hit the speed bag and skip rope. But after he was persuaded to spar, he joined the Detroit Athletic Association at the Brewster Community Center and began competing as an amateur, even winning the city Golden Gloves in 1933 as a lightweight. Among his teammates was Joe Louis—the man I'd set out to be like. Remember? The next Joe Louis.

Well, Eddie told me about the original Joe Louis:

"When I first saw Joe Louis I was not too impressed. I expected something more flashy. I didn't know enough to realize he was a real gem. But as I continued to be around him, I was amazed at his quickness and sound boxing ability. He was such a good puncher that people overlooked his boxing ability.

"As I became more experienced, Joe started asking me to spar with him, even though I was a lightweight. I once told him, 'Why don't you get one of the middleweights if you're looking for speed?' He said, 'If I hit you with anything, I know I'm sharp.' Well, he hit me with that right of his one day, and put me through the ropes. That was enough for me, but the next day Joe persuaded me to spar with him again. He told me, 'I'll just use the jab, Eddie.' Well of course his jabs were like machine-gun bullets.

"But I was a clever fighter and caught on to Joe's ways. I'd sit out-side and watch every move of his. Joe didn't telegraph anything. But he had a little circumference he'd work, and he wouldn't punch beyond that distance. As long as I was beyond the edge of that circle, I was okay. I'd circle to the left, I'd circle to the right. He wouldn't punch unless both of his feet were on the canvas. So I kept moving and turning. That meant he was moving and turning and picking his feet up. I never let him get set."

A heart murmur ended Eddie's amateur career, but led to his be-coming a trainer, first of amateurs and later professionals.

With Yank gone, Eddie became *the* man in my corner.

But the question remained—What the hell was I going to do with Foreman ducking a rematch? The answer came in a phone call a few days later with Teddy Brenner, the matchmaker at Madison Square Garden.

"How about you and Muhammad again?" Brenner asked.

"Do it," I told him.

There were issues to be resolved, like what to do about Jack Kent Cooke's claims on the rematch—he and Jerry Perenchio had promoted The Fight in '71—and about the nasty tax bite that New York State took out of our purses the first time Clay and I fought—four hundred thou-sand dollars apiece. If the Garden was to get Frazier–Clay II, I wanted a little relief from New York's taxman.

Well, eventually the Garden tidied things up, and came back of-fering Clay and me the same deal—a guarantee of $850,000 or $32^{1}/_{2}$ percent of the net receipts, whichever was greater. That suited the both of us. The fight was on for January 28, 1974.

So there we were, me and damn Clay again.

Back to the North Broad Street Gym I went, to get myself ready to do what I had done before—whup that scamboogah.

And back to the bullshit went Clay.

I'd just stepped into the Garden's Hall of Fame Club, for a news conference to announce the fight, when across the room I heard Clay screaming at me: "I'm sick and tired of you living on my name. I'm gonna whip you like I'm Willie Pep, you Uncle Tom."

Pep was a featherweight from the 1940s and 1950s, who was so skillful a boxer that he'd once told reporters that he'd win a round without throwing a punch. And he'd gone out and done it by making the other guy look foolish by missing him with practically every punch.

Clay might compare himself to Pep; I could care less. But that "Uncle Tom" reference—man, that steamed me up.

"Tom, huh?" I said. "My skin is blacker than yours. Maybe you're really a half-breed." As Clay sneered, I went on: "He talks out of one side of his mouth to blacks, and the other side to white folks."

"You the white man's champ," he shouted. "You the white man's champ and they got them other champs. George Foreman is the other champion. James Ellis was the other champion. Joe Frazier was the other champion. I'm the real champion with the people."

When I made a move to hit him, Clay pretended to go for me but let bystanders restrain him. Good thing they did, too, because he might have gotten more than he bargained for. I was real, real tired of his mouth. His was the mouth that roared, and it never stopped.

On January 17, a week and a half before the fight, Clay turned thirty-two. In honor of the occasion—and to get extra publicity mileage—the Garden threw the joker a birthday party and asked me to show up.

I wasn't all that crazy about being there. So when somebody asked what I'd brought for Clay's birthday, I mumbled, without much sincerity: "Happy birthday."

"That's all?" the guy asked.

"That's all. On the twenty-eighth I'll give him another present, but that's all now." To Clay: "You thirty-two?"

"That's right," he said. "We're getting old, Joe."

He was right about that. Five days earlier, I'd turned thirty. The Garden threw me a private party and then invited the public to join me on my morning's roadwork. To accommodate those folks, I'd bumped my training run from 5:30 to 7:30 A.M.

Anyway, back at the party, someone asked: "How do you feel about Ali's claim that he really won the first fight?"

"He say that?"

"It's just my opinion," Clay said.

"He's always dreaming," I told these folks. To Clay: "You oughta look at the film a few times."

"I've looked at it a hundred times."

"Learn anything?"

"You took a terrible beating, Joe."

"For a guy that was down, you talk a lot—"

"That don't mean nothin'. I been down a lot of times. You had Joe Bugner down but they don't stay down. You in trouble, Joe."

"Do I look scared? Look at me shaking. Any other questions, gentlemen?"

And it went on from there, with the both of us whipping off our jackets at one point and acting as though we were going for each other.

A week later, we weren't playing.

🥊   🥊   🥊

On Wednesday, January 23, five days before the rematch, ABC Sports invited us to their studio on West Sixty-sixth Street for an advance taping for *Wide World of Sports.* Howard Cosell was going to show a tape of Frazier–Clay I and we would comment after each round.

Clay showed up in a vested pin-striped suit; I wore a suede jumpsuit. There were others there too, many of them from the media. For an hour we looked at the 1971 match and mildly needled each other. Then, as we watched the tenth round and noted Clay's swollen jaw, the mood changed.

"That's what he went to the hospital for," I said about the jaw.

"I went to the hospital for ten minutes," Clay said. "You went for a month."

"Be quiet," I told him. "I was resting. I was in and out."

"That shows how dumb you are. People don't go to a hospital to rest. See how ignorant you are."

"Why you think I'm ignorant? I'm tired of you calling me ignorant all the time. I'm not ignorant."

Angry, I threw my headphone to the floor and stood.

"Why you think I'm ignorant? Stand up, man."

At that moment Clay's brother, Rudy—who went by the Muslim name Rahaman—came out of the audience toward us. This sucker Rudy had been jiving and heckling during the taping. Every time Clay landed a punch on the tape, he'd go: "Amen. Praise Allah. There it is again." He was getting on my nerves. So when I saw him moving in my direction, I said, "You in this too?"

That's when Clay stood up. And suddenly it looked like they were going to two-on-one me. So as Clay grabbed for me, I threw him down. We rolled off this carpeted platform we'd been sitting on, and onto a cement floor. They broke us up before I could punch Clay, and a good thing. Because I was ready to rock and roll. It wasn't a gimmick fight, like a lot of people thought who watched it. I wanted a piece of him.

As Eddie Futch led me out of the studio, Clay shouted, "See you Monday night."

"Be on time," I told him.

In the limo heading back to Philadelphia, I didn't feel a bit embarrassed. I was tired of his bullshit and showed him that.

"Did you see how wide Clay's eyes opened up?" I said. "Now I really got him scared."

Days later the New York commission fined Clay and me five thousand dollars apiece for conduct that "demeaned" boxing. The chairman of the commission, Edwin B. Dooley, said there would be more fines if a similar incident occurred at the weigh-in. But the Garden had taken measures to head off a repeat of the scuffle. Clay and I would weigh in separately.

While the Garden's twenty-thousand-odd seats had been sold out for weeks, the incident figured to boost closed-circuit ticket sales on the potential 1.8 million seats . . . and increase the satellite TV audience in places like Malaysia and Singapore. But that wasn't what triggered my going after Clay; I just hated what came out of his mouth. And when his brother Rudy interfered, I had to act.

🥊　🥊　🥊

Anyway, that was over with, and now came the fight. Once again the celebrities turned out: Streisand, George Jessel, Jean-Paul Belmondo, Milton Berle, John Jr. and Caroline Kennedy, Toots Shor, Emile Griffith, Foreman.

And once again the fans leaned in toward the aisle I came walking down, shouting words of encouragement to me.

But on this night, Clay didn't want to rumble. His strategy was to limit the action. He would do his damnedest to make the fight a nonfight, to make the night a punch-and-grab show as if we were fighting under the rules of the World Wrestling Federation rather than of the Marquis of Queensberry.

Afterward, Eddie Futch watched the film of the bout and counted 133 clinches that Clay instigated. During the fight, Eddie complained to the referee, Tony Perez, about the excessive holding, and so did I. But Perez just let Clay throw his octopus arms around me and freeze the action, or press his forearms down on my neck so I couldn't punch.

Perez said later that what Clay was doing was not illegal. Had he hit and held, then he could have penalized him, he said. But that was bullshit. Officials routinely handle jab-and-grab fighters by slapping away their gloves to free both fighters from a clinch, and by saying, "Let's go. Quit holding." In cases where the clinching is extreme, as it was that night, they may even deduct a point from the offending fighter's scorecard.

But Perez wasn't going to do that with Clay, 'cause like a lot of people he was blinded by the so-called "Clay mystique." Yeah. The loud-mouth had made himself a big celebrity with all his talk, and it gave him an edge when he walked into the ring. So while Clay was holding me as often as he could, ole Perez was adopting a hands-off policy.

The punches Clay did throw were mostly pittypat, with the exception of a right to the side of the head late in the second round. That one shook me, but as I struggled to get myself together I caught a break. Perez thought he heard the bell ending the round, and stepped between Clay and me. Then the timekeeper got Perez's attention and shouted up to him that the bell had not sounded. By the time the round resumed, I had recovered.

The fight would come down to this: Clay threw a lot of punches without any steam on them. They were punches that were strictly for show, and reminded me of the way amateur fighters move their hands in a blur, and get credit for punches that barely make contact with the opponent. There's even an expression for that bogus busy-ness in the amateurs: it's called "shoeshining."

Well, Clay's offense was a shoeshine deluxe. In fact, during the fight I kept telling him: "You don't have no sting in your punches." My offense? It was what it usually was—punches meant to put dents on the other guy.

What it came down to was what weight, what value you'd give to Clay's half-baked blows.

Some pretty respected sportswriters saw through Clay's game. Red Smith, for instance, would write in the next day's *New York Times*:

> *Matches like these almost always stir debate, for followers of the fancy never have agreed on a basic question: does aggressiveness and heavy hitting cancel out several light shots when the shooter is running away?*

Smith's scorecard had me winning seven rounds to five. His *Times* colleague Dave Anderson also scored the fight for me—six rounds to five with one round even. Anderson wrote:

> *Joe Frazier thought he won. So did this ringside seat's scorecard, which had him ahead . . . . Perhaps the referee and the two judges, in their unanimity, were influenced subconsciously by Ali's persistent dispute with the 1971 verdict. Ali threw more punches that night, too, and for three years he kept shouting that he had. Perhaps he had the referee and the judges more aware of the number of punches, rather than their effect, than they usually are.*

Yeah, the decision went to Clay. Unanimous. Judge Jack Gordon voted eight rounds Clay, four rounds Frazier. Judge Tony Castellano had it seven rounds Clay, four rounds Frazier, one even. And Perez called it 6–5–1, Clay.

It was not the first and for damn sure wouldn't be the last time Clay got a gift from the judges. Norton had beaten him in the rematch nearly five months earlier, but had been robbed by the judges. Now me. And down the road there would be Jimmy Young and Norton again in their third bout. We were all victims of Clay's popularity.

But I didn't make a big fuss about the decision. That wasn't my way. I was no crybaby like Clay was after the first one, talking his bullshit and trying to persuade folks that he hadn't gotten his ass kicked. In boxing you take the good with the bad, and push on. The outcome of the fight was not what it should have been. But it turned out that with our percentage of net receipts, the scamboogah Clay and I made out better than we did for the 1971 bout: Each of us ended up with $2.6 million.

After the bout, the press was ready to write my boxing obituary—they were asking me if I thought it was time to retire. Florence wanted me to, but I still felt capable of winning back the title. For sure, this rematch with Clay wasn't the proof of my deterioration that some of these media guys thought it was. Hell, I was convinced I'd beaten Clay—it was his public image that had gotten him over with the judges. I hadn't been shucking him when I'd told him during the bout that his punches hadn't anything on them.

But the loss to Clay had impact, putting my chance to fight again for the title on hold. Extreme hold. For the next twenty-one months, other men would be center stage of the heavyweight picture—first Foreman, who stopped Norton in two rounds in Caracas, and then Clay, who, using a shock-absorber strategy he called "rope-a-dope," drained Foreman of his energy and then knocked him out in eight rounds in Zaire in October 1974.

With the title once again his, Clay did not come rushing back to fight his old nemesis, Smokin' Joe. No, as 1975 unfolded, he fought other men—scoring technical knockouts over Chuck Wepner and Ron Lyle and then decisioning Joe Bugner in a rematch.

During that time, I fought twice, knocking out Quarry and Jimmy Ellis. But the popular impression of Joe Frazier was that I was no longer the fighter I'd been—that I was damaged goods. And you know what? More than those critics knew, they were right.

I was hurting. The cataract in the left eye had grown worse. Dr. Yanoff ran tests after each fight that now came back with increasingly negative results. Not that those results were any surprise to me. I knew. Fight by fight I was having a more difficult time seeing. The vision in my left eye was almost completely gone, and my right eye was starting to fail.

Dr. Yanoff told me that if I had surgery on the cataract, I would then have to wear contact lenses or Coke-bottle glasses. Obviously, I couldn't go into the ring with eyeglasses. Mr. Magoo wouldn't ever get licensed. And while the boxing commissions would never allow a man to fight with contact lenses, they were difficult to detect. So it was likely I could do it without the commissions' being any the wiser for it.

But for now, I decided to put off cataract surgery. The way I saw it, there was but one fight more for Smokin' Joe, and that was the grand finale against goddamn Clay. *If*—and it was a big "if"—the sucker wanted any more of what I had for him.

Wasn't no fun fighting me, and for all his talk about dancing fifteen rounds—the older he got, the less able he was to do that la-de-dah stick-and-move of his. Which meant the sucker had to get in the trenches with me. And he wanted that as much as he wanted polio.

I figured for that one last fight I could make do with my eyes as they were. With my right eye, I could see enough to get in close against Clay and beat on him.

But my eyes were not the only physical problem I had. My orthopedic man, Dr. Joseph Fabiani, was keeping busy, holding me together for this stretch run of my career. For starters, there was that crooked left arm, which over the years would grow arthritic, and with the hard training I did, often developed water on the elbow. It doesn't sound like a big deal, but when your elbow is full of fluid it is not only painful—like a toothache in your arm—but it limits what that arm can do. The range of motion is severely reduced. Since I was missing 30 percent range of motion to begin with because of my boyhood accident with that raging hog, it made my left arm no damn good to me until Dr. Fabiani drained the fluid and injected it with cortisone.

The same thing happened with the heads of the knuckles of my index and middle fingers—they developed water and thick calluses. Dr. Fabiani explained it by saying that the fourth and fifth bones of those fingers—or what we call knuckles—were shorter than they should have been. As a result those knuckles absorbed more of the impact of my punches than was good for them. The remedy? When training, I'd pad the hands over those vulnerable places. And when problems developed, Dr. Fabiani would drain the water and inject cortisone. We did this during the six or so weeks of training, with the last treatment typically coming a week out from the fight.

And then there was my back, which flared up from time to time and gave me problems. I remember in '68 waking up one morning and being unable to get out of bed because of spasms in my back. Dr. Fabiani came to the Marriott Hotel in Philly where I was staying and gave me a shot. That was the first time, but there would be many others. Dr. Fabiani's trusty hypodermic needle would usually solve the problem—a shot of novocaine in my back or xylocaine (which is an anesthetic with cortisone) and I'd be up and moving.

These were injuries that we kept the lid on; we didn't want anybody knowing my business. You make your problems public, some people think you're setting up excuses in case you lose. That wasn't my style. Problems or not, I fought the best I could. And keeping quiet about physical troubles made sound business sense. You broadcast it that you're up to your elbows in pain, you're encouraging boxing commissions to take a closer look in their medical exams. With my eye problem, I didn't really want that. I accepted the hurt, and damage, as the price of being the best. I saw myself as a warrior who was obliged to carry on through thick and thin. I wasn't the best athlete in the world, but I had that fire in my belly. And I was reckless in my determination.

But I knew that I wasn't getting off scot-free—knew that the price to pay would run beyond the years I was fighting. Today, for instance, my right eye is deteriorating and I have trouble with my right shoulder and other joints. Dr. Fabiani tells me the right shoulder is worn out—that circulation to the shoulder is dying. I have pain there all the time. Pretty soon, I'm gonna need an operation so that a steel replacement joint can be put in. Back in the 1970s I was aware that the business I was in there could be problems later. But I was willing to make the sacrifice to be the champion I became—and to have the life I had. A small price to pay.

Having beaten the Butterfly, I now have some time to relax on my plantation in South Carolina. Here I am with my black anguses.

As I tell the boxers I train today, you always have to do your roadwork. I'm practicing what I preach on my plantation, filling my lungs with that sweet country air.

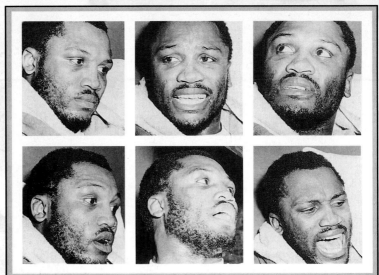

The different faces of Smokin' Joe Frazier . . .

And a very familiar one.

Throughout the years, I've done lots of work for charities; here I'm playing with some children from the Sickle Cell Anemia Foundation, with Yank by my side. *Courtesy New York Daily News.*

The Heavyweight Champ entertains and answers questions for the kids from the Madison Square Club. *Courtesy New York Daily News.*

The Smokin' Joe Frazier Revue, in 1973.

It all began for me here—in Philadelphia, the home of so many great boxers. Here I am in front of Independence Hall in the early 1970s.

Being heavyweight champ means there's always someone looking to take the title away from you—so you have to keep in top shape, which means doing roadwork.

Working out for the Terry Daniels bout. On January 15, 1972, I put him on the mat in four rounds. *Courtesy United Press International.*

Weigh-in with Ron Stander, before the May 25, 1972, fight. Stander lasted five rounds before I KO'd him.

George Foreman was an uncommonly strong opponent when we fought on January 23, 1973—and he still is today. I couldn't get it right that night and ended up losing the heavyweight crown to the big guy in just two rounds. This is a post-fight picture of me. *Courtesy A.P. Wire Photo.*

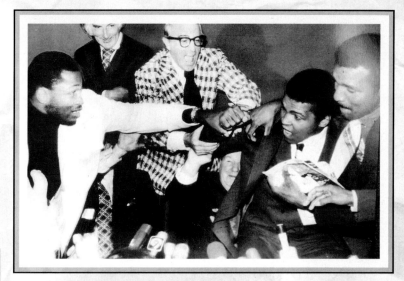

Having a little fun at a press conference before Frazier-Clay II. *Courtesy New York Daily News.*

Fight II, on January 28, 1974, at Madison Square Garden. *Courtesy George Kalinsky.*

The end of that match-up. I've got my arms raised in victory, but the judges that night didn't see it that way. *Courtesy George Kalinsky.*

Punching the stuffing out of tough Jerry Quarry on June 17, 1974, as my idol, Joe Louis, officiates. *Courtesy George Kalinsky.*

The press greets me as I arrive at the New York press conference for The Thrilla in Manila. *Courtesy New York Daily News.*

Eddie Futch and me, 1974. *Courtesy Boxing Illustrated.*

Frazier-Clay III. *Courtesy Neil Leifer/Sports Illustrated.*

The weigh-in—and the stare-down—for my second fight with Big George. *Courtesy George Kalinsky.*

The rematch between me and the big guy, June 15, 1976, in Uniondale, New York. I think I gave George the idea that bald is beautiful. *Courtesy George Kalinsky.*

For the love of boxing I had fought George Foreman again, this time secretly wearing contact lenses because of my eye problems. This is what I looked like after the fight. *Courtesy Boxing Photo.*

Here I am training my son Marvis, in the "gentleman's art" around 1980 in my gym. As an amateur, Marvis would beat Tim Witherspoon and then as a pro he'd step into the ring with Holmes and Tyson.

My talented son Hector, who fought under the name, "Smokin' Joe Junior."

Singing has always been a passion for me, and you can still catch my act today. *Courtesy George Kalinsky.*

At the 20th Anniversary Dinner for The Fight of the Century, Clay was performing for the press, as usual. *Courtesy Webster Riddick.*

My son Marvis and me. *Courtesy George Kalinsky.*

Here I am among friends of honor, integrity and community—(from left) Walter Fauntroy, Arthur Ashe, Butch Lewis, and Nelson Mandela. *Courtesy Webster Riddick.*

World Heavyweight Champions Michael Spinks, actor Jon Amos, Larry Holmes, Cassius Clay, and Floyd Patterson helped me celebrate my 50th birthday at the Trump Taj Mahal, 1994. *Courtesy Webster Riddick.*

The Frazier family today—(seated) my wife Florence, (left to right) Natasha, Jo-Netta, Marvis, Weatta, and Jacqui. *Courtesy Webster Riddick.*

J oe Fraizer — Still Smokin'. *Courtesy Webster Riddick.*

In 1975, I didn't know the specifics of what the physical tax on me would be twenty years later, but sure as hell I knew I'd be showing the effects of a decade of swapping punches with the biggest and baddest guys in the universe. It was why when Marvis, fourteen years old at the time, started talking about becoming a fighter I wouldn't have any of it.

I'd *had* to become a boxer: There wasn't any other way for me to get ahead. Being poor is all the motivation I needed to take a punch in the face. But Marvis didn't have that problem. As a boy, he'd had everything a kid could want—GI Joe toys, pinball and video machines, pool tables, a stereo system, TVs, and a seventeen-thousand-dollar backyard swimming pool. Not to mention a trust fund that would enable him to go to college or start a business.

But let me backtrack.

Florence and I raised Marvis and his four sisters to be responsible, respectful, and kind to one another. They had chores to do, rules to mind. I was a stickler for these things. I didn't want them growing up to be slackers.

Marvis, like his sisters, was a good kid. If all kids grew up to be as decent as this boy, being a father would be a breeze. Yeah, he made it easy. Not to say that every so often Daddy Smokin' didn't have to get in his face.

We called the cellar of our house "The Zoo." One day while I was at the gym, Marvis, who was ten years old at the time, got into a fight with his sister Jacqui. Florence sent him up to his room and told him: "Wait there 'til your father gets home."

Well, I came home and got the news that Marvis had been beating on his younger sister. I went up the stairs and banged on his door.

Poom poom poom. No answer. "Get up, boy. You ain't asleep."

Marvis gets up and opens the door, pretending like he's been sleeping.

"What's this I hear about you hitting girls?" I ask.

"No, Pop. I was just—"

"Just nothing. We're going to The Zoo. Get the gloves."

There were two pairs of boxing gloves in his room.

Marvis starts going "I'm soorrrry," and gets to crying.

I wasn't buying any of it. "Get them gloves on," I told him.

Down to The Zoo we went. He raises his hands. And when I start jabbing him—hard enough for him to know he's being punished, but soft enough not to really hurt him—he covers up.

"You want to hit girls, huh?" Jab, jab.

"No sir."

"You know how much strength you've got?" Jab, jab.

"I'm sorry, Daddy," he says, in this pathetic whiney voice.

"I'll teach you what to be sorry for, you sissy." Jab, jab.

That was the last time Marvis hit a girl. Fact of the matter is there weren't many times I had to get rough with the boy. Like I say, this was a very good guy, who knew right from wrong.

And, as it turned out, he grew up to be a damn fine athlete. At the age of fourteen he was six foot one, 190 pounds—built a little longer and leaner than his daddy. At Plymouth-Whitemarsh, a public school, he played baseball (catcher), football (fullback), basketball, and he wrestled. But when his grades fell, we made him do the tenth grade at a private school, the Wyncote Academy. Since Wyncote had no sports programs, it forced Marvis to concentrate on his studies.

But with no teams at Wyncote to play on, he asked if he could work out at the gym to keep in shape. Florence and I decided to let him in the gym as long as he kept up on his studies. Well, Marvis became a regular there, working hard on the bags, on the skip rope, and on his floor exercises. Unbeknownst to me, he got the boxing bug. As he later would tell reporters: "I knew after three months in the gym, it was boxing for me."

That's when he asked me whether he could spar.

"What for?" I asked him.

" 'Cause I think I want to be a fighter."

"Say what?"—pretending like I hadn't heard right.

"I'd like to try boxing."

"No you don't. You don't need to fight. Chase the girls. Have a good time. Be a doctor . . . a lawyer. It's why your daddy took the lumps and bumps—so you wouldn't have to."

But the more I said no, the more he seemed to want it.

I gave him another lecture: "This is nothing to play with. You've got to be serious. Guys are in there to tear your head off. No one gets in there unless he's serious."

Well, he showed he was serious.

He began getting up at 3:30 in the morning to pick up his cousin Russell, who lived in North Philadelphia and was training to be a fighter, and then the both of them would join me in the two-and-a-half-mile route I ran around Fairmont Park.

Russell had a style like mine, so I was partial to him. But Russell didn't always attend to his training as diligently as he should have. Whereas any time I spied on Marvis in the gym, the boy was working like a pack animal. So one Saturday, when they were both in the gym, I turned to Marvis and said, "Let me see what you got."

Russell and Marvis climbed into the ring, and Marvis started tagging him and then getting out of the way of Russell's left hook. Well, I gotta admit I felt a jolt of pride to see my blood looking like the real McCoy. And 'cause Russell had been slackin', it pleased me to no end to see that Marvis, working hard as he'd been, had caught up to his cousin as a boxer.

"Don't want to do your roadwork?" I needled Russell. And to Marvis: "Go on. Hit him to the body."

$$\text{\textdagger} \qquad \text{\textdagger} \qquad \text{\textdagger}$$

While Marvis' boxing future at this point was uncertain, mine was growing clearer. On July 2, 1975, the day after Clay beat Joe Bugner in Kuala Lumpur, Malaysia, the both of us met the press down there to announce the third go-round between us—a fight that would come to be known as "The Thrilla in Manila."

Clay, as champion, was guaranteed $4 million against 43 percent of all bout-generated money. My guarantee was $2 million and a percentage of total revenues. A Manila promoter named Tommy Oh told the reporters that the Philippine government had put up $4 million of the $6.5-million guarantee, with half a million bucks going to Don King, a black American promoter who'd only recently gotten into the fight game.

By now I was used to Clay's big mouth. But accustomed as I was to his baloney, I still despised him for trying to misrepresent me to the public. No one gave his heart, and soul, to his sport as I did. And yet the message that the bigmouth sent out was that I was a caveman with gloves, too stupid to get out of the way of punches.

And while *he* could barely read, he took real pleasure in making *me* out as an ignoramus.

In Malaysia, after the scamboogah had his say, I got up to speak. I began, "I'm gonna—"

"I'm going to, man," Clay cut in. "It's not 'I'm gonna.' It's going to. Talk intelligent."

Trying to ignore the boy, I said: "I'm gonna go into training—"

"Not inta," he said. "Into. How far did you go in school?"

"As far as you went."

Later, Clay told the press: "This ain't publicity. We don't like each other."

"That's right," I said. "I want you like a hog wants slop."

"Ain't no Baptist gonna beat no Muslim," he said.

It never ended with this chump. Nonstop bullshit. While the public found it amusing, I guess, and came to view him as a good guy, I knew different. This was a nasty, envious, mean-spirited egomaniac, who still couldn't stand the fact that in the biggest fight of his life I'd put him on his ass, I'd whupped him in front of God and the world.

And but for three blind mice who judged the second fight between Clay and me, it'd have been two wins in a row for me over the scamboogah.

A couple of weeks later, back in the States, I had a press conference in New York to promote the fight. In the midst of it Clay and several of his cronies come barging in, all of them wearing black T-shirts with a picture of a gorilla on it. And here's Clay shouting: "It will be a killer and a chiller and a thrilla when I get the gorilla in Manila."

And that was to be his gimmick for our third fight. He'd had me as a white man for the first two, and now he was gonna make me a cartoon of a nigger, a knuckle-scraping baboon-man. Gorilla. Frazier the gorilla. And because he was so loud and different and quotable, the news guys couldn't resist it. Most of them presented it as if it was a big joke, but they reported it to the world.

It wasn't any joke to the Frazier children when classmates would tease them that their father was a gorilla. They'd come home crying.

And it wasn't a joke to me when I'd show up at a Clay fight, like when he fought Wepner in Cleveland, and get booed. Booed 'cause Clay had folks, black folks especially, believing that I was a traitor to my race.

Most of the press just let him be the trash-talking bozo he was without nailing him on his real motives. Only a few guys, like Dick Young of the *New York Daily News*, called it the way it was. Reporting on the booing I'd gotten in Cleveland, Young wrote:

> *Several things happened here the other night that disturbed me. Most of all, it was the booing of Joe Frazier. They were booing class. There were cheers, too, for Smokin' Joe, but the hooting was much too audible as he was introduced in the pre-fight ceremony. Black people boo Joe Frazier, unthinking black people, people who have let themselves be influenced by Muhammad Ali and his often crass exploitation of racism.*
>
> *Muhammad Ali has said, "I am the black people's champion."*
>
> *Joe Frazier has said, when he held the title, "I am champion for all the people."*
>
> *That is why some blacks boo Joe Frazier, a pretty pitiful reason. He does not appeal to their prejudices, their weakness, the way Ali does. Ali, early on, learned the favorite trick of all demagogues, peddle hatred to a downtrodden people. It is an easy sell.*

Yeah: Frazier the gorilla. That would be big with this scamboogah Clay this time around. In August, when the press visited him at his training camp in Deer Lake, Pennsylvania, he had a big stuffed gorilla on display and was spouting that thriller-killer-gorilla nonsense.

He'd also gotten hold of a Joe Frazier Challenge the Champ pop-up toy—a balloonlike punching bag sold to kids. In his Deer Lake ring, Clay began shooting jabs at it, saying: "See how it came back for more. Just like the real Joe Frazier. He gets angry if you miss him."

And in case they didn't get his theme—that I was a primitive sort of black man—he recalled our TV studio run-in like this: "I told him he was dumb and he jumped me, like an animal. That's what he is, really. He goes around wearing big diamonds on his fingers, buying Cadillacs, has a leopard-skin rug in his gym and a brain about the size of one of the rings he wears. He won't come on a television program anymore because it embarrasses him when there's a meeting of our minds. Mentally, my diction is so much more educational. . . . Besides, he's ugly."

🤽   🤽   🤽

In September, I arrived in Manila first, bringing Marvis with me. When Clay flew in a few days later, Marvis went out there to meet and kid him a little by singing a song written by Van McCoy, "First-Round Knockout":

> *. . . He was down, he was down,*
>
> *Lord knows he was down . . . .*

Clay took it in the joking spirit Marvis intended, but naturally he couldn't keep quiet for long. As Marvis sang, Clay interrupted, saying: "He's better-looking than his father, and he makes more sense."

But Marvis paid no mind to him, singing on:

> *. . . You tried to shake it off,*
>
> *but you just couldn't do it.*
>
> *'Cause there was a soul power in my punch*
>
> *and like a good left hook I threw it.*
>
> *One minute you were standing so tall,*
>
> *the next second you began to fall.*

"Hey, that's good," said Clay. "He even talks better than his father."

Marvis turned fifteen in Manila. We gave him a party, with a birthday cake that had figurines of two sumo wrestlers sitting on it. That was in recognition of Marvis' junior Olympic wrestling championship.

But it was a fighter that he gave every sign of wanting to be now. In the early mornings, when we'd do roadwork, Marvis would get up and run with my sparring partners and me. We'd had to get special permission from the Philippine government of Ferdinand Marcos to go out there during the 1:00 A.M. to 4:00 A.M. martial-law curfew. We did it because Philippine fans of mine would meet me when I stepped out of the Hyatt-Regency Hotel and run along with us, making it harder to go the pace and distance we wanted.

So we'd hit the streets of Manila about 3:30 in the morning, when the natives still had to be inside. Soldiers would be moving along the streets, with machine guns at the ready. A few of them in jeeps, or special agents on motorcycles, would follow us as we ran along the waterfront of the city.

By the time we were heading back, the curfew would be over, and the sun would be coming up. We could see the city coming awake. Folks on bicycles, heading off to work. Others pushing carts. Women already doing their wash in the bay.

Once Clay got into Manila, there was a news conference. No surprise, he produced a small black rubber gorilla and said: "This here is Joe Frazier's conscience. I keep it everywhere I go. This is the way he looks when you hit him."

Clay proceeded to smack the gorilla doll, saying: "All night long, this is what you'll see. Come on, gorilla, we're in Manila. Come on gorilla, this is a thrilla."

"We've got something for you," I said. "Your head and your body."

I told the crowd there that I didn't want to knock out Clay—that I would rather hurt the son of a bitch for the full fifteen rounds. It wasn't just prefight make-believe, I really wanted to make him suffer.

He interrupted, saying, "I'm going to hit you on the head and straighten out your nose . . . . Joe Frazier's so ugly his face should be donated to the Bureau of Wildlife."

When newsmen came to my hotel room, I'd point to the picture of my kids on my dresser and say: "Look at my beautiful kids. Now how can I be a gorilla? That's a dirty man, talking that stuff. . . . Well, I guess he's gonna talk, and ain't no way to stop him. But there will come that moment when he gonna be all alone, when he gonna hear that knock on the door, gonna hear it's time to go to the ring, and then he's gonna remember what it's like to be with me, how hard and long this night's gonna be."

Meantime, Clay was creating a minor scandal by carrying on in public with a woman. When President Marcos invited us to the presidential palace ten days before the fight, Clay brought a model named Veronica

Porche with him and didn't correct Marcos' mistaken impression that Veronica was his wife.

"Your wife is quite beautiful," Marcos said.

"So is yours," Clay replied.

And later that day, he was introducing Veronica to Filipino newsmen as his wife.

In fact, Clay's actual wife and mother of his four children, Belinda, was back in the States, where she was reading about her man's gallivanting about with this other woman.

Veronica was a tall, pretty gal, who Clay had spotted a year earlier at the beauty contest to pick the ring-card girls for "The Rumble in the Jungle," as his fight against Foreman would be called. She ended up being among the four contestants chosen to go to Zaire.

Veronica had been in Kuala Lumpur, Malaysia, when Clay fought the rematch with Bugner, but Clay had been cool about it there. In Manila, though, the boy just didn't seem to give a damn if folks knew he and Veronica were heating it up.

Far be it from me to trash him for it. I was my father's son, and had done my share of partying through the years as a fighter and would continue to do so. But as much as I played around, I kept my goings-on private; very few people knew my business. Few knew, for instance, that not long after Marvis was born, my other Beaufort lady, Rosetta, gave birth to a daughter of mine, Renae. And in October 1962, a son of mine named Hector was also born to Rosetta.

Clay, he just didn't seem to care that by carrying on so publicly he was humiliating Belinda. At another palace function that both of us attended, I teased him: "You done lost your mind, Clay, introducing this woman as your wife."

"Think so?" he said.

"Oh, yeah. You gonna get two ass whuppings. I'm gonna have to get in line behind Belinda. She's gonna be on your butt like white on rice."

"She don't run me, Joe Frazier."

"You're crazy, boy. What can you be thinking about, running around like that with Veronica?"

"I'm the champion," he said, like he was the king of England or some such. Meaning he could do what he damned well pleased. That was how he said it. And then, when it came out in *Newsweek* magazine about Veronica and him, he couldn't leave it alone. No, he brought it up first thing with the press that very day:

"Anybody who worries about who's my wife, tell them, you don't worry who I sleep with and I won't worry about who you sleep with. This is going too far. They got on me for the draft. They got on me for my religion. They got on me for all sorts of things. But they shouldn't be able to get on me for having a girlfriend. I could see some controversy if she was white, but she's not. The only person I answer to is Belinda Ali and I don't worry about her."

Well, the next day Belinda was on a plane, heading to Manila.

Florence and my four daughters were on the same flight, out of San Francisco, and they reported that she looked mean enough to bite the bumper off a Buick. Yeah. Sat there on that long flight just staring ahead, like she was about to go to war.

And from what we heard, Belinda gave Clay hell in his suite at the Manila Hilton, throwing furniture around and cursing him and threatening to whup his lady friend if she caught her sniffing around. But Belinda didn't stay long enough to get it on with Veronica. After an hour of jabbering away at Clay, she got into a limo and flew back to the States.

Next time I saw Clay, I kidded him: "I told you she'd be up your butt, chump."

"No big thing."

"Not the way I heard it."

"I'm still here, bro'."

"That's good. She saved your half-breed ass for me."

"Get real, man. You ain't got it no more, Joe Frazier. You're too slow, too old. Your time is past."

I don't know whether he really believed that or if he was just whistling in the dark. Besides, he was two years older than me. But he kept telling anybody who would listen that I was a ghost of what I'd been.

ALI: FRAZIER IS WASHED UP. A headline in the *New York Post*.

ALI WATCHES JOE: HE'S TOO SLOW—HE'S FINISHED. A headline in the *New York Daily News*.

One writer put it like this: "As expected, Blowhard Ali filled the tropical city with enough hot air to start a new front moving across Asia."

As the clock ticked down on the fight, Clay was running around, talking shit, making a ruckus wherever he could—barging in on my workouts, or hollering up to me outside the Hyatt-Regency. The sucker even showed up one night around three-thirty in the morning with a toy pistol, shouting, "I want Joe Frazier. Where's Joe Frazier?" And when I walked out onto the balcony nine floors up to see what he was doing, he aimed it at me and the hammer went *click click click click*—Clay snapped that gun four or five times. I wasn't too happy about that. I don't feature fooolin' around with guns, and from where I stood there was no way I could tell whether it was a real gun or not.

But Clay—he thought it was a big joke. He told the news guys that he had learned the trick from Sonny Liston, back when he had fought him. It seems like Liston came up to him one night when Clay was in a casino in Las Vegas and pulled a gun on him. As Clay recalled it: "I was so afraid I jumped up on a craps table."

Well, I just threw a fistful of my publicity photos and then a pillow at him and went back to sleep.

And all the while, Clay really seemed to believe that I was a shot fighter. "What kind of man can take all those punches to the head?" he would ask reporters.

As for me, I was getting ready, working like a beast. And when I wasn't training, I was killing time playing blackjack with Marvis and my sparring partners, or sitting alone thinking my thoughts while staring out across Manila Bay.

Three days before the fight, Dr. Fabiani came up to the room and removed fluid from my elbow joint and gave me a shot of cortisone.

At the weigh-in, when Clay came in at 224¹/₂ pounds, in contrast to my 215¹/₂ pounds, my guys needled him: "Too heavy."

"You're in trouble, boy," my brother Tommy hollered to Clay.

But that was just talk—a way of messing with his head. And I knew that it didn't faze a guy like Clay one bit.

As for all *his* nasty talk, it only served to build the anger in me. I told Marvis: "Who does this son of a bitch think he is, talking about me the way he does? I ain't no goddamn gorilla. Enough is enough. I'm gonna warm his ass good; make him suffer."

"Do it, Daddy. Smoke him."

The fight took place in an arena in Quezon City, just outside Manila. As we drove up, the sun was blazing overhead, and there wasn't a hint of wind blowing in from the South China Sea to take the bite off this hot and humid morning. Even though the arena was supposed to be air-cooled, once the seats filled up with live bodies the air-cooling system would prove useless. The air in the place would be thick and moist as a sauna.

The fight was scheduled to begin at 10:45 in the morning. An unusual starting time in a business where headline bouts normally go off after dark. But the early start time was to accommodate closed-circuit TV locations back in the States. There was a twelve-hour time difference between New York and Manila. While it was morning here, it was evening there.

With tickets priced up to $333, there were twenty-seven thousand folks in the arena when I entered the ring in a blue denim studded robe, with Marvis alongside me. For the first time in his life he was working my corner, acting as a bucket carrier.

Clay followed in a white satin robe trimmed in blue.

At ringside, President Marcos and his wife, Imelda, were seated in red-upholstered gold chairs—the lifestyle of the rich and famous (or infamous, depending on your politics).

Willie (the Worm) Monroe for some reason ended up sitting near Clay's corner. So in the minutes before the fight he saw Clay look down at his manager, Herbert Muhammad, and say, "Just another day's work. I'm gonna put a whuppin' on this nigger's head."

When the referee, a Filipino named Carlos Padilla, gave his instructions, Clay began jabbering away, as he always did—that bugeyed bullshit of his.

"Joe Frazier, I'm gonna kick your ass," he said. "I'm gonna whup you."

I just gave him a cold smile and said, "I'm gonna kill you Clay. You're dead."

The opening bell rang and Clay came out flatfooted. Through the weeks leading up to this fight, he had repeatedly told newsmen I was long-gone as a fighter and that he would knock me out early.

Well, he tried. He began trading shots, and he discovered Joe Frazier was no slouch. I was smokin'—I put a hurting on his butt, going up one side and down the other. Through the first three rounds we went at it toe to toe, and it didn't take Clay long to realize he was in a real fight.

On this morning, he wasn't clinching the way he had in our previous fight. Padilla, to his credit, wouldn't let him. So when he wanted to slow things down, Clay would stretch out that long left arm of his and stick it in my face, moving it around like a feather duster.

But for me the fight was just beginning. I began to rev the engine.

In taking on Clay, you have to crowd him and accelerate the tempo—not let him work at the pace he wants. Hurry him, and he would begin to huff and puff. Slow the scamboogah down, and it became a battle of survival—now that's my kind of fight.

In front of twenty-seven thousand mostly Filipino folks, and before God, from the fourth round on I got in his face and, snorting the way I do, kept whipping the left on him. He fired back, but found that it wasn't the one-sided deal he figured it would be. I was making the fight, and he didn't dig the pressure I was putting him under.

"You dumb chump, you," he snarled, as if annoyed that I wasn't going to fold up like an accordion.

Gotcha, baby, I thought. *I'm not quite the dead man you figured.*

Before the fifth round, the crowd began to chant, *"Ali, Ali,"* and Clay stepped away from his corner to wave to the voices. As he did, the chant of *"Frazier, Frazier"* rose up, just as the bell signaling the start of round five sounded.

In the fifth round, I drove Clay to the ropes, and whacked him with both hands to the body and head, jarring him at one point with a left hook that brought more chants of *"Frazier, Frazier."*

In the sixth, I staggered him with left hooks and knocked his mouthpiece out. They were big hurting shots, and I'm told when they landed Imelda Marcos looked down at her feet. She couldn't stand to see her pretty ole Clay eat the hook the way he was.

Clay retreated to the ropes, and lay there, taking punches the way he had against Foreman. But was no dope he was gonna rope this time. Sit on the ropes, and he was gonna pay. I hit the chump wherever and whenever, the way Marciano used to do to guys. Arms, ribs, whatever was exposed, I beat on it.

"They told me Joe Frazier was washed up," Clay said to me when we came out for the seventh round.

"They lied," I told him.

In those middle rounds, seven through eleven, we battled. Clay hadn't the legs to dance anymore, so he had to stand there and fight. He took some mighty big shots from me, and answered back. But the edge was mine. I was hurting him, and grinding him down. You could hear it in the voices that came from his corner, Bundini's and Angelo Dundee's:

"Stop playing, Champ."

"You got to float like a butterfly."

"He'll call you Clay from now on. Make him call you Muhammad."

"Fight for God, fight for Allah."

In the tenth round, Clay wobbled when I nailed him with a left hook to the side of the head. I could see he was running down. Between rounds, as his handlers attended to him, he sat with his head lowered. When he raised up, he rolled his eyes as if to say: "How much more can I take?"

"Go down to the well once more," Bundini screamed at him.

He'd have to dig deep down if he were going to beat me. Through ten rounds Padilla and judge Larry Nadayag had the fight dead even, four rounds Clay, four rounds Frazier, and two even. The other judge, a hard-of-seeing local named Colonel Alfredo Quiazon, had it 5–3–2, in favor of Clay. I was the stronger man after ten rounds, but my face had begun to swell some. That didn't alarm me. I'd been lumped before, and I accepted it as part of doing business. But for me, this night was a trying one, given how damn hot it was in that arena. One hundred ten degrees, they said. It felt closer to 120 to me; when I'd suck in air, it was like walking into a pizza oven.

Urged on by Bundini and Dundee, Clay roused himself, scoring several times with his right. But I took him to the ropes and continued to smoke him. Things were going my way, but then my face betrayed me.

I'd come to the bout with a virtually sightless left eye—my vision had deteriorated that badly from the cataract. So when the swelling on my face worsened around the right eye, limiting vision there, it left me in a real jam. The blood trickling from my mouth was nothing to me. But as the right eye began to close, it meant that I was fighting Clay in a kind of haze.

From Clay's corner, it looked as though suddenly I was running on empty.

"Look at old Frazier," Dundee shouted. "He's dead."

Not really. I had firepower, still. But I no longer had the ability to see clearly. And because of that, I had to step back to get a bead on Clay with my limited vision, which put me at a distance where I became a target.

Clay hit the target. In the thirteenth he knocked my mouthpiece out, and sent it flying into press row. I fought him best I could. I could barely see; I was fighting on instinct, bobbing and weaving. But Clay was timing me. Late in the round he shook me with a right as we stood in the center of the ring. When I got back to the corner, Milt Bailey, my cut man, pressed the ice pack against my eyes to hold back the swelling. But it didn't help.

"I can't see much," I said, when Eddie Futch asked me how I was doing.

The swelling was bad, my sight was decreasing dangerously. The left eye was closed shut. But I figured if I could get close enough to Clay, I might be able to nail him. What the hell. He was no fresh daisy. I'd put the scamboogah through the wringer.

As I walked out for the fourteenth round, Futch, who knew about the cataract, turned to his assistant, George Benton, and said, "I don't like him taking the shots he's taking. If he keeps getting hit . . ." and he shook his head.

Well, I kept getting hit. Without any use of the left eye, I couldn't track his right hand. In that fourteenth round, Clay hit me directly on the right eye. The punches were coming at me, and I just couldn't make them out.

A few days later in Philly, Doctor Yanoff would test me and find that my left eye was legally blind. Two weeks later, he would run another test. This time my vision was slightly better: the left eye recorded 20–70, which in Pennsylvania means you're prohibited from driving at night.

In Manila, all I knew was that Clay was a fuzzy vision, and the less I could see of him the more it cost me. But I fought on. There was nothing else to do. There was always a chance that I could fire the big one on him. Tired as he was, if I could nail him once more, who knows? He might fall, as he had in 1971.

When I got back to the corner after the fourteenth round, Padilla (66–60) and the two judges, Quiazon (67–62) and Nadayag (66–62), had me behind in the scoring, and needing a last-round knockout to win. But Eddie Futch had come to the conclusion that I'd had enough. He was afraid that I could be seriously hurt, given how little vision I had. He'd been in the arena the night Davey Moore had died in a world feather-weight title bout in 1963 in Los Angeles, and he'd been in arena the night Jimmy Doyle died fighting Sugar Ray Robinson in Cleveland in 1947.

"What's with his right hand?" he asked me.

"I can't see it. I can see the left, but when I move away, I get hit with the right."

"I'm going to stop it," he said. "You're taking too much punishment."

"No. No. Don't. You can call the shots out to me. I want him, Boss."

I rose in protest from the stool. But Eddie laid his hand on my shoulder and said, "Sit down, son. It's all over. No one will ever forget what you did here today."

From across the ring, Willie the Worm was eavesdropping on Clay's corner. He heard Clay say, "I ain't going out there. That man's crazy." And then Bundini: "Come on, Champ. You can make it."

As Worm watched Eddie restrain me, and saw me sit back down on the stool, he began shouting to Eddie: "No no. Don't stop it. Don't stop it." He felt there was a good chance Clay might not come out for the fifteenth and final round. But the crowd noise drowned out his voice.

And so when Eddie notified the referee the fight was over, Clay slumped to the canvas and lay there on his back. "The closest thing to death" was what he called these fourteen rounds, later.

Me? I wanted to go out on my shield. I was willing to take my chances with my body, to absorb the pain for a last shot at Clay. But the man in charge of the corner—well, his word rules. I wasn't happy with the fight being stopped. But you gotta take the good with the bad. And I knew Eddie didn't make his decision lightly.

Back in the dressing room, Eddie couldn't help but second-guess himself. He asked George Benton, and then Marvis, had he done the right thing. They both told him yeah, he had.

The dressing room was quiet. I was disappointed, and a bit angry still, that the fight had been stopped. I had all I could do to keep from bursting out in tears. Losing hurt.

I had no idea of how the world would come to perceive those fourteen rounds, no idea that The Thrilla in Manila would go down as a classic match, leaving Clay and me as the measuring stick for heated boxing rivalries.

Yeah, even as I sit here looking back twenty years, the current edition of *Sports Illustrated* is running this line about another heavyweight rivalry:

> *In only 94 minutes of boxing, Bowe and Holyfield have been delivered straight into Ali–Frazier country, their careers forever defined by their repeated and concussive collisions.*

Bruised, weary, and dehydrated in that dressing room in Quezon City, I wasn't thinking about the place in history this fight I'd just fought would have. I had lost, and that was as deep as my reality went.

While I sat there, applying the ice pack to my eyes, word came from Clay's dressing room that he wanted to see Marvis. When Marvis got over there, Clay was lying on a padded table. His skin was ashy and his right eye was discolored. His lower lip was scraped pink. There were welts and bruises all over his body. He looked like a wax museum version of himself.

When he saw Marvis, he struggled to sit up and shake his hand. Then he said, "Tell your father all the stuff I said about him—I didn't mean it. Your father's a helluva man. I couldn't have taken the punches he took tonight."

Well, it may have satisfied Clay's conscience to excuse his years of trashing me like that. And it may have touched Marvis' heart to hear it from the scamboogah's lips. But it didn't change a doggone thing for me. Why tell it to Marvis? Why not be man enough to say what you feel to me, to my face? Yeah, he'd proven himself in the ring—I'd give him that. He'd stood up to punches that would have put holes in concrete. But as a man, Clay was so kneedeep in ego that in the end he couldn't bring himself to do the right thing.

What the right thing for me to do was—whether to keep fighting or retire—remained to be seen. That night, as I soaked my face in warm water and Epsom salts in a sink back at the hotel, the family was huddling and trying to figure what buttons to push to make me give up boxing.

Florence told me: "Now you can retire. And spend time with us."

Marvis said: "You've got all the money you're ever going to need."

Jacquelyn added: "Why not enjoy yourself? You've worked hard enough and long enough."

All of which was true.

That night, in the lowdown mood I was in, I told them: "Okay, we shot our shot. I'll hang them up."

But a retirement promise from a hard-core fighter is right up there with "The check is in the mail" for industrial-strength bullshit.

When morning came, I was back in business.

8

Hanging Up the Gloves

And eight months after The Thrilla in Manila, there I was, hunkered down in my dressing room in the Nassau Coliseum in Uniondale, New York, waiting for that knock at the door that would tell me it was time to rumble again.

Rumble against that heavyhanded fella, big George Foreman.

The Fraziers of Philadelphia were right about one thing: I didn't need the one million dollars I was guaranteed for this night's work.

After a decade of fighting, I had secured a future for my family and me.

There was the house in Philly; the plantation in South Carolina; the real-estate investment in Bucks County; a half-million-dollar pension fund that earned interest at between 8 and 10 percent; and trust fund investments totaling nearly four hundred thousand dollars.

The garage to my home now held a gray and black '74 Rolls-Royce, a pearly-white '72 Lincoln Mark IV, a maroon '75 Cadillac Royal Brougham, a purple '62 Corvette with a custom-built engine, a black 1964 Austin taxi, a 1934 Chevrolet sedan, a 1975 Kawasaki fifteen-hundred-cc motorcycle, a Harley-Davidson road bike, three snowmobiles, and one helluva gas bill. Oh, yeah, and there was a powder-blue Cadillac Seville on order for Marvis.

All that, and my nine years of splitting purses with Cloverlay was behind me. That deal had ended in December 1974, which meant that by 1975—with the Jimmy Ellis return match and The Thrilla in Manila—I had no partner divvying up my purses. All the money went to me, and from that purse I paid sparring partners, trainers, and manager.

No, it wasn't financial need that kept me going. It was competitive need. I had the warrior's appetite for battle—which is a rarity these days. With the big money to be made on the pay-per-view end of boxing promotions—leading to fighters earning as much as $24 million to $25 million a fight—guys flame out like Fourth of July sparklers now.

Yeah, once they get the dough-re-mi, they grew fat or uninterested. They didn't want to sacrifice anymore. Riddick Bowe, Buster Douglas, Lennox Lewis, Ray Mercer, Michael Moorer—these are all guys whose skills went south as soon as the big money rolled in. They lost interest.

A couple of years ago, I remember being at the Boxing Hall of Fame banquet, up in Canastota, New York, seated at the head table along with such boxing greats as Carmen Basilio, Gene Fullmer, Willie Pep, Bob Foster, Carlos Ortiz, Rubin Olivares, and dozens of others. And along with them was the then current heavyweight champion, Michael Moorer.

Sometime during the dinner, Moorer said to me: "I'd like to fight someone soon." And so, looking up and down the head table, I said to him, "Hell, there's a whole table of champions. Why don't you fight one of them now?"

The reason for my needling remark was I'd remembered the last time Moorer fought—and didn't really want to. This was the fight against Evander Holyfield for Holyfield's heavyweight title. On this night Holyfield was not the nonstop punching machine he'd been in the past. It was clear to everybody in the arena that Holyfield was short on stamina—that he'd aged as a fighter and was ready to be taken.

But Moorer fought as though he wasn't really interested in doing what he had to do to win. It got to the point where Moorer's trainer, Teddy Atlas, sat on Moorer's stool between rounds and asked would he rather Teddy Atlas go out there and fight Holyfield instead. I mean, here was a man fighting for the heavyweight championship of the world and he acted as though he was bored.

Me? A whole other story. I loved the combat, whether in a sparring session on North Broad Street, with maybe a passerby peeking in from outside, or in the main event at Madison Square Garden, with a sellout crowd roaring like God's own engine. That full-contact challenge was, and is, the best damn experience I can think of. Or as I'd once told a sports columnist, "The most thing is, I love to fight."

However you want to put it, there was nothing like that man-to-man combat for me. And the pleasure stood apart from the money to be made. I loved the sensation of applying what brute force, and technique, I had against bigger men—and seeing them diminish round by round. And I loved the attention, and respect, that went to the guy who was champion of the world. Not to mention the lifestyle it gave you. Oh, yeah, boxing—that was "the most thing" for sure.

🥊　🥊　🥊

But after the bout in Manila, it was obvious that for me to continue fighting something had to be done about the cataract in my left eye. For about a year, I'd taken eye drops before fights to make the pupil bigger and enable me to see better around the cataract during the action. But the eye had now deteriorated to the point where surgery was necessary, no ifs, ands, or buts about it. The hitch was that if word leaked to the boxing commissions, I'd be through. Once they found out, they'd use their test procedures to make me an ex-fighter. It made it crucial to do the surgery on the sly.

I came up with the idea of shaving my head, thinking it would change my look enough so that people wouldn't recognize me. Doctor Yanoff had arranged for the surgery in New York. But when I hit the streets of the city with my Kojak look, folks said, "Hey, Joe. How ya doin'?" Or, "Nice head, Joe." Or, "Yo, Joe. Mr. Clean."

So much for traveling unrecognized.

On November 19, 1975, on Long Island, Dr. Charles Kellman successfully performed surgery on the cataract. But for the eye to function I now had to wear contact lenses in and out of the ring. That made things a lot more dicey for Smokin' Joe the fighter than for the civilian Frazier. For not only were contact lenses prohibited by the commissions, but there were no guarantees even if I made it into the ring with lenses.

I mean, it's no late-breaking news that contact lenses can be jarred loose. Anybody who has watched basketball is familiar with that scene where players and officials walk stooped over, looking for a contact lens that has been dislodged from a player's eye. And hell, if it can happen in a so-called noncontact sport like basketball, chances are it can happen in a no-holds-barred game like boxing. But for me it was a chance worth taking. I wanted to keep boxing.

🥊   🥊   🥊

After a match as grueling as the one in Manila, it would have been easy, and acceptable, to take on a patsy. But that wasn't for me. At this stage of my career, if there was no challenge involved, I couldn't get psyched. Besides, I needed to beat a name opponent to prove I deserved another title shot. Next to Clay, Foreman was "it"—the biggest name out there. Even though Foreman had lost to Clay in Zaire, and had had to climb off the canvas to beat Ron Lyle in January 1976, he still was regarded as a holy terror—a wrecking ball in boxing trunks.

More than that, he was the only man who had made me bounce up and down off the canvas like a damn basketball. Six knockdowns. Nobody had handled me so easy. Clay had fought to the point of exhaustion—"the closest thing to death." By contrast, for Foreman, fighting me had been a day at the beach.

I didn't believe back then, and more than three years later still didn't believe, that Foreman was the better man. He'd beaten me, yeah. But I was convinced that it had been an off day—that I had not been all there, so to speak. Mentally and physically. Nobody could dominate Smokin' Joe like that.

Anyway, for the Frazier–Foreman fight, Jerry Perenchio would resurface as promoter, working with Caesars Palace. Perenchio intended to put the fight originally in seventy-thousand-seat Yankee Stadium. In fact, in April, *The New York Times* had run a story headlined: FRAZIER VS. FOREMAN/ AT STADIUM JUNE 15. In the article Perenchio announced the bout would be the first at Yankee Stadium since Ingemar Johansson took the title from Floyd Patterson in 1959.

But even though dozens of major fights—thirty-seven, according to Perenchio—had been held at Yankee Stadium over the years, this time the facility suddenly became unavailable. See, Perenchio hadn't counted on the Yankees' principal owner, George M. Steinbrenner, vetoing the deal, which he was entitled to do during the baseball season. The Boss, as he later would be known, claimed that the ringside seats that would be placed onto the field would leave the grounds a mess afterward.

A Steinbrenner aide told the press: "The last time a fight was held in the stadium—Johansson versus Patterson—was the only year in ten the Yankees lost the pennant. The field was terrible after that fight. We're not against holding a fight. But we don't want some guy coming in from California telling us what to do. And then when the fight's over he's gone and we have to clean up the place."

Perenchio? He took note of the fact that the Knicks and Rangers had not made the playoffs for the first time in ten years and wished the Yankees better luck, adding, "I hope that Steinbrenner's toupee turns green and flourishes."

And guess what? A Yankee spokesman responded, denying that Steinbrenner wore a toupee.

Crazy, right?

Steinbrenner—so it was said—wouldn't even take phone calls from New York's mayor, Abe Beame, to discuss the matter, and that created a few more headlines. Beame wanted the fight to land in the city because of the across-the-board revenues a big match like Frazier–Foreman would bring in: taxis, restaurants, hotels, what-have-you. But long before Steinbrenner was firing managers and insulting players, he was showing a knack for stirring things up. He wouldn't give in to Perenchio.

No matter. Perenchio simply kept the June 15, 1976, date, and shifted the site to the Nassau Coliseum out on Long Island.

In the buildup for the fight, he had George and me dress up in various costumes—Foreman as Teddy Roosevelt, Abe Lincoln, Sitting Bull, and Paul Revere, me as Sitting Bull, Ben Franklin, and General Douglas MacArthur for a series of TV spots that would air across the United States and in Canada.

As Paul Revere, Foreman said, "Listen my children and you shall hear/ Joe Frazier knocked on his ear."

Dressed in drag as Betsy Ross, I promised folks Foreman would be seeing stars when I hit him.

The bout was called "The Battle of the Gladiators," and to emphasize the point Perenchio also had us dress up in Roman gladiator gear that had been used in MGM's 1959 film *Ben Hur.*

It was in my dressing room at the Nassau Coliseum that while awaiting that knock on the door that night, I sat thinking about the strategic changes Eddie Futch had devised to help me beat this big guy Foreman.

Eddie had taken the tactics used by Clay in Zaire and changed them for me. Obviously, I hadn't the height and reach that Clay did, not to mention the distancing jab. But Eddie's approach had the same objective—work the guy and fatigue him. The thinking about Big George was that if you could take him into the late rounds, you could count on his grinding down. The man didn't have the best gas tank.

For me it meant being less rambunctious. The full-tilt forward-march attitude was replaced by a more cautious, tactical approach—more circling, bobbing, ducking, covering up. That reduced the chance of running into the punch that had ruined me the first time around—Foreman's right uppercut. And it improved my chances of tiring out Foreman.

So instead of charging straight in, like a tank with a left hook, I would counter Foreman, and punch from long range and, when I wasn't punching, be sure to move my head so as not to be an easy target. If the opportunity arose where I could slip inside, and whack him with my left, I'd do it but not linger. Not until he was tired and ready to be had.

In the dressing room before the bout, on an impulse I had decided to shave my head—that Kojak look again. Can't explain why. Just decided to do it right there in the dressing room. I tried to persuade Marvis to go baldy too. But he wouldn't take it to the extreme. He got a close haircut, but not the chrome-dome that I did. He had himself a girl-friend, Daralyn—the woman he would end up marrying—and felt that the billiard-ball look wouldn't go over big with her.

Finally, there was a knock at the door, and the man was saying: "Main event. Joe Frazier."

And here we go again—down the aisle toward the ring, with Marvis alongside me.

The crowd was smaller than what would have turned out at the Garden: some 10,300 paying customers, among them celebs like Liz Taylor, Norman Mailer, Dick Cavett, James Caan, Julius Erving, Jim Brown, and Elliott Gould.

Like I say, I had tactics, and I had a plan. And for a while I thought it might get me over. The Foreman who'd gone bombs-away and blitzed me that first time found me harder to hit on this night. In fact, in the first round, as I saw he couldn't zero in on me as easily, I dropped my hands to my sides and stuck my bald head out there as a target, laughing at him when he couldn't hit it.

When the bell ending the first round sounded, my grin widened.

In the second round, I hit him four solid left hooks, the punches sending a fine spray of his sweat shooting off his face and into the air.

"I'm gonna get you," I told big George.

I got him—not just with the hook, but with straight rights and lefts too that Eddie Futch had worked on with me. But George had a few tricks in his bag. His trainer, Gil Clancy, had anticipated my being prepared for that Foreman right uppercut, and he had Big George mixing left hooks in with straight rights, and going more to my body. Besides that, George was showing a piston-jab that he had neglected against Clay in Zaire, and against Lyle in Las Vegas.

Big George was hitting me, but not dead-on as he had in Kingston. Still it was enough to let me know it would be a rough evening. But as we moved through the third round and into the fourth I felt that if I could keep punching in bursts and avoid George's heavy shots, the guy would lose wind and be there for the taking.

The crowd was for me—wall-to-wall Frazier fans that shouted encouragement throughout the evening. I gave them something to get happy about when I nailed Foreman a left hook in the fourth round—a shot that should have made George's legs turn to putty. But he was in shape, and he didn't wobble. It surprised me because Lyle had put Big George down twice in January with punches that had less smoke on them.

Still, his punches seemed to be more labored now, and Clancy was shouting from the corner: "Keep your right up, George."

Trouble was my face was getting puffy by the fifth round. At this point in my career, the bumps and welts seemed to rise like yeast, as if they had a life of their own. The left eye was now swollen, and George was targeting it. One of his punches knocked the contact lens off the pupil and troubled my vision.

He seemed to sense that. And like that, he became bolder, moving in and firing away. Big punches that hurt. A left hook split open the skin above the eye. Another left hook and a right, and I was sprawling into a neutral corner, my eyes glassy and blood oozing from between my lips. Big George hovered over me, as though he was going to hit me while I was down. But the refeee, Harold Valan, grabbed his hand and led him to a neutral corner.

"I don't think Foreman realizes what's going on in the ring," Valan told reporters afterward. "He's like some kind of animal in there. All he wants to do is punch."

I was up by the count of four and took the mandatory count of eight.

"Are you all right, Joe?" Valan asked.

I told him I was. But that's what a fighter says, even when he's in serious trouble.

Foreman hit me a vicious right, and down I went again. I was up by seven, but by then Eddie Futch was climbing up onto the ring apron on a mission of mercy and I was trying to push Valan away and continue. But Eddie reached through the ropes and grabbed me, as Valan was signaling that the fight was over.

"Joe, that's enough," Valan told me. "You were a great champion."

To Futch, the referee said: "It's over, Eddie."

"That's good, Harold."

And for me, at two minutes twenty-six seconds of the fifth round, it was over.

After eleven years and thirty-six professional bouts, of which I'd won thirty-two, after fighting for wages all over these United States and across both oceans, I knew it was the end of the line as Marvis helped me to my corner.

"I think it's time to put the gloves on the wall," I told the press afterward.

It seemed strange to be saying those words. But it had to be. I'd hoped that with a lens in my eye I could keep fighting—I didn't know the damn thing was going to pop out. I really didn't want to get out of boxing. But with that eye problem that the world knew nothing about, I was at too great a disadvantage.

Was I sad that the end had come? Not really. I'm the sort that takes things as they come, without getting hung up on could-have and should-have. Still, I couldn't help but wonder what life after boxing would be like.

✗ ✗ ✗

Well, in the beginning it turned out to be about my music.

Through my years as a fighter there had been gigs here and there—in the States and abroad. But with a booming career as a fighter, "Smokin' Joe and the Knockouts" couldn't be but a part-time deal.

Lots of fun it was, and the money didn't hurt. But the reason for doing it was the pleasure of making the music—of setting in there with an audience and feeling them react to your sounds. Yeah, you couldn't help but diggin' that.

In the very beginning, starting out in the 1960s, we'd played in tiny clubs in North Philly for chump change . . . and were happy to get it. But as time went by, and Smokin' Joe became a name known the world over, the music went where the name went . . . and for better dollar.

Hell, for a while I'd even had a recording contract with Capitol Records. And with the jobs in Vegas, in Atlantic City, and in Europe, it was a world removed from the smoky dives where we first started playing.

But face it—the music was always a distant second to boxing. Had to be that way. I loved music, but I lived boxing. Now, having announced my retirement from the fight game, I figured, let's give the music a real shot and see what happens. I moved to New York—got myself an office on Broadway and West Fifty-fourth Street, and an apartment a few blocks away. And set about to put together "The Smokin' Joe Frazier Revue."

There was lots to do besides just singing when the lights came on. Holding together an eleven-piece revue is a heap of work. Besides drumming up jobs, there's equipment to worry about, travel arrangements to be made, wardrobes, musical charts, a payroll to get out for the performers and the technicians.

That work load became mine, and the money to keep things moving was boss Joe's too. I hired Henry Letang to choreograph our show, and began studying with a voice teacher, Carlos Menotti, to get a better sound. For a few years, beginning in 1977, Smokin' Joe's Revue worked regularly, hauling our own equipment in a truck and traveling in a van and in my own personal car, which I drove.

I spent a lot of money on the best sound equipment. I was a bug on that. You don't have to be Streisand or Sinatra to make the sound come out right. And I'd hired an ace audio technician, who could hook up Italy and blow up America at the same time—I mean, this cat could solve any problem that came up.

By February 1977, we'd made it to the Rainbow Grill, atop Rockefeller Center in New York—a kind of fancy place—and ended up with great reviews. John Wilson in *The New York Times* wrote:

> *Mr. Frazier is preceded by three singers and three dancers who stir up some slick, polished action that keeps the eye and ear occupied but leaves Mr. Frazier with nothing too great to overcome when he makes his entrance. When he does, however, wearing a silver-textured jacket that gives the effect of a coat of mail, he establishes his new credentials very quickly.*

> *"Once I was a fighter," he says, "but tonight I'm going to sing for you."*

> *And he gets right down to a rock and soul performance that has the ease and assurance that one might expect of a seasoned pro in this field. He has a warm and pleasant voice and an easy, gracious manner. His timing is exemplary. And, singing with expression and feeling, he builds such a rapport that when he reaches his own version of "My Way," a song that has been worn threadbare by innumerable singers, he has his listeners in the palm of his hand.*

> *With dancers and singers behind him, Mr. Frazier's performance was reminiscent of the showcases at the old Copacabana. Even on his first time out, Mr. Frazier would have deserved the Copa bonnet that the club used to award to its top stars.*

I was not the first fighter to perform in public, and I doubt I'll be the last. Sugar Ray Robinson had headed a revue back in the 1950s, and was even booked in France, where Parisians fussed over him. And before him, in the 1930s, Max Baer had been the singing star of a movie called *The Prizefighter and the Lady*, opposite Myrna Loy.

Plenty other fighters had appeared in movies—usually playing boxers or tough guys. Jersey Joe Walcott was a corner man in *The Harder*

They Fall. Tony Galento and Abe Simon were among many fighters who played dock workers in *On the Waterfront.* Joe Louis, Carlos Palamino, Tommy Morrison, Mark Breland, Clay, Tex Cobb, Marvelous Marvin Hagler, Evander Holyfield, Eddie Mustafa Muhammad—they'd popped up in one film or another.

Smokin' Joe's Revue played all over. New York, Vegas, Tahoe, Atlantic City, Virginia Beach, upstate New York. Just about every week, there was a job for us to do, usually two shows a night on weekends. The old habits of being a fighter die hard, though. On the road, I could *not* keep from working out. From a night's gig at the Rainbow Grill, I'd slip out of those slick threads and into work clothes and heavy boots, and run the streets of New York in the wee hours until I made it back to the hotel.

And it was the same in Vegas as it was in New York. I remember riding home in a classic Rolls-Royce at 7:30 in the morning after a gig. Suddenly I jumped out and began running the Strip—that long stretch of neon-lit casinos—with the Rolls following at five miles an hour and the sun reflecting off my black patent leather shoes.

In truth, I really never strayed too far from boxing. When I wasn't performing, or in New York, I was back in Philly at "Joe Frazier's Gym" out there on North Broad Street, hard by Amtrak's North Philadelphia station.

Yeah, the old Cloverlay gym was now mine. On retiring I'd bought it for $75,000—getting the gym and the fighters Cloverlay had under contract, which at that time included heavyweights Duane Bobick, Mike Koranicki, and Marty Monroe, and middle-weight guys like Willie the Worm.

That made me a fight manager. As a fight manager, I tried to be a hands-on kind of guy, jumping into the ring from time to time to make my points with the fighter. But I found that for whatever reason, there was resistance from them to what I had to say. And from early on.

I can remember gloving up Bobick one afternoon as he was getting ready to spar. Bobick was a white heavyweight with a 38–0 record but a reputation for fighting tomato cans. One sports columnist insisted he had climbed into the rankings "by beating old ladies, roundheeled has-beens and clowns moonlighting in the Shrine Circus." Anyway, not paying a whole lot of attention, I ended up slipping a right-handed glove halfway onto his left hand. It was an honest mistake, and I realized it right off. But Bobick looked at me like I was a leper and said disgustedly: "Yeah. And you want to be a trainer."

I climbed down off the ring, and never talked boxing to Bobick again. When Bobick was offered a network TV prime-time fight against Ken Norton, I thought it was a bad fight for him—that Norton would destroy him. I told that to Eddie Futch, who once had trained Norton but now trained Bobick and my other fighters. Futch disagreed. The fight was made, with Bobick guaranteed $250,000. Norton stiffed Bobick in one round. And Bobick never really got back into the picture after that.

My office at the gym was up a short flight of stairs. From there, through a wide window, I could look down at the action on the floor and see what I wanted to—my fighters as well as the young amateurs that flocked to the gym.

At that time, in the late 1970s, the city was alive with lots of great amateurs—Tyrell Biggs, Myron and Meldrick Taylor, James Shuler, Curtis Parker, Robert (Bam Bam) Hines, and, would you believe, Marvis Frazier. Yeah, with my Smokin' Joe Revue out on the road a lot, the job of training Marvis had become George Benton's. And under Benton, my son was turning out to be a well-schooled amateur heavyweight.

I got a lot of kicks out of helping the amateurs develop—offering instruction to them or keeping them afloat by giving them shoes and equipment and funding an amateur team so they could travel to all the competitions. There were trainers in the gym including Van Colbert and Sam Hickman who worked with them and, when I could, I'd put in my two cents as well.

Between the Smokin' Joe Frazier Revue, the action in the gym, and a limousine service and restaurant ("Smokin' Joe's Corner") that I owned, I stayed busy. All the while, I did roadwork in the mornings with the fighters and worked out enough in the gym to keep within hailing distance of a comeback.

And from time to time, there'd be a news story indicating that Smokin' Joe was thinking about a return to boxing. To fight Earnie Shavers. Or Scott LeDoux. Or Gerrie Coetzee. Or Kallie Knoetze. I listened to the offers and didn't always discourage them.

You know by now there wasn't anything more natural, or pleasing, to me than standing in the four-squares and boxing another man. But for one reason or another, these comeback fights would go up in smoke. The closest I came in those first few years after retiring was a May 1978 match against Knoetze, a South African policeman who had knocked out Bobick earlier in the year in Johannesburg. Knoetze and

I were scheduled to fight in Las Vegas, but before the two of us could get it on I contracted hepatitis and had to cancel.

The hepatitis slowed me down, and forced me to spend more time at home, which was okay with me. The kids were growing up, and it was good to see them shaping up so nicely. While over the years I'd spoiled them with material things, neither Florence nor I believed in a household where anything goes. The Frazier kids had to mind their p's and q's, and were expected to give best effort in school.

And while I might have been a hellraiser at their age, you better believe I wasn't playing that as their daddy. Oh, we had our fun together. Some nights I'd come home and throw money on the table for them to divvy up so all of us could sit around there and play blackjack. And in Smokin' Joe's gambling parlor, the boss made sure there were no losers. Whatever I won I'd spread among the ones that weren't doing as well.

At Christmastime, I'd put out so many bright lights and Yuletide decorations that the Frazier house was as eye-catching as Las Vegas Boulevard, with all its blinking casino neon. In fact, folks would drive by in such numbers that the police would assign an officer to keep traffic moving.

But on certain things I was a stickler. When the kids were young, I didn't allow overnights at their friends'. Since I didn't always know what kind of homes their friends came from, I figured let their friends hang out at Joe Frazier's—there were so many fun things to do in our place anyway.

As for dating, my girls weren't allowed to until they were at least sixteen. And I'd find out who the guy was. There were rules for the Frazier girls: Be home by two on weekends and no sitting out there in the driveway in the car with the lights cut out. Uh uh. Didn't want no smooching in the yard.

One young fella dating Jacqui tried car sitting, as I was arriving home one night. I cut the engine, got out of my car, and told him, "Take Jacqui in the house." When he came back out, I had his car keys and some advice for him: "I don't want no car sitting. If you got to make pit stops, do it outside. Once you're on my property, bring her in the house and get out. If you can't do that, then don't come back." Well, he came back, but hipped to Daddy Joe's rules.

When Marvis turned sixteen, I gave him a silver, sky-blue 1976 Cadillac Seville and some advice.

"Son," I said, "if the speed limit is thirty, you drive twenty-five."

I'd grown up in the South, where a black man driving an expensive car is an invitation for a police officer to pull him over. And some lawmen, I knew, got nervous around young blacks. I didn't want no trigger-happy accidents where my kid was concerned.

I told Marvis: "If you're ever stopped, step out of the car with your hands up. And if you're with buddies, you make sure they cut out the laughing and you pay attention to what that officer is saying. And if you're asked any questions, always say 'yes sir' or 'no sir.'"

Well, Marvis did get stopped once in Philly. And when he stepped out with his hands up, the officer seemed puzzled.

"What are you doing with your hands up, son?" he said.

"That's the way my daddy said to do it if I ever got stopped."

"Who's your daddy?"

"Smokin' Joe Frazier."

"Well, give him my best. And get back in the car."

By the late 1970s, Marvis—six foot one and a half inches, two hundred pounds now—had become the top amateur heavyweight in the country. Busy as I was with the Smokin' Joe Frazier Revue, I didn't get to see all of his matches. But through his trainer, George Benton, I kept up with how he was doing.

In all, Marvis would go 56–2 as an amateur, beating the likes of Tim Witherspoon, James (Bonecrusher) Smith, Tony Tubbs—that's three guys right there who went on to become world champions—as well as future contenders like Mitch Green, Phil Brown, and David Bey. Benton had him as a slick boxer, which was what Benton had been when he was a middleweight contender. Marvis was considered a good bet to represent this country at the 1980 Olympics in Moscow.

Up to 1980 my input with Marvis' boxing was minimal, the biggest contribution being a terrible dream I had—a nightmare, really—in which

I saw my family caught up in the flames of an airplane crash. It was so powerful a dream that when I heard Marvis was supposed to fly to Europe for an international competition I wouldn't let him go. I absolutely, positively forbid it.

Well, on March 14, 1980, eighty-seven people, including twenty-two members of the American boxing team, were killed when that jet crashed in Poland.

There were times, I know, when Marvis must have felt odd, and maybe even a little hurt, by his famous father not being at major tournaments he was in. When he won the national Golden Gloves title in Indianapolis in 1979, people kept asking him where's Joe, where's Joe? Well, Joe was in the lounge of the Pittsburgh Holiday Inn with his revamped eighteen-member song-and-dance troupe.

For Marvis, being Son of Smokin' was no easy deal. As a schoolboy, he had gotten whupped and had his lunch money snatched up by older kids who figured it made them big shots by beating on a fighter's son. Eventually, Marvis started hauling along his German shepherd when he returned for after-school activities.

Then there was the fact that I wasn't around that much when Marvis was growing up. When he was four years old, he had met me at the airport when I returned from Tokyo with the gold medal. He barely knew me. I'd been up north, getting started as a fighter; he'd been with Florence in South Carolina.

And through the glory years, I wasn't around a whole lot either. If I wasn't training, I was out there boogieing between fights, having fun while I could. It was a normal response for a guy who'd been holed up in a training camp for five, six weeks, denying himself pleasure and torturing himself with a disciplined training regimen every day. It was a normal response for a guy who would be going back to that routine sooner than a body wanted to.

While I was not exactly an absentee father, there were large holes in my kids' lives when Daddy was just a voice on the phone. Yet Marvis turned out damn good. I'd like to think he got enough of Daddy to know what was right, and what was not. For sure Florence did her part in raising him up right. This was a god-fearing and responsible child. A yes-ma'am, yes-sir polite sort of fellow—still is—who never got to acting uppity or like the rich boy he was.

Come spring, he'd be out there mowing our two and a half acres with a hand mower. At night he'd put out the garbage, and see to it that the dogs were settled in their kennels. And he was always a regular at church—Monday nights choir practice, Wednesday nights Bible study, and on Sundays church services. Marvis practiced what the religion preached: no smoking, no drinking, and moderation in all things. He was the real McCoy about it, too; there was no shamming with Marvis.

In fact, I sometimes called him "The Deacon" and teased him about being un-Frazierlike in his love life. My daddy and I were busy with the women, but Marvis was more conservative. A one-woman man. Had only two girlfriends in his life, and the second one he married. And no matter how much I kidded him that the chip fell near the block, he stayed a one-woman man.

Once he began fighting amateur, Marvis moved out of the house to a room over the gym, on the second floor, where a few other fighters had rooms too. For them, a rent-free room was a nice deal, and maybe an improvement on where they were living. Not for Marvis, who had all the creature comforts back where he lived. But for him it was a way of showing his commitment.

Florence was not crazy about his taking up boxing. She'd been hoping he'd get himself a wrestling scholarship, and a college degree.

"Seeing your husband get hurt is one thing," she told a reporter. "Seeing your baby get hurt is another."

But in the Frazier household, it's the man who runs things. If Marvis wanted his shot at the four-squares, the boy was gonna get it.

By 1980, as the Olympics drew near, he and I were spending lots more time together. Back then, the CB radio craze was going strong, and we were part of it. My handle was KO-1, he was KO-2. Say I'd walk into the office and greet him with: "It ain't nothing but a party," Marvis would reply: "Up to snuff and powder puff," which was CB talk.

The Olympic dream that Marvis, and others, had got waylaid when President Jimmy Carter decided the U.S. would boycott the 1980 Olympics in Moscow. The Russians had sent troops into Afghanistan and that got Carter into a lather. But the U.S. Olympic folks still held a competition in Atlanta to decide which fighters would be named to the team.

In the semifinals of these Olympic trials, Marvis was knocked down by a fighter named James Broad less than a minute into the bout. Marvis sat there on the canvas, unable to move, though his eyes were clear and he was quite conscious. It was as though he was paralyzed. Marvis would later say his whole body felt like a "funnybone"—that tingling kind of sensation. A sensation that trapped him and wouldn't allow him to get up. He was counted out by the referee. And though he quickly recovered from the effects of the punch, it was a mystery to us why it had happened.

For Marvis it was more than a mystery. As he told a reporter: "It was a big blow, but my religion held me together. God doesn't give you any more than you can stand. After the loss, I was trying to figure out what God was trying to tell me. Then I heard this song on a gospel station I listen to with the line, 'I don't believe He could bring me this far just to leave me.' "

Well, Marvis' faith would be tested when, during routine sparring in the North Broad Street gym, a punch again left him "frozen" on the canvas. We hurried him over to the doctors this time. Their examination produced this explanation: Under certain conditions, a nerve in Marvis' neck was being pinched by a muscle. Surgery fixed it so that the problem never occurred again.

But the injury led me to become more involved with his career. As I studied the situation, I realized that George Benton was becoming increasingly busy with other pro fighters of his, at a time when Marvis needed close personal attention to develop into a successful pro. That meant Son of Smokin' would have his daddy to train and manage him.

9

FATHER'S FOOTSTEPS

Over the years that followed, there would be a whole lot of talk about whether Joe Frazier did right by Marvis. Start with the very notion of a father knowing what's best for his son the fighter. Among boxing people, fathers are traditionally seen as being too emotionally involved to make the correct decisions. By this view, too often boxing fathers use their sons to make up for their own past disappointments.

You all know that wasn't the case with me. I had been world champion, and earned millions of dollars. But that still didn't cut me any slack with critics who wondered was I hellbent on making Marvis over in my own image. The controversy was laid out by the guy in *The New York Times,* who wrote:

> *Under Smokin' Joe, the style changed. As Marvis tells it: "The only thing Pop added was my standing my ground a little firmer. Rather than my being so defensive, a little more offense was added." That "little more offense," which in Marvis' account sounds rather like a quarter-turn of the wrench in a subtle mechanical refinement, has struck others as radical retooling—a change of psyche, and outlook.*
>
> *"Joe's only fault," said Lou Duva, a manager and trainer, "was trying to make a replica of himself rather than letting the talent come out of the fighter's own style. George (Benton) had*

Marvis cuter, more defensive. See, a guy like Marvis Frazier shouldn't be going in to a fighter and trading. He should box and be cute. It'd make him a better fighter. . . ."

Talk to Joe Frazier about how he has influenced his son's style and he will deny molding him in his own image. "You can't make guys like yourself," he said.

Understand this: A lot of heavyweights that are hot stuff in the amateurs, where a pure boxer has an edge in the way a bout is scored, don't cut it as pros. From my era, look at Mathis. A top gun in the amateurs, where they went nuts for his fat-man dancing act, he wasn't diddlysquat as a pro. Pros is a tougher game for heavyweights. Pros is a more physical, brutalizing deal. You can only go so far with slip-and-slide jive as a professional heavyweight.

Four years after Marvis went to the Olympic trials, look what happened. The heavyweight gold medalist at the 1984 Games in Los Angeles was Henry Tillman, and the super heavyweight gold medalist was Tyrell Biggs. Both stick-and-move guys who couldn't knock down the price of a serape in a Tijuana flea market.

And guess who couldn't even make the Olympic team in 1984? Michael Gerard Tyson is who.

Tyson, badass Tyson, became the world champion. Tillman and Biggs were busts in the pros. Tyson, who couldn't get a decision in two tries against Tillman in the Olympic boxoffs, knocked him out in the pros—had him folding up like a Slinky toy. And Biggs too; Tyson knocked him out and then boasted how Biggs was wimpering like a woman when he hit him with those wicked body shots.

For Marvis to make money—and that's why a fella fights, for money and for glory—it would take a bit more than what Georgie Benton had given him. That was my thinking at least. And critics be damned, I knew a few things about Marvis they didn't.

Main thing was Marvis hadn't the tunnel vision, the singlemindedness his daddy did. Maybe in the beginning it was there—the quest to bring the title back to the Frazier family. But once he got married to Daralyn in 1983, by his own account he wasn't into boxing with that at-all-costs gotta-have-it urgency that I had. As Marvis put it: "I was about family. From 1983, I wasn't there mentally the way I had been."

Family and religion. Marvis would become a licensed minister—in his words, "knocking 'em out for the Lord" at the Faith Temple Church of God in Christ in Philly. All well and good. Marvis Kirk Frazier is as decent as they come—a fine husband and a great father to his daughters, Tamyra, twelve, and Tiara, ten. And I'd get as big a kick reading, or hearing, the nice things people said about him as a man as I did hearing praise for my son the fighter.

In one newspaper account, Mort Sharnik, who used to run boxing for CBS-TV, was quoted as saying: "Boxing is so remote from his character and instincts. He is such a gentle man, such a godly man."

In the same article, a promoter named Sam Glass told of how Marvis stopped by to see him after fighting on a card of his: "He thanked me for having him on the card and said he hoped I was satisfied with how he performed. He was uncommonly gracious. Fighters just don't do that sort of thing."

In a way Marvis' niceness worked against him as a fighter. The best fighters are self-involved, self-absorbed; me-me-me is how they think. Marvis wasn't built that way. That—and the fact that he was a small heavyweight who was skilled but without the really big punch—made my job as manager a bit tricky.

But you know what? It was satisfying. And soon, some of my nephews started coming into the gym. Before you knew it, I was managing and training a whole slew of fighting Fraziers. Smokin' Joe Frazier's Gym produced some great talent—and still does—but the "Fighting Fraziers" dominated the gym.

Besides Marvis, there was Rodney, a heavyweight who was the son of my sister Rebecca; Mark, a super middleweight who was the son of my brother Tommy; and finally, Hector, who was a junior welterweight and my son by Rosetta.

It was Marvis who brought Hector into the fold. While talking by phone to Rosetta's daughter Renae, who was Marvis' sister, he found out that Hector was hanging out in New York.

"How's he doing?" Marvis asked.

"Not so good," said Renae. "Somebody ought to get a hold of him."

Marvis, who was two years older than Hector, tracked his brother down, and drove to New York to pick him up. It was the first time the two had met, even though they had talked by phone over the years.

Through the years, I didn't have a lot of contact with Hector and Renae. Rosetta was married, and I knew the children were well-cared for and in a good family. I wanted to be closer to the children, but the situation was difficult.

In the gym, Hector worked hard and showed promise, fighting with an aggressive style a lot like mine. The similarities between me and Hector are amazing considering the distance between us when he was growing up: We look, walk, talk, and often think alike. On top of that, he has a great sense of humor. The other fellas called him "G-man" for "Gas, girls, giddy-up, got it, and gone." As the name suggests, Hector was as busy a fella outside the ring as he was in it.

After four or five amateur fights, I turned him pro because of his talent. Bing bang, in his first year as a pro, in 1983, he won seven straight fights, all by knockout After a few years, though, the G-man started running with the wrong crowd and got himself into trouble. We didn't hear from him for awhile, but now we're back in touch and he's getting himself together.

By 1983 I'd made the gym pretty much a closed shop—mostly for Fraziers. I'd been disappointed by the way the amateurs I'd been so good to—the Meldrick Taylors, the Tyrell Biggses—didn't even let me make them an offer to manage them. So I hung up a sign by the door that said, "Starting Jan. '83, any trainers that do not have fighters for Smokin' Joe Frazier must and will pay $250 a year for gym dues. Thank you. [signed] Joe Frazier."

At the time, other gyms in the city, such as the Percy Street Gym and McCall's Gym, did not charge trainers' dues. But I'd reached the point where I didn't want to invest time and money in fighters, and have them turn their backs on me just when I could earn back a few of the dollars I'd spent on them.

As I told a news guy: "You don't go to General Motors, build a car, and say it's yours. Same thing at my gym. If you come here and learn, I want to make money back. You belong to us."

Well, that didn't make me the most popular gym owner in the city of brotherly love, but I didn't give a damn. My way or the highway. I was happy, real happy, just working with my blood. I'd be in the gym every day, training them, sparring with them. What more could I ask for? Boxing and family.

Early on, working mostly with Marvis, I got so into the training that I even came out of retirement for one fight—a draw against an ex-convict named Floyd (Jumbo) Cummings in December 1981 in Chicago. The consensus among family and friends was that the smoke was just about out. I didn't like to hear it. Or believe it. But I guess deep down I knew they weren't shucking me. So that was it: I never fought again.

Instead, working with a partner named Joe Verne, I concentrated on moving the Fraziers, and another fighter of mine, a heavyweight named Bert Cooper.

Remember that TV show I was watching the night before I whupped Clay? *The Naked City.* Well, they used to open that show by saying, "There are eight million stories in the Naked City."

The same holds true for boxing. A whole lot of stories about men rolling the dice—staking their blood, sweat, and tears against the chance that they could hit the jackpot. Well, over eight years, from 1980 to 1988, Marvis would fight twenty-one bouts and earn more than a million dollars, most of it in the only two bouts he lost—to Larry Holmes in 1983 ($750,000) and Mike Tyson in 1985 ($300,000).

There were some who said I screwed up big time when I put Marvis in against Holmes in what amounted to Marvis' eleventh fight. "Too soon," they said.

Well, I felt about his fighting Holmes like the guy did who climbed Mount Everest. They asked the man, why would you want to climb all that mountain? 'Cause it's there, he said. Same thing with Holmes. Why fight him? 'Cause he and that $750,000 were there. And in boxing you got to grab your chance while it's there.

I mean, in this game things can go south in a hurry. Tyson versus Holyfield, November 1991, was supposed to be the biggest-grossing fight in boxing history—one hundred million dollars, some predicted. Well, first Tyson injures his ribs, causing the fight to be canceled. And then he gets himself into a jam on that rape charge in Indianapolis, and it's adios big money, the fight, and Michael Gerard.

Same thing with Bowe and Lennox Lewis. At one point, that was the biggest match out there—a projected $80-million, $90-million gross. But rather than getting it on when they should have, Bowe fought veterans like Michael Dokes and Jesse Ferguson and then lost his WBA/IBF title to Holyfield, while Lewis deteriorated fight by fight until Oliver

McCall knocked him out and took his WBC title. And a fight that once was a huge payday became a big nothing.

Happens all the time. Tommy Morrison, due for a $7-million payday against Lennox Lewis, decides to take a tuneup fight and blows his pot of gold when the tuneup guy, Michael Bent, knocks him out.

Marvis was injury prone. Besides the pinched-nerve problem, he had been sidelined seventeen months, from September 1981 to February 1983, with an ear infection and then with viral hepatitis. He didn't fight at all during that time. As his father and manager, I couldn't help but wonder if trouble was gonna keep calling. And if that were the case, it made grab-it-while-you-can even more logical.

Besides, earlier that year, 1983, Holmes had barely beaten Tim Witherspoon, a fighter Marvis had whupped in the amateurs. Holmes was thirty-four, old for a fighter, and at this point was fighting more for the money than out of the passion that Marvis had.

Before the bout, there were smart boxing guys like Teddy Brenner, the Garden matchmaker, who were quoted as saying they believed in Marvis' chances. When Holmes knocked out Marvis in one round, it was easy to call me a dummy *after* the fact.

But there were a few who recognized the realities. Two years later, David Wolf, who'd managed Boom Boom Mancini, the WBA lightweight champion, and Donnie Lalonde, the WBC light heavyweight champion, would tell reporters: "Any time you're offered the amount of money he got to go after Holmes in what was a no-lose situation, you take it. Marvis was not a whole lot less marketable afterward, because nobody expected him to win. And beyond that, Joe hasn't matched Marvis poorly in any other fight. He successfully resurrected his career by picking good opponents."

Among those opponents was Bonecrusher Smith in February 1986. In that fight Marvis got his jaw busted in the fifth round, but he hung in there and beat the scamboogah by decision. That December Bonecrusher would knock out Witherspoon to win the WBC heavyweight title and then in March 1987 would go the twelve-round distance while losing to Tyson.

That victory over a heavy puncher like Smith, in adverse circumstances, said to me Marvis was ready for a Tyson. Again, though, there were folks who thought I'd overmatched him. Me? I figured for $300,000 it was worth taking the chance. Besides, he'd suffered another injury—a detached retina that made me want to take the money and run. As David Wolf told reporters, for Marvis to make the kind of money he was getting for Tyson, he'd have to fight five bouts against quality opponents. And as Wolf said, there were not so many network fights those days that Marvis could say to himself, "I'll fight every other month because I'm Marvis Frazier." It turned out Tyson was too much for Marvis. Two uppercuts and a flurry of lefts and rights, and Marvis was knocked down . . . and out in thirty seconds of the first round. Once again, the critics slammed me for mismatching Marvis. But hell, two years later promoters would pay Michael Spinks more than $13 million to fight Tyson because they thought he could give Tyson a competitive match. Did that make them fools when Tyson knocked out Spinks in ninety-one seconds? Not really. Because that's how it went when you fought Iron Mike back then.

Bottom line, in boxing's Naked City, Marvis' was a success story. More than one million dollars he'd made in only twenty-one fights.

🏃 🏃 🏃

Besides Marvis and Hector, I've fathered four other sons that I love and am very proud of—Joseph Rubin, sixteen, Joseph Jordan, thirteen, Brandon Marcus, twelve and Derek Dennis, five—and have taken responsibility for all of them. My thinking was: If I'm that strong enough to make 'em, then I'm strong enough to take 'em as my responsibility.

By 1985, Florence and I filed for divorce. As these things go, it ended amicably. I left her the house, and moved into a six-thousand-square-foot loft apartment.

Folks asked: What happened with the marriage? I'd tell them: When a marriage is gone, it's gone. Hey, I wasn't easy; I know that. I tended to go where I wanted, when I wanted. I was restless in the house. Still, I did the best I could. The proof is in the pudding: The proof is in those kids. When Marvis retired from boxing in '88, he moved into the Frazier family business. For a while he took over the limousine operation. These days he runs Smokin' Joe Frazier, Inc.—the endorsements and card show bookings that his daddy gets—while doing double duty as a preacher who also counsels young folks. He is in charge of the gym and Frazier's Golden Gloves, a youth boxing program in Philly. Renae is a word processor in New York City. Jacquelyn got to American University on a basketball scholarship, and went on to earn her law degree at Villanova.

Weatta is a professional services representative for Blue Cross. Jo-Netta works as a finance coordinator for a medical insurance consulting company. And Natasha assists Marvis in the management of all the Smokin' Joe Frazier, Inc., businesses.

These kids have done okay, and I'm proud of them. In a world where trouble is around every corner, they avoided it. Do Florence and I deserve credit? Some. But I know for damn sure that when you're a parent there's luck and God's will involved, too.

🥊   🥊   🥊

Take Bert Cooper, a young cruiserweight that signed on with me. Cooper was from a good family—in fact, his father didn't want him to be a fighter at first. I had to persuade the old man that he'd be doing his son a real injustice by holding him back—the boy was a natural hitting machine. A little raw when he walked into Joe Frazier's Gym, but with a punch that went *ker-boom* from day one.

I tried to explain to the father what a diamond in the rough this boy was, and what a future he had. And I wasn't blowin' smoke at him. As with me, you put somebody in front of Cooper, well, he just beats him up. A natural fighter. I'm not talking boxer; I'm talking an asskicking straightahead brawler. And a boy who figured to grow into a heavyweight about the same size I was.

Cooper turned pro at the age of eighteen in 1984. By the end of 1986, he'd won fifteen of his sixteen bouts, all of them by knockout, including a victory over Henry Tillman for the NABF cruiserweight title.

In his first fight in '87, he stepped up to heavyweight against a Canadian, Willie De Wit, who the promoters up there were building into a hot attraction. De Wit was undefeated (one draw) in fifteen fights, and favored to beat Cooper. Well, Cooper destroyed him—stopped him in two rounds. Gave him the kind of beating that should have sent De Wit to a vocational counselor after.

But with a bright future ahead of him, Cooper was blowing it. He let the wrong people into his life—cocaine-sniffing scamboogahs that derailed the boy. He just didn't care enough about the gift he had, and the life it could make for him. He wasn't dedicated. Other voices took him someplace else. Following one fight, his urine sample came up tainted with drugs.

Marvis and me tried to set him right. Long talks to which he'd always give respectful responses.

"I ain't playin' no drugs, Bert," I told him.

"Yes, sir."

To keep him away from the easy access he had to drugs in Philly, we sent him down to South Carolina to train. Damned if the boy didn't find a source for cocaine like *that*. In his next fight, against Carl Williams that May for the USBA heavyweight title, Cooper looked pitiful—a ghost of the fighter he was—and quit on his stool after eight rounds.

"That's it," I told him. "If you can't respect yourself, and the work we've put in—I don't want you around me."

Well, if you follow boxing, you know he never changed. Three years later, against my old comebacking friend George Foreman, Cooper quit on his stool again after two rounds. Afterward, he tested positive for cocaine, and was fined twenty-five thousand dollars, eight thousand dollars more than his purse.

And yet in November '91, he still had enough left, in spite of the cocaine and in spite of being out of shape, to show up as a last-minute replacement and damn near knock out Holyfield for the heavyweight title. Remember how he knocked Holyfield into the ropes and had him glassy-eyed that night at the Omni in Atlanta? Had the referee, Mills Lane, let Cooper follow up, he might have finished Holyfield off. Instead, Lane ruled that the ropes had held Holyfield up, which technically meant a knockdown. That mandatory count of eight saved Holyfield, who went on to stop my old protégé a few rounds later in a brutal, brutal fight.

Eight million stories in this naked city.

🥊　🥊　🥊

What with Marvis, Hector, and the others—even Cooper—I got a chance to stay in boxing. I can't ask for any more than that. I loved boxing when I first walked into that PAL gym. All these years later, I'm still crazy for the game, which is as crazy a game as there is.

It's a business that uses its fighters, too often leaving them short of the money that should have been theirs. Compared to some of the guys I fought, I'm lucky. Real lucky. I got my money, and I still walk, talk, and laugh like a normal guy. And if I don't speak too fast, you can understand me.

Sadly, I can't say the same for some of them that I rumbled with.

Buster Mathis died this past September (1995) of a heart condition. He seemed to have nothing but medical troubles from the time he retired in 1972, after a loss to Ron Lyle. He suffered from high blood pressure, diabetes, strokes, kidney failure, and heart trouble that forced him to wear a pacemaker.

Jerry Quarry. The news clips sent me say he's suffering from *pugilistica dementia.* That's the fancy way to say he's punch drunk. For lots of people "punch drunk" is an expression that is a cue to make jokes. But what's happened to Jerry is no laughing matter. He was a courageous fighter, and if he didn't cut so easy, he could've been a world champion. His brother Jimmy, who takes care of him, was quoted in the *Los Angeles Times* as saying: "We've lived in this house for four months, and he can't find the bathroom or his bedroom. He's walked out and we've had to call the police to find him. He'll leave at 5 o'clock in the morning, so he has to be watched 24 hours a day. . . . If he gets milk out of the refrigerator, he can't remember where it goes back. He's not violent. He's happy. He lives in a small world."

And so it goes. Eddie Machen, gone. Bonavena, gone. And that sleepy scamboogah Clay—well, everybody knows the troubles he's seen.

It'd be easy for me to fall in line and act as if Clay was some fuzzy ole saint to me, like he is to so many others. I know that's what people would like to hear. Forgive and forget.

But I'd be shuckin' you if I told you that.

Truth is, I'd like to rumble with that sucker again—beat him up piece by piece and mail him back to Jesus. No, I ain't forgiven him for what he said and did. I stood up for him when few others did. Told the boxing officials, "Let the man fight." Then, when he got what he needed, he turned on me and said everything bad that he could. Called me the white man's champion to get the black men to turn on me. Called me a Tom and an ignoramus to demean me in public.

Now people ask me if I feel bad for him, now that things aren't going so well for him. Nope. I don't. Fact is, I don't give a damn. They want me to love him, but I'll open up the graveyard and bury his ass when the Lord chooses to take him. You see what the Lord did to him: He shut him down, that ungrateful scamboogah. Clay always mocked me—like I was the dummy. Gettin' hit in the head. Now look at him: He can hardly talk and he's still out there trying to make noise.

People don't understand this guy, don't understand what he's all about. Well, I'll tell you: He's about himself more than anything. Yeah, Clay—he was so busy being *THEE* greatest, he couldn't see the snakes that were holding up his pants. Well, all that talk of his don't amount to much anymore. He's a ghost, and I'm still here.

Now let's talk about who *really* won those three fights. . . .

10

I'm Still Smokin'

Yeah. Here I am—fifty-two years old, a man with a bum shoulder and a bit of an eye problem. But after all these years in the fight game, I can still do everything but walk on water.

I still hit the streets and do roadwork every now and then. My weight stays at 230 pounds—only eight pounds heavier than I was when I last fought Big George. I still wear size 46 regular suit. God's been good to me.

For a while I drank too much. Courvoisier, Christian Brothers, and ginger ale—all in the same glass. I would drink four guys under the bar, and look for the fifth one.

The doctor brought me in, said my blood pressure was 250 over 132. He told me: "The good news is you're still alive, but barely. The bad news is you got to quit drinking. Anything to say?"

Told him: "Yeah. I thought you were going to tell me—'Quit having sex.'"

Got to laugh. Sometimes you just have to laugh.

I had my times when I was dead serious, and still do. But I keep a light step now, mostly.

I go here, I go there. And sometimes they pay me to.

I sign autographs, posters, this and that. It's nice. It means the people remember, and like what they remember.

Mostly what they remember is me and Clay.

We were, I think, what is good about boxing—skill and passion, and the both of us tapping deep into ourselves for that extra effort. In that ring, we brought the best out of each other.

But that's the past, and much as I feel good about it, I try not to live there too much.

Yeah. I like to set out there for whatever adventures today's got in store. It doesn't always have to be a grand situation. A soul-rockin' song on the dashboard radio. A blue-sky day. A pretty girl shooting me a smile. That little five-year-old boy of mine reaching out to Daddy. Whatever it is, just bring it. Bring it on to me.

You know, fifty-two is just a number, and the way I feel about it is—hell, I'm still smokin'.

The Fight Record Of Smokin' Joe Frazier
32–4–1, 27 KO's

1965

Aug. 16	Woody Gross, Philadelphia, PA	KO	1
Sept. 20	Mike Bruce, Philadelphia, PA	KO	3
Sept. 28	Ray Staples, Philadelphia, PA	KO	2
Nov. 11	Abe Davis, Philadelphia, PA	KO	1

1966

Jan. 17	Mel Turnbow, Philadelphia, PA	KO	1
March 4	Dick Wipperman, New York, NY	KO	5
April 4	Charley Polite, Philadelphia, PA	KO	2
April 28	Don Smith, Pittsburgh, PA	KO	3
May 19	Chuck Leslie, Los Angeles, CA	KO	3
May 26	Memphis Al Jones, Los Angeles, CA	KO	1
July 25	Billy Daniels, Philadelphia, PA	TKO	6
Sept. 21	Oscar Bonavena, New York, NY	W	10
Nov. 21	Eddie Machen, Los Angeles, CA	TKO	10

1967

Feb. 21	Doug Jones, Philadelphia, PA	KO	6
April 11	Jeff Davis, Miami Beach, FL	KO	5
May 4	George Johnson, Los Angeles, CA	W	10
July 19	George Chuvalo, New York, NY	TKO	4
Oct. 17	Tony Doyle, Philadelphia, PA	TKO	2
Dec. 18	Marion Conners, Boston, MA	KO	3

1968

March 4	Buster Mathis, New York, NY	KO	11

(Won vacant New York Heavyweight Title)

June	24	Manuel Ramos, New York, NY	TKO	2
Dec.	10	Oscar Bonavena, Philadelphia, PA	W	15

1969

April	22	Dave Zyglwicz, Houston, TX	KO	1
June	23	Jerry Quarry, New York, NY	TKO	7

1970

Feb.	16	Jimmy Ellis, New York, NY	TKO	5

(Won vacant World Heavyweight Title)

Nov.	18	Bob Foster, Detroit, MI	KO	2

1971

March	8	Muhammed Ali, New York, NY	W	15
July	15	Cleveland Williams, Houston, TX	Exh	3
July	15	James Helwig, Houston, TX	Exh	3

1972

Jan.	15	Terry Daniels, New Orleans, LA	TKO	4
May	25	Ron Stander, Omaha, Neb	TKO	5

1973

Jan.	22	George Foreman, Kingston, Jamaica	TKO	by 2
		(Lost World Heavyweight Title)		
July	2	Joe Bugner, London, England	W	12

1974

Jan.	28	Muhammed Ali, New York, NY	L	12
		(For NABF Heavyweight Title)		
June	17	Jerry Quarry, New York, NY	TKO	5

1975

March	1	Jimmy Ellis, Melbourne, Australia	TKO	9
Oct.	1	Muhammed Ali, Manila, Philippines	TKO	by 14
		(For World Heavyweight Title)		

1976

June	15	George Foreman, Uniondale, NY	KO	by 5

1980

Elected to the Boxing Hall of Fame

1981

Dec.	3	Jumbo Cumming, Chicago, IL	W	10

INDEX

ABOUT THE AUTHORS

Smokin' Joe Frazier is a member of the Boxing Hall of Fame, and he was honored with the WBA Living Legend Award in 1995. The 1970–1973 Heavyweight Champion of the World is the cochair of the annual Jesse Owens Dinner and the United Negro College Fund Sports Ball. He regularly attends many charity functions across the country. A strong supporter of the community, Frazier works with amateur and professional boxers in Smokin' Joe Frazier's Gym in Philadelphia, where he also runs Frazier's Golden Gloves youth development program.

Currently, in between his singing engagements, Frazier is working with his son Marvis to produce a documentary of his life.

Phil Berger is one of the country's most noted sportswriters. Both his *Miracle on 33rd Street: The New York Knickerbockers' Championship Season* and *Blood Season: Tyson and the World of Boxing* have become classics of the genre. Berger's other book credits include: *The Last Laugh: The World of the Standup Comic, Punch Lines: Berger on Boxing* and two novels, *Big Time*, and *Deadly Kisses*. A former boxing correspondent for *The New York Times*, Berger's award-winning work regularly appears in the pages of a variety of publications, including *The New York Times Sunday Magazine, Playboy, Esquire, The Village Voice, Penthouse, Sports, Inside Sports* and *The Washington Post*.